# Amuse-bouche. The Taste of Art

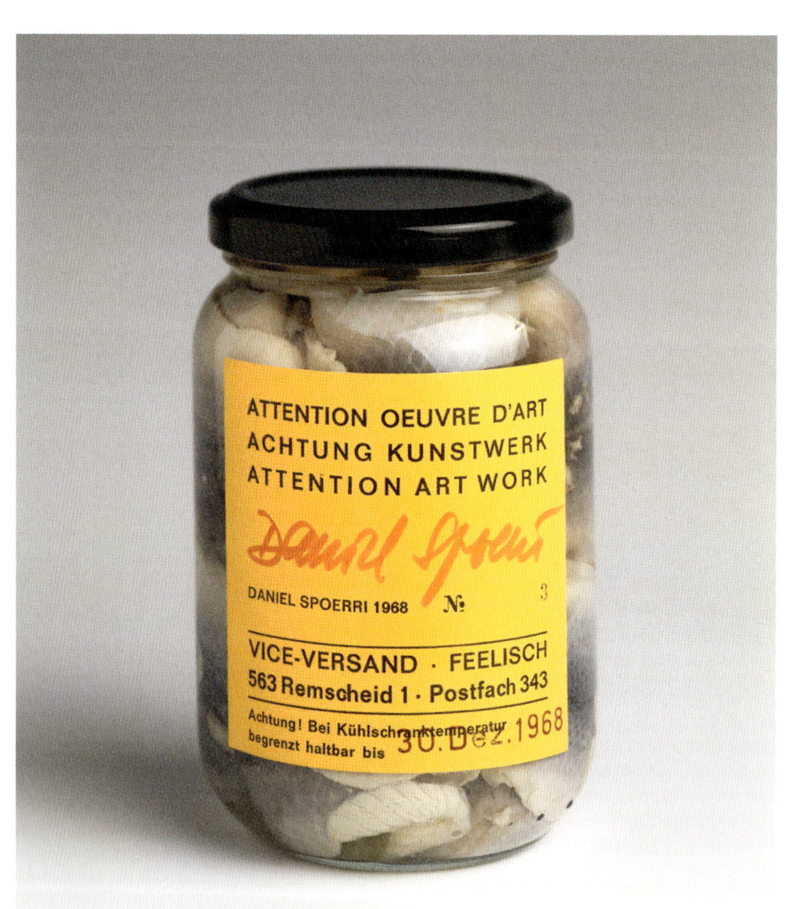
ATTENTION OEUVRE D'ART
ACHTUNG KUNSTWERK
ATTENTION ART WORK
DANIEL SPOERRI 1968
N: 3
VICE-VERSAND · FEELISCH
563 Remscheid 1 · Postfach 343
Achtung! Bei Kühlschranktemperatur
begrenzt haltbar bis 30. Dez. 1968

# Amuse-bouche
# The Taste
# of Art

**Interdisciplinary
Symposium on Taste
and Food Culture**

HATJE
CANTZ

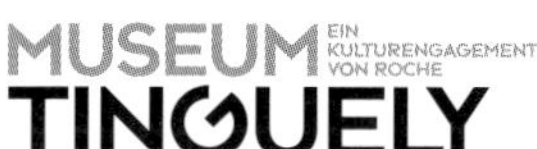

**Contents**

# Amuse-bouche.
# The Taste of Art   Foreword

Multisensorial perception plays an essential role in the experience of Jean Tinguely's works of art. His kinetic pieces create physical empathy and have a tactile appeal; they have an acoustic aura and enable spatiotemporal visual experiences. Working with smells and tastes was also important for Tinguely and the artistic circle of the Nouveaux Réalistes. This is why we, at Museum Tinguely, decided to present a series of exhibitions on the human senses and their role in the visual arts. It began in 2015 with *Belle Haleine – The Scent of Art*, followed by *Prière de toucher. The Touch of Art* in 2016. We are now continuing this series with *Amuse-bouche. The Taste of Art*, and in the coming years we will also explore the two "higher" senses: the visual and the auditory.

Sensual experiences are always multisensory. They cannot be reduced to a single sense. This is particularly pronounced with regard to the sense of taste, since the gustatory can hardly be separated from the sense of smell, nor from sight and touch, and even the sense of hearing is part of a comprehensive incorporation process, not only in haute cuisine. At the same time, it is revealing how the changing perspective, which focuses on only one sense at a time, leads to different observations which portray individual sensory reception processes and their consequences. Through its openness and propensity for interpretation, the field of art offers a fascinating approach to understanding these complex processes.

One of the most productive aspects of this engagement with the human senses from an artistic perspective is the dialogue with different fields of knowledge, which is often already present in the works themselves. Within the framework of each of the three "sense exhibitions," we have organized an interdisciplinary symposium that opens up questions touching on multiple disciplines and fosters discussion on these issues with leading experts. We then publish the results for each of the five senses in a symposium volume, which also serves as an accompanying publication for the respective exhibition.

While the exhibition *Amuse-bouche* concentrates on the sense of taste, the symposium on April 5–6, 2019, focused on facets of culinary culture(s) to examine the sensual dimension of taste, to reflect on discourses about identity and migration, and to assess the diversity of symbolic actions and iconographic references related to eating.

Following an introduction to the exhibition by the curator Annja Müller-Alsbach, the empirical sciences form the first section of this volume, as they did during the symposium. In his contribution, the biochemist Wolfgang Meyerhof explains the development of taste sensations and describes how our brain uses this information to control our eating behavior by developing taste preferences and aversions.

Culinary preferences and aversions also play a role in the research conducted by Charles Spence. In his text, the psychologist focuses on the history of colorless dishes—clear, white, or black—and on the curious role that the experience of color plays in the enjoyment of food.

Jeannette Nuessli Guth and Maren Runte shed light on descriptions of tastes from a food-sensorial and linguistic point of view. They explain the challenge, on the one hand, of a standardized verbalization of sensory experiences and, on the other, of identifying which concepts for taste experiences are actually in circulation and how their use differs markedly in different languages.

Elisabeth Bronfen also focuses on the verbalization of taste. The literary scholar and passionate cook describes the role of imagination in cooking and how the desired taste experience can be expressed in words.

Offering a glimpse into the culinary practice of a star chef, Stefan Wiesner describes in an interview how, among other things, gourmet menus can be created with products from the forest—or with fire, wood, and stones. The question arises: Where are the boundaries between gourmet cuisine and artistic intervention?

Further texts are devoted to the experience of taste in the fine arts. Karin Leonhard contributed to this volume as an author after the symposium. The art historian describes in her text how still life painters of the seventeenth century knew to stimulate the viewer's taste buds through visual means and even to suggest culinary compositions.

In a survey spanning several centuries, art and cultural historian Ralf Beil examines symbolic moments of incorporation, from Allan Kaprow and Meret Oppenheim, via propaganda in National Socialism, and back to Lucas Cranach. Beil demonstrates how, in addition to aesthetic questions, the most diverse issues, whether of a power-political, religious, mythical, or sociological nature, are connected with food intake and incorporation.

Is there a difference between cooks who experiment and artists who cook? Using numerous examples, such as the Italian Futurists, Daniel Spoerri's Eat Art, and star chef Ferran Adrià, the cook and gastronomic art historian Felix Bröcker takes a look at the interfaces between art and gastronomy, where craft meets reflections on the cultural significance of food.

The next section of this publication is dedicated to Daniel Spoerri's experiment *Nur Geschmack anstatt Essen* (Tasting, Not Eating), which was first realized during the *Amuse-bouche* symposium. A statement by the artist and photographs illustrate Spoerri's experimental setup, the aim of which was to isolate taste and confuse the senses.

The last thematic section contains texts from the fields of anthropology and cultural studies. Here as well, one contribution has been added after the symposium: based on his experiences with "thick sauces" and their connection with (in)harmonious coexistence among the Songhai in the Republic of Niger, Paul Stoller presents a survey of the history of anthropology and the ethnology of taste. What role do savoring and taste play in describing and analyzing human relationships, hierarchies, memory formation, identity, and social change?

Antje Baecker investigates what happens when a new food is added to the culinary repertoire of a hitherto agriculturally autonomous region. Based on her field studies in the Colca Valley in Peru, the ethnologist describes how noodles find their way into Andean cuisine as a decidedly feminine and socially connective foodstuff.

Thomas Macho's contribution picks up the concept of metabolic reason. The appropriation of the foreign in every act of food intake is the starting point for his reflections on the connection between food and alterity, the consumption of the other, or a kitchen of fusion and migration.

The final contribution of both the symposium and this volume was made by the Portuguese artist Marisa Benjamim. Her work revolves around the consumption of plants that usually do not find their way onto menus. In this book, she uses sketches to present her work *Hortus Deliciarum*, which can be seen in the exhibition *Amuse-bouche. The Taste of Art* at Museum Tinguely from February to May 2020.

The exhibition curated by Annja Müller-Alsbach—I would like to take this opportunity to thank her, and also Lisa Ahlers, who edited this symposium volume—returns in its conception to the fundamental differentiation of the sense of taste as the five physiologically distinguishable tastes: sweet, sour, salty, bitter, and "umami." They form the background for a thematic tour through the exhibition with over eighty works by international artists, which Müller-Alsbach explains in the ensuing contribution. A list of the exhibited works, the performative and participatory contributions within the framework of the exhibition project, along with an overview of all persons involved in the exhibition and publication can be found at the end of this volume.

**Roland Wetzel**
Director, Museum Tinguely, Basel

# Amuse-bouche: Insights into an Exhibition on the Taste of Art

Annja Müller-Alsbach

The ingesting of food is first and foremost existential, deciding over life and death. Our ability to perceive different aromas through the senses can, however, also making eating a pleasurable experience. For centuries, therefore, food and the act of eating, along with the associated cultural and social aspects, have been the subject of fine art. Our culinary culture, how and what we eat, opens up heatedly debated areas of discussion that, especially today, can also be ethical in nature.[1] So it is not surprising that in recent years there have been numerous art exhibitions about food as artistic material, Eat Art, or a historical examination of the transformation of our culinary culture.[2]

In contrast, *Amuse-bouche* focuses rather on the sense of taste. In what form can this fascinating sensorium—with which we take manifold facets of the universe into the body through the mouth, tongue, and nasopharynx—become part of the aesthetic perception of art at all? This show breaks with the usual museum practice of addressing primarily the sense of vision and instead offers a diversity of art-historical, phenomenological, and empirical encounters with our sense of taste. Several of the works can be experienced in a participatory way and tried out as part of special tours and performances. In addition, however, works of art are represented that evoke the experiences of taste solely with the aid of the viewer's imagination.

"You eat with your eyes first," as the saying goes, and indeed our sense of vision plays a crucial role in assessing the taste of food. That our perception of taste is influenced by a number of multisensory impulses has long since been known and proven scientifically by studies of the psychology of perception like those of Charles Spence (see also his contribution, p. 30). How does our gustatory sensorium, which is closely linked to our memories and emotions, operate when it is activated solely by visual stimuli, that is, when we view food or the act of eating in works of art as rendered only? Does a new level of aesthetic experience really open up when we try to taste art visually on the basis of our storage of knowledge, personal experience, and feelings? What does a work of art taste like when we are allowed to lick it with our tongues, when we can drink and eat the ingredients from which it was produced?

In the exhibition *Amuse-bouche*, we encounter situations that we know from our daily life and come across works of art from the past and present, though they are not arranged chronologically. Their arrangement is based rather on the common tastes that we can perceive via different receptors: bitter, sour, salty, sweet, and umami—the latter a term coined by the Japanese scientist Kikunae Ikeda in 1908, which can be best described in English as "savory" or "rich" (on this, see the discussions of Jeannette Nuessli Guth and Maren Runte, p. 40). The works shown produce a whole spectrum of evocations, from pleasure to disgust, from "sugar-sweet" to "bitter earnest." For example, the sweet section of the exhibition has works made of chocolate or sugar, as well as *Ein Pfund Erdbeeren* (A Pound of Strawberries, 2005) by Hans-Peter Feldmann, a seductively fruity-sweet work composed of thirty-four color photographs, and *Gib mir Honig* (Give Me Honey, 1979) by Joseph Beuys. By contrast, assembled in the bitter section are exhibits that begin with the objects illustrated and the materials used to address disgust, processes of decay, and death. At the same time, accents have been placed on themes such as "The Taste of Desire," "Sensory Deception," and "The Taste of the Other."

At one point on the way through the exhibition, Urs Fischer's *Noisette* (2009, **fig. 1**), a realistic-looking pink tongue, suddenly sticks out of the wall at eye height, having been triggered by a motion sensor. The effect of the motif in Janine Antoni's *Mortar and Pestle* (1999, **fig. 2**) is equally disturbing. With unapologetic directness, the photograph points the eye toward an intimate scene between two people: one sees an extreme close-up of one person touching and licking another person's eyeball with her

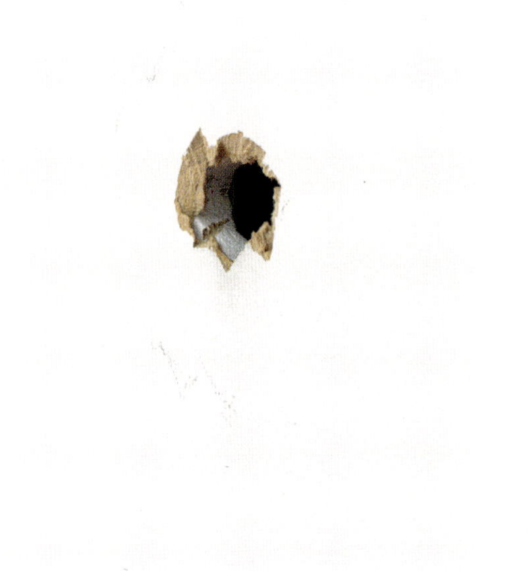

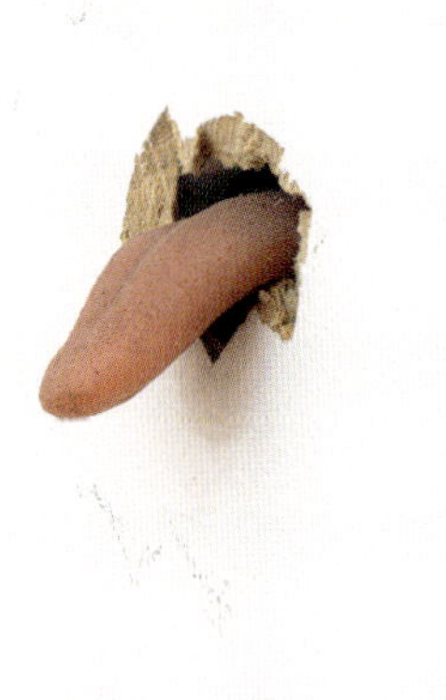

**Fig. 1** Urs Fischer
*Noisette*, 2009
Hole in the wall, silicone,
motion sensor, electric
motor, mechanism,
Dimensions variable,
Private Collection,
Courtesy of the Artist

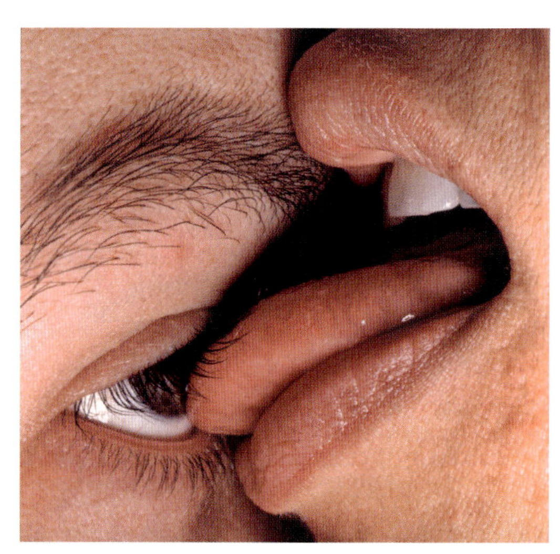

**Fig. 2** Janine Antoni
*Mortar and Pestle*, 1999
C-print, 121.9 x 121.9 cm
Courtesy of the artist
and Luhring Augustine,
New York



**Annja Müller-Alsbach**

tongue. The work's title lends the moment captured a taste of physical violence. Yet the eye is open, and so the tongue appears to be touching it so gently that the eyelid does not reflexively protect itself by closing: "I thought that I was making a very sweet and tender image. [I wanted to] taste [my] husband's vision,"[3] as the artist herself describes her intention. In *Mortar and Pestle*, mouth and tongue seem to take over the task normally reserved for vision: capturing the world. Is it going too far to read this work as symbolizing the contribution of vision to our sense of taste?

### Seductive Tasting and Lustful Noshing: Of Gingerbread and Flowers

Even before entering the exhibition proper, an installation on the outer longitudinal wall of the exhibition architecture invites us to nosh. Around twenty-two meters long, one can try to nibble on the work *Goosebump* (2011, **fig. 3**) by the Australian artist Elizabeth Willing, which is made of gingerbread cookies and white icing. It turns out to be more difficult than it looks, because the small, round gingerbread cookies with icing are firmly glued to the wall and can only be bit off where they protrude. Gradually, the sweet-and-spicy gingerbread cookies of this interactive and temporary work of art are eaten up by the visitors, and the initial white relief structure in a uniform linear pattern is transformed over time into a wall with irregular brown remnants of the gingerbread and the traces of eating and impressions of bodies that remain. The artist was inspired by the gingerbread house from the fairy tale *Hansel and Gretel*. The work's title, *Goosebump*, also refers to the polarizing moment of good and evil in the story by the Brothers Grimm: the threat of Hansel and Gretel dying inside the house due to the witch's cannibalistic intent is countered by the seduction of the sweet shell.

On the front wall of the exhibition architecture is *Hortus Deliciarum* (Garden of Delicacies), a new project by Marisa Benjamim on the taste of flowers (pp. 126–31). Here, Benjamim has installed a temporary "kitchen" consisting of a raised bed of flowers in the form of a table, standing in front of a wall clad in floral tiles—showing deference to the traditional buildings of her Portuguese homeland. From the "flower kitchen," one looks out through the window façade onto a greenhouse in neighboring Solitude-Park. Various edible plants and flowers are growing there, which the artist has turned into sample canapés. Benjamim wants to encourage us to think about our relationship to plants, nature, and their resources. Perhaps we have already eaten flowers, which we saw as colorful

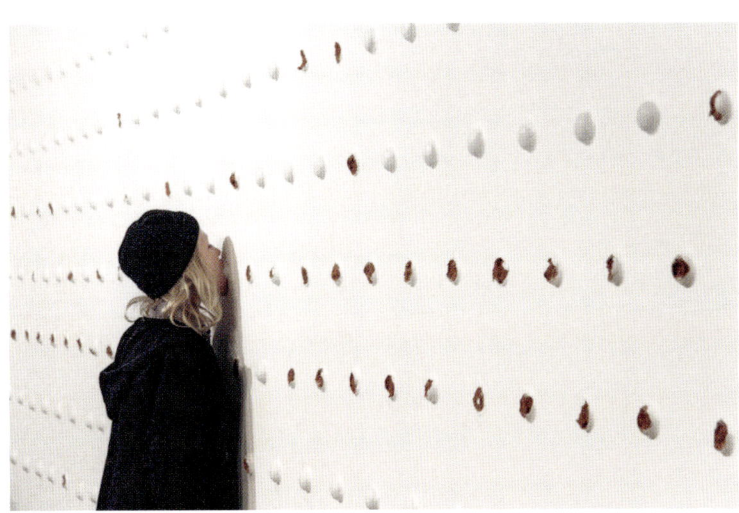

Fig. 3 Elizabeth Willing
Installation view of the interactive work *Goosebump*, 2011
Pfeffernüsse (frosted gingerbread) and icing on a wall, dimensions variable
Courtesy of the artist and Tolarno Galleries, Melbourne

decoration on dishes. But the idea of eating a dish consisting entirely of flowering plants—however seductive and beautiful it may appear—might fill us with mistrust. Valuable knowledge about flowers that are actually edible and delicious has been lost, and not just in our cities. During her performances in Benjamim's "flower kitchen," we have the opportunity to taste plants such as cowslip, clover flowers, broadleaf plantain, or the seductively sweet and almondy meadowsweet.

### The Taste of Desire: Of Bananas and Pomegranates

In allegorical depictions of the sense of taste and in still lifes, foods often symbolize seduction, excess, and lack of inhibition. Often these images feature a close connection between, if not an equation of, the gustatory sense and erotic pleasure. Assembled at the very beginning of the exhibition, in a section titled "The Taste of Desire," is a selection of related works from the sixteenth and seventeenth centuries and documents of the avant-garde from the early twentieth century, for instance by Marcel Duchamp and the Futurist Filippo Tommaso Marinetti. Found here is also artwork from the 1960s, such as *Mario Banana #1* (1964) by Andy Warhol, and works by contemporary artists. Baroque depictions of the senses suggest that the animalistic sense of taste, which largely evades reason, has a dangerous seductive aspect. In allegories of *gustus*, an often tightly embracing pair of lovers, feeding each other sweet fruit, unmistakably points to the close tie between the gustatory and sexual lust. In a copperplate engraving by Peter Overadt from the first half of the seventeenth century, this negatively connoted sensual-physical desire, whose temptation is supposed to be resisted, is further underscored by a depiction of the biblical scene of the Fall in the left background of the image **[fig. 4]**. Over time, representations of personifications of the sense of taste were replaced by other images, in the form of genre scenes of still lifes. The virtuosic skill of painters such as Jan Davidsz. de Heem sometimes went so far as to make the food seem so real in terms of its color, materiality, and consistency that one's mouth literally waters (on this subject, see also the contribution by Karin Leonhard, p. 68).

Works in which food and its eating are to be read symbolically are found in art history not only in the Baroque era. In her photographs and videos, the artist Farah Al Qasimi, born in the United Arab Emirates, works with a symbolic visual language that triggers the sense of sweetness and exoticism. One example of this is *Lunch* (2019, see the cover illustration of this publication), in which the artist presents above all sweets and exotic fruits spread out seductively on a cloth in pastels and floral patterns, including bananas, a cut papaya, and a pomegranate, which for centuries has been a famous symbol of female fertility. In *Pomegranate* (2016), too, Al Qasimi focuses our gaze on a freshly cut pomegranate, the temptingly streaming red juice of which promises a syrupy sweetness.

### Gustatory Illusions: From Sugar-Sweet to Bitter Earnest

Our vocabulary for describing specific aromas is relatively limited (on this, see also the contribution by Jeannette Nuessli Guth and Maren Runte, p. 40). At the same time, in our ordinary language, we employ metaphorically countless expressions related to taste in order to describe mostly emotional states, for example, "went sour" or "bittersweet." German commonly uses such formulations as *zum Fressen gern haben* (loving a person enough to eat him or her), *in den sauren Apfel beissen* (lit. "biting the sour apple," meaning "biting the bullet"), *Honig ums Maul schmieren* (lit. "smearing honey around someone's mouth," meaning "buttering someone up"), *süsses Nichtstun* (dolce far niente), or *bitterer Ernst* (bitter earnest). The question of shifts in meaning also comes up in several works in the exhibition *Amusebouche*: in works of art whose sugar-sweet taste suggested by the material becomes bitterly earnest with an eye to the history

                    **Annja Müller-Alsbach**

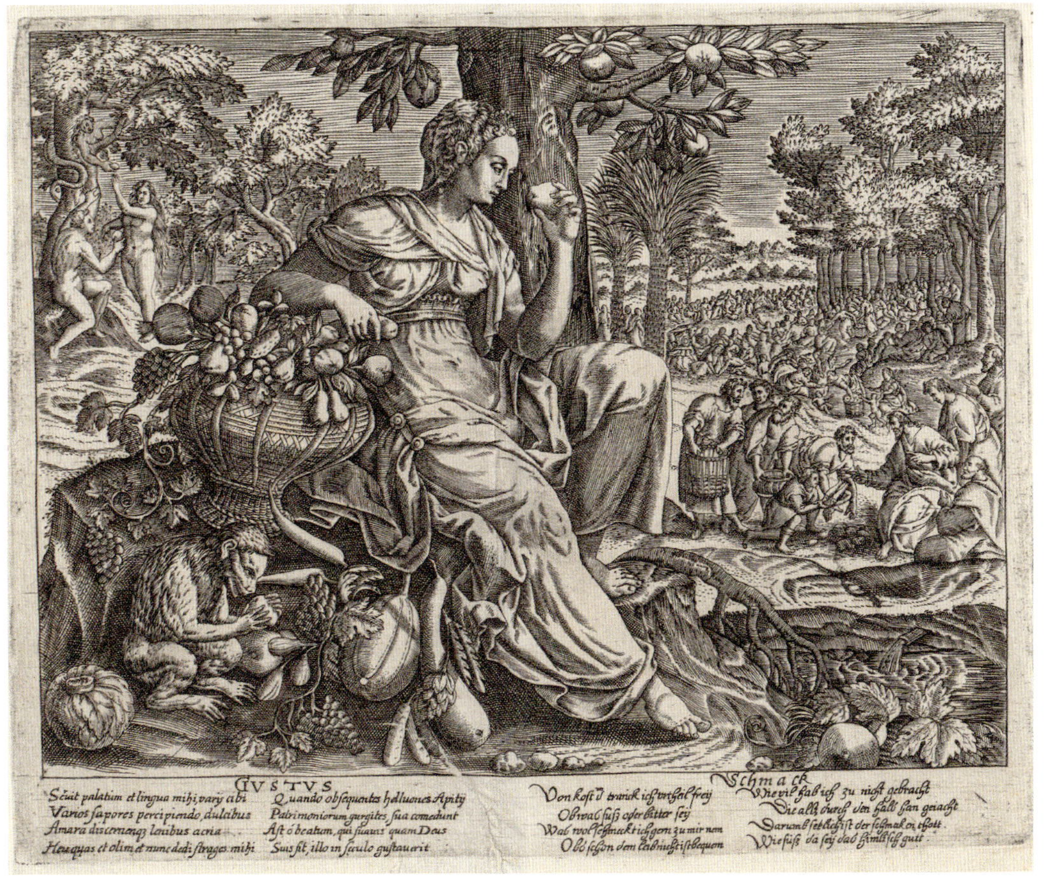


**Fig. 4** Peter Overadt
"'Gustus' or Taste", plate
from the series *The Five
Senses*, ca. 1600–50
Copperplate engraving,
25.2 × 29 cm
Graphische Sammlung,
ETH Zürich

of the work's origins. For example, the minimalist pieces by the Yugoslavian conceptual artist Mladen Stilinović, for which he employs sugar as an artistic medium. The titles of the works are correspondingly simple—a monochrome white board covered with a layer of crystalline sugar or a metal ladle filled with sugar cubes and chewing gum: *Secer* (Sugar). From the first moment, the viewer intuitively gets a feeling of seductive sweetness. But this is way off the mark. For the artist, who realized these works in the early 1990s in the middle of the war in Croatia, the white monochrome symbolizes emptiness, loss, and pain. "What is the color of pain?" Stilinović asks. "White is the color of silence, very intimate, and pain is an intimate thing."[4]

Daniel Spoerri has engaged with the illusory maneuvers of our sense of taste. The founder of Eat Art deliberately tracks down the arcane, the inverted, and the abnormal in order to play with our familiar view of things and to call it into question (see also the contribution by Felix Bröcker, p. 88). In his performative *menus travesti*, which he has already served a number of times in different ways, everything tastes different than it looks. The palate plays against the eye. His new experiment *Nur Geschmack anstatt Essen* (Tasting, Not Eating), first presented on the occasion of our symposium (see pp. 96–97), aims to perplex our senses: it is a four-course menu composed of identically colored cubes of aspic. Probably no artist of the twentieth or twenty-first century has engaged as intensely with food and the act of eating as Spoerri. As Karl Gerstner aptly wrote: "Spoerri saw eating neither as only a need, nor as only a feast of the senses. That, too, but above all as a reflex of the spirit."[5]

**Taste between Life and Death:**
**Of Milk Fat, Mold, and Bitter Poison**
Revealingly, our life outside the womb begins instinctively, not yet seeing properly, usually just feeling and smelling, absorbing vital nutrition in the form of breast milk through close physical contact (see also the contribution by Thomas Macho, p. 118). Normally, we cannot remember what it tasted like; it seems strangely foreign to us. In *Butter* (2019), the Basel-based artist Alexandra Meyer works with precisely this fatty source of energy. She processes breast milk, which she mixes with animal milk, into a roughly shaped clump of butter, which she presents on a cooling base along with a depiction of the Roman Charity and a brief video. The latter shows a close-up of the butter being scraped from the block very slowly by a special blade pulled continuously, resulting in a wavy form that is pushed out of the field of vision.

Although the title of the exhibition is *Amuse-bouche*, it does not just contain tasty, appetizing bites of art. Our sense of taste famously also serves to indicate to us insalubrious, spoiled, even poisonous and life-threatening food. This is associated with negative emotions, including disgust and even existential aspects of our life, such as decay and death. These taste experiences with negative associations are manifested, for example, by Dieter Roth's *Grosses Schimmelbild* (Large Mold Picture, 1969, **fig. 5**). Whereas in that case years have passed in which organic material has transformed into a dark, undefinable mass, the process of decay can be followed in time-lapse photography in the fascinating video *Still Life* (2001, **fig. 6**) by Sam Taylor-Johnson. The motif of a platter of fruit recalls a Baroque still life with fruit and reflects on the vanitas theme of such a *nature morte*. A clever use of time-lapse photography enables the viewer to experience in just under four minutes how a once seductive mountain of ripe and sweet fruit decomposes and collapses on itself. As they decay, the fruits increasingly dissolve into initially round, cloudy, soft-looking forms of mold. In the course of the process, fruit flies flit rapidly past the screen. The looped playback multiplies the decay, calling attention to the constantly repeating cycle of life and death. The only thing that does



Annja Müller-Alsbach

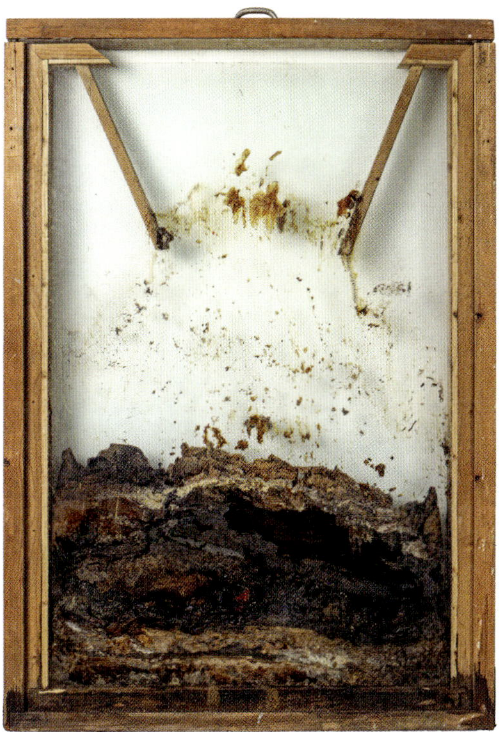

**Fig. 5** Dieter Roth
*Grosses Schimmel-bild*, 1969
Wooden frame covered with glass on both sides, layers of moldy organic materials of different colors, 121 x 82 x 8.5 cm
Kunstmuseum Basel, gift of Emil Wartmann, Basel, 1986

not change during these four minutes is the blue plastic ballpoint pen at the lower right corner.

### Of Famous Flavor Enhancers and the Unfamiliar Taste of Kola Nuts and *Sufferhead Original*

There are several unmistakable aromas that have made an unimaginable march of triumph across the whole globe, especially since the second half of the previous century until the present—despite all of their alleged negative health effects. In *Amuse-bouche*, one encounters the famous bottle of Maggi seasoning, which in the edition *Ich kenne kein Weekend* (I Know No Weekend, 1971) by Joseph Beuys forms a pair with the Reclam edition of Immanuel Kant's *Kritik der reinen Vernunft* (translated as *Critique of Pure Reason*). And looking at Andy Warhol's series of prints *Campbell's Soup II* (1969, **fig. 7**) usually evokes in us, despite the many ingredients listed on the label, the uniform aroma of meaty, bouillon-tasting monosodium glutamate.

Perhaps one of the most famous tastes in the world is "the real taste of Coca-Cola." While preparing for this exhibition, I ran across a whole series of interesting attempts to come to terms with Coca-Cola in art, for example, the critical, political action *Coca-Cola Project* (1970) by Cildo Meireles.

We are astonished when we first perceive on our tongue the bitter taste of the kola nut, which was once used to produce Coca-Cola. Compared to the taste of Coca-Cola anchored in our minds, the bitter taste seems very strange. The kola nut is also the subject of *Contained Measures of a Kolanut* (2012–ongoing) by the Nigerian artist Otobong Nkanga: a multimedia installation that is activated by her in performances with the public [**fig. 8**]. It is based on artistic, anthropological study in which Nkanga uses botanical drawings, maps, and photographs in various narrative strands to tell us the historical journey of the kola nut. This journey leads from West Africa to the remote world of the commodities of colonial states, which

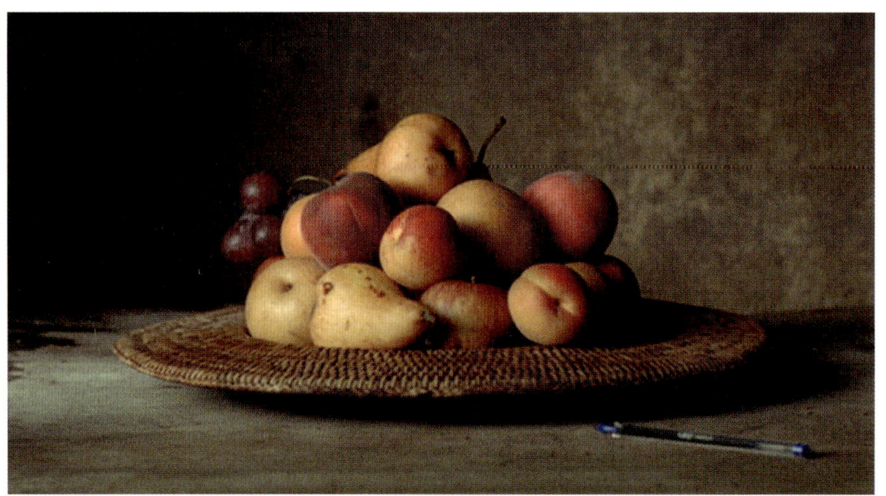

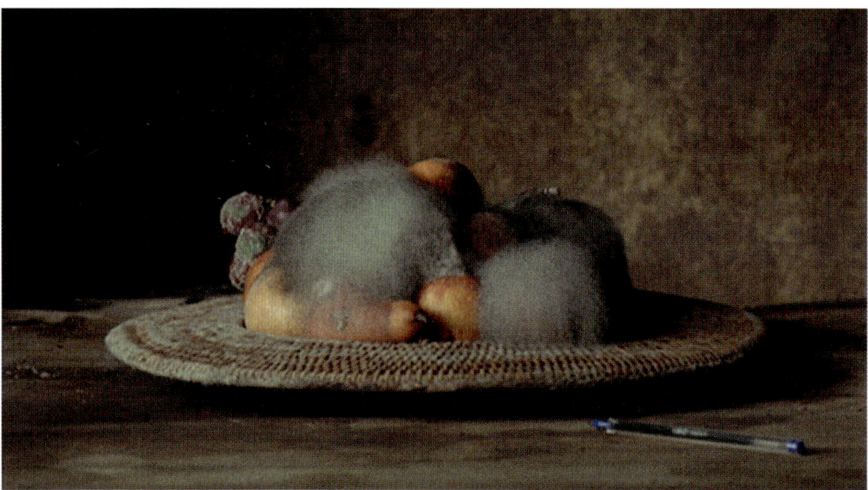

**Fig. 6** Sam Taylor-Johnson
*Still Life,* 2001
One-channel video
(color, no sound) on
monitor, 3′44″ loop
Edition 5/6
Courtesy Sammlung
Goetz, Munich

          Annja Müller-Alsbach

annexed the fruit out of purely financial and economic interests. The artist, who wears white gloves during the performance, reverently opens a fresh kola nut and begins to eat it in a concentrated way, sharing it with the person in the audience sitting opposite her. As she does so, Nkanga explains the motifs and the content of the many reproductions and maps placed on nine tables in the room. The kola nut, a natural resource full of energy with a high percentage of caffeine, antioxidants, and other substances, is explained to the audience during the performance with regard not only to its botanical quality but also to the complex role that the fruit plays in the social interactions of the Igbo.

Finally, the Berlin-based Nigerian artist Emeka Ogboh is also interested in explosive sociopolitical subjects related to the taste of the strange when he asks the question in the new Basel edition of his ongoing project *Sufferhead Original*: "Who's afraid of black?" With his stout beer brand *Sufferhead Original*, which is produced using different ingredients depending on where it is brewed and is accompanied by ads he shoots himself, Ogboh addresses the themes of immigration, moments of arrival, assimilation, transformation, and fusion of cultural identities and taste preferences.

Going through the exhibition, one encounters works of art that evoke in us memories of familiar aromas and give off completely foreign ones. According to our personal preferences, we find attractive but also aversive tastes. *Amuse-bouche* is intended to offer us an opportunity to experience our fascinating sense of taste in its sensually direct, complex, and reflective qualities. The sense of taste that remains at the end can best be described as *dulce malum* (sweet bitter)[6] and moves between the poles that determine our lives: Eros and Thanatos.

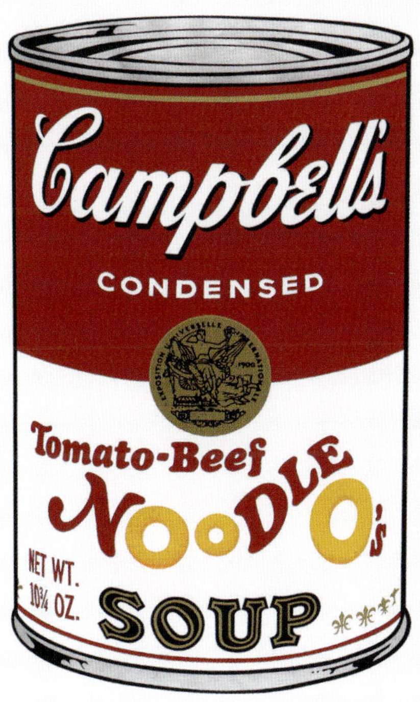

Fig. 7 Andy Warhol
*Campbell's Soup II: Tomato-Beef Noodle O's Soup,* 1969
Screenprint on paper, 81 × 47.6 cm
Staatsgalerie Stuttgart, Graphische Sammlung, acquired in 1988 with lottery funds

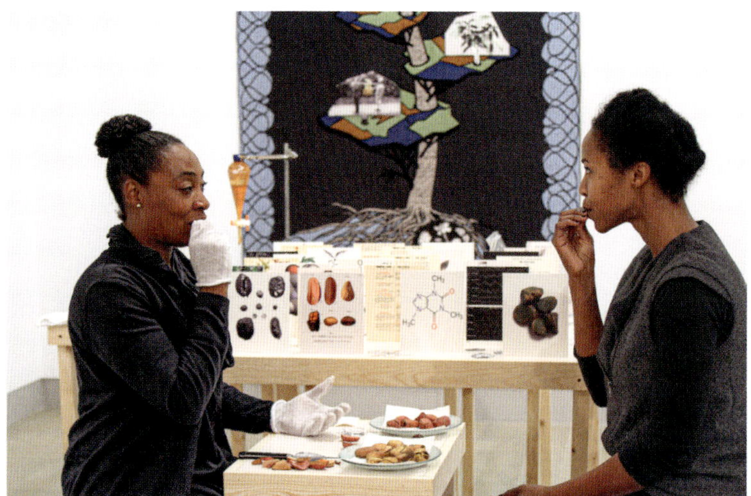

                    Annja Müller-Alsbach

**1** Of the many available publications, we mention here only a few representative ones: Harald Lemke, *Szenarien der Ernährungswende: Gastrosophische Essays zur Transformation unserer Esskultur* (Bielefeld, 2018); Harald Lemke, *Über das Essen: Philosophische Erkundungen* (Munich, 2014); Wolfger Pöhlmann, *Es geht um die Wurst: Eine deutsche Kulturgeschichte* (Munich, 2017).

**2** We mention here just a few publications accompanying these exhibitions: *Eating the Universe: Vom Essen in der Kunst*, exh. cat. Kunsthalle Düsseldorf, Galerie im Taxispalais, Innsbruck, and Kunstmuseum Stuttgart (Cologne, 2009); *Food: Produire, manger, consommer*, ed. Adelina von Fürstenberg et al., exh. cat. Musée des civilisations de l'Europe et de la Méditerranée (Milan, 2014); *Daniel Spoerri: Eat Art in Transformation*, ed. Susanne Bieri et al., exh. cat. Centro culturale Chiasso, M.A.X. museo, Chiasso (Milan, 2015); *Arts & Foods: Rituals since 1851*, ed. Germano Celant, exh. cat. Triennale di Milano (Milan, 2015); *FOOD: Ökologien des Alltags*, ed. Susanne Gaensheimer et al., exh. cat. 13. Triennale Kleinplastik Fellbach (Berlin, 2016).

**3** Victoria Tellechea-Rotta, "Artist Janine Antoni on her sweet, soapy sculptures," *The GW Hatchet*, February 12, 2015, https://www.gwhatchet.com/2015/02/12/artist janine-antoni-on-her sweet-soapy-sculptures (accessed November 16, 2019).

**4** Quoted in Branka Stipančić, "Does the World Seek a White, Total, Lasting Absence?," in *Mladen Stilinović: Nula iz vladanja / Zero for Conduct*, exh. cat. Muzej Suvremene Umjetnosti, Zagreb (Zagreb, 2012), p. 162.

**5** Karl Gerstner, "Hommage an Daniel Spoerri, der die Nahrung zum Thema der Kunst machte," quoted in *Aufgedeckt, aufgetischt: Rezepte und Konzepte der Kunst im Umgang mit Essen*, exh. cat. Kunsthaus Langenthal (Langenthal, 1995), p. 194.

**6** Very much in the sense of Ovid's topos of *dulce malum*; see P. Ovidius Naso, *Ars amatoria*, 2.9.26.

# Swallow or Spit: On the Origins of Taste Perception

Wolfgang Meyerhof

Our sense of taste ensures the supply of our body with nutrients vital to life and prevents us from ingesting substances harmful to our health. It quickly decides during the short time span we chew if we swallow a bite or spit it out. Wrong decisions could be fatal, if poisons remain unnoticed, or increase disease risk if the putative presence of poisons leads us to refuse food. This daily service is that much more astonishing when one considers that dozens, hundreds, or even more different chemical molecules can be present in the mouth when chewing [**table 1**]. The discussion that follows is intended to describe how we taste and how our brain uses the taste information to control our eating behavior.

### The Taste Apparatus

Two areas in the mouth are sensitive to taste: the tongue and the palate. There are special structures on the tongue responsible for taste: namely, the taste papillae.[1] Located on the front of the tongue are the fungiform papillae, which are easily recognizable as they stand out from the surface of the tongue. On the back of the side edges, the less visible foliate papillae can be seen as folds, and in the center of the back of the tongue we have the circumvallate papillae, which are barely visible. The taste papillae and the mucus membrane—the epithelium—of the palate contain the true taste organs: the microscopically small taste buds whose tips end in a recession of the mucus membrane called a "pore" [**fig. 1**]. Their number varies considerably in human beings, between around 4,000 and 10,000. They decline in number with age, which usually goes hand in hand with a limited sensitivity to taste.

These collections of around a hundred cells interact in the pore, with the taste compounds dissolved in the saliva.[2] In addition to immature progenitor cells, taste buds have five types of chemosensory cells [**fig. 1**], each being responsible for one of our basic tastes: sweet, sour, salty, bitter, and umami (savory, the taste of certain protein components).[3]



**Table 1:** Selected Taste Compounds

**Bitter**  Alkaloids, amides, amines, amino acids, carbamides, carbonyl bonds, crown ethers, diterpenes, glycosides, hydroxy fatty acids, L-tryptophan, lactones, mineral salts, nortriterpenes, peptides, phenols, secoiridoids, sesquiterpene lactones, urea bonds

**Salty**  Table salt (NaCl), sodium acetate, sodium bromide, monosodium glutamate, lithium salts

**Sour**  Inorganic acids such as hydrochloric, sulfuric, and phosphoric acid; organic acids such as acetic acid, benzoic acid, citric acid, lactic acid

**Sweet**  D-tryptophan, neohesperidin dihydrochalcone, peptides, mono-, di-, and oligosaccharides, mono- and diterpenes, glycine, halogenated sugars, L-alanine, lead and beryllium salts, phenols, polyols, sesquiterpenes, saponins, sulfamates, sulfonylamides, sweet proteins such as brazzein, thaumatin, monellin

**Umami**  Monosodium glutamate, alapyridaine, (S)-monelid

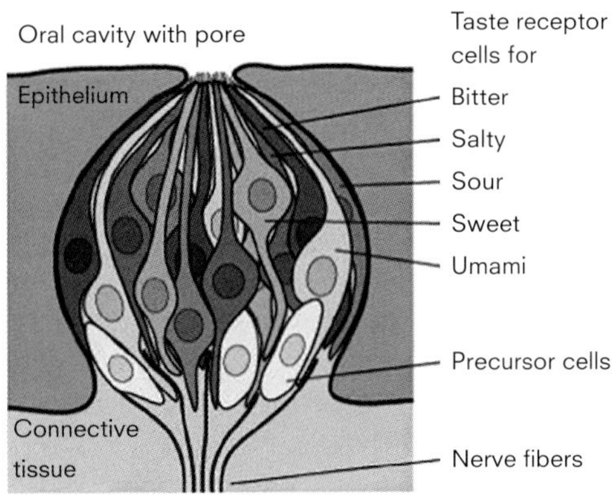


**Fig. 1** Schematic representation of a taste bud

**Table 2:** Significance and Properties of Our Basic Tastes

| Quality | Pleasure | Substance | Threshold (M) | Function |
| --- | --- | --- | --- | --- |
| **Bitter** | Aversive | Denatonium benzoate<br>Sodium saccharin<br>Quinine sulfate | 0.000000035<br>0.009<br>0.000008 | Avoiding potential toxins |
| **Salty** | Attractive at low concentrations, aversive at high ones | Sodium chloride | 0.01 | Regulation of electrolyte balance |
| **Sour** | Attractive at low concentrations, aversive at high ones | Citric acid<br>Hydrochloride | 0.0030<br>0.0037 | Acid-base homeostasis, warning of noxae from acids |
| **Sweet** | Attractive | Sodium saccharin<br>Saccharose | 0.000023<br>0.01 | Intake of calories in the form of carbohydrates |
| **Umami** | Attractive | Monosodium glutamate | 0.01 | Intake of calories in the form of protein |

     **Wolfgang Meyerhof**

Each of our basic tastes has its own significance and characteristics [**table 2**]. The five types of cells have special protein molecules on their surface known as taste receptors with which they recognize their cognate taste compounds. Substances in our mouth that do not bind to any taste receptor are tasteless. By contrast, all substances that, for instance, our sweet receptor recognizes stimulate the cell type responsible for sweet, and all of those that bind to one of our twenty-five bitter receptors stimulate the cells responsible for bitter. The five types of cells of our taste buds thus define the number of our basic tastes and explain why we can very easily distinguish tastes from one another.[4] Only when a substance binds to different types of taste receptors may categorization be difficult to achieve. That is the case, for example, with the widely used sweetener saccharin, which binds both to the sweet receptor and to two of our twenty-five bitter receptors, hence giving rise to a clearly perceptible bitter off taste.[5]

The interaction of the taste molecules with the receptors of the taste cells triggers electrical impulses through intracellular biochemical reactions.[6] These rhythmic changes of the charge of the cell membrane, known as "action potentials," contain information about the chemical nature of the stimulating taste molecule. The taste receptor cells thus perform the indispensable function of transforming information about chemical structure into biological signals [**fig. 2**]. Nerve fibers running through the taste buds take up the electric signals and the information encoded in them and transmit them to various areas of the brain. The brain integrates the taste information with other information about the food—olfactory information, for example—to make appropriate decisions about dietary intake.[7] The brain is also able to decode the encoded taste information about the chemical structure, concentration of flavor, nutritional value, and pleasure value of food molecules. Among other things, the activity of nerve cells in a specific area of the cerebral cortex reflects the basic taste sensed in the mouth. For example, sugar molecules in the mouth from eating fruit bind to the sweet receptor and stimulate our sweet cells. The stimulation of sweet cells is taken up by the nerve fibers and transmitted to the corresponding taste region of the cerebral cortex, where some of the nerve cells cause the sensory impression "sweet." If we drink tonic water, by contrast, the quinine dissolved in it binds to oral bitter receptors and stimulates the bitter cells. This stimulation is processed analogously to the description above resulting eventually in the sensory impression "bitter." In vitro and in animal experiments, this has been studied in detail, but the regions of the brain that process taste information can also be shown in human subjects using modern clinical imaging systems.[8]

### Innate Taste Preferences and Aversions

Observations of the so-called gustofacial reflex reveal that newborns already have the ability to taste.[9] In these tests, taste solutions are dipped on the baby's lips, and the baby is observed to see how his or her face reacts. When sweet solutions are applied, the babies' faces show clear signs of pleasure and attraction. By contrast, if bitter solutions are applied, their faces show clear signs of discomfort and rejection. Their reactions to other basic tastes are more difficult to interpret, since their facial expressions are less clear. It must be assumed, however, that newborns are also able to perceive the other three basic tastes. All mammals that have been studied reacted with analogous behavior to "sweet" and "bitter." These observations demonstrate two things: first, the ability to taste is innate; second, taste is inseparably connected to the level of enjoyment of a taste molecule or food. Thus, the brain links the processing of taste information with attracting and avoiding behaviors. The higher-order brain activities involved in cognition are not required for these. Even babies with hydrocephalus—abnormal damage of the frontal part of the brain—are able to demonstrate the gustofacial reflexes.[10] Physicians have also reported on the case of a patient with abnormalities in the frontal brain who was unable to identify the basic tastes but still had a distinct preference for "sweet."[11] As the term "gustofacial reflex" indicates, it is a reflex-like behavior controlled by the brain stem. This region of the brain, which is phylogenetically very old, controls the vital bodily functions such as breathing and heartbeat. This demonstrates the great biological value that innate taste preferences and aversions have. They ensure appropriate nutrition even in primitive animals that are not capable of higher-order cognitive brain functions or in young animals and babies that have not yet learned to consume appropriate food.

### Hereditary Fructose Intolerance

The innate preference for "sweet" is extremely strong and can be observed in humans from all ethnic groups. For babies in particular, sugar has a calming, even consoling and analgesic effect, and it helps people with addictions overcome their withdrawal symptoms. This is because sugar activates the reward system of the brain strongly, even compared to other components of food with great pleasure value, causing a comparatively robust release of the pleasure hormone dopamine. Nevertheless, even such strong preferences for food are by no means completely rigid and can turn into their opposite.

This is common, for example, in the case of hereditary fructose intolerance. In this genetic anomaly, the fructose ingested with food is incompletely metabolized. A metabolic by-product accumulates and inhibits the metabolism of glucose. Those affected suffer from extreme hypoglycemia and present with vomiting, diarrhea, dizziness, and lethargy. This sickness can be life-threatening if not diagnosed. Patients usually attract attention after weaning from breastfeeding, because breast milk contains no fructose. The young patients first ingest fructose with solid food, and the symptoms of the illness soon appear. Many of those affected develop a clear, biologically sensible aversion to everything sweet, which strictly limits their consumption of fructose and protects them from the serious consequences of the illness. The innate preference for sweet thus transforms into an acquired aversion.

### Learned Food Preferences and Aversions

Observation of fructose intolerance thus leads to the fundamental insight that innate taste preferences are not immutable but can

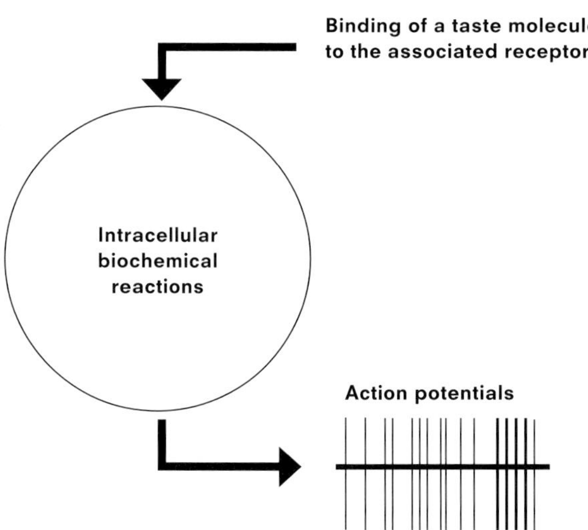


**Fig. 2** Principal function of a taste receptor cell

　　　　Wolfgang Meyerhof

change. Furthermore, it appears that the organism learns to connect physical experiences with earlier taste impressions.[12] In the case described above, a connection is rightly made between the taste impression "sweet" and the discomfort that follows it. Such discomfort can certainly be seen as "punishment," which we want to avoid as much as possible. We eat nothing sweet so we are not exposed to any discomfort. The formation of food preferences and aversions is thus also based on the classical learning principle of "punishment" and "reward." The organism associates the taste impression of a foodstuff with the physical consequences of eating it and stores this in so-called taste-recognition memory.[13] Upon renewed contact, the brain "remembers" the taste and its consequences, and the food is now quickly and effectively rejected or accepted. It is understandable that extreme discomfort leads to rejection more quickly and lastingly than mild unpleasantness does—with the whole spectrum in between. Not only digestive problems play a role in acquiring aversions to food—in principle all "punishments" work in this context. The threat "If you don't eat your soup, you can't play on the computer for a week" will therefore usually lead to the opposite of what is intended. Associating soup with punishment puts it on the list of disliked dishes.

But the opposite principle becomes equally clear. Rewards lead to a preference for consuming a food. The reward "If you eat your soup, you can play on the computer for an extra hour" leads to the soup being eaten and becoming part of the menu. Normally, the calories contained in food can be seen as a reward, since they eliminate the feeling of hunger and give us a satisfying feeling of satiety. When we become full without any discomfort, then we like to eat the food in question. Examples of other "rewards" include the stimulating effect of caffeine, which causes us to overcome our innate aversion to bitter things. The case of alcohol is similar, with its initially beneficial effects causing us to enjoy drinking bitter beer.

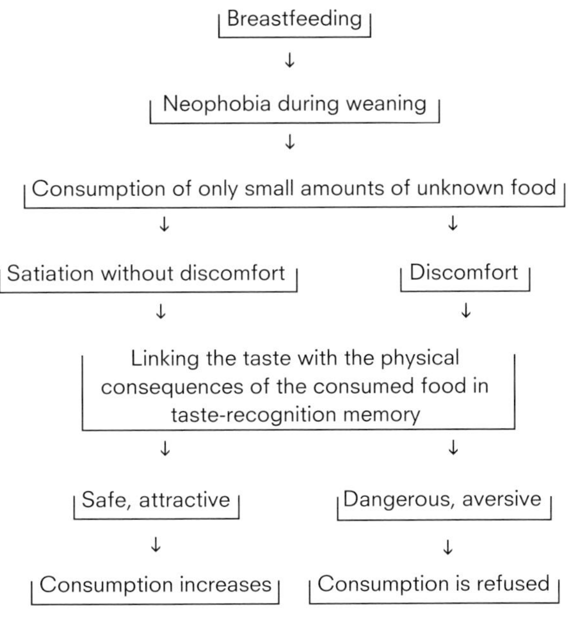


**Fig. 3** Development of taste preferences and aversions

These two principles—reward and punishment—determine what we do and do not eat [**fig. 4**]. Naturally, they become important with weaning since from that point on small children and young animals are neophobic, that is to say, averse to everything new.[14] Because they have no experience with solid food, however, this neophobia protects them from the possibly fatal ingestion of large quantities of food that could be poisonous. Small children and young animals protect themselves from food poisoning by first eating only tiny quantities of unfamiliar food. Tiny quantities of poison may not be fatal, but they do lead to digestive or other discomfort. If what they eat fills them up, without causing any discomfort, then they will consume more such food in the future. Conversely, they stop eating food that has caused discomfort. In this way, step by step, we condition ourselves to certain ways of eating, including both favorite foods and dishes we simply do not like. The critical times for this condition are in childhood, but it occurs throughout all of our lives.

In observing the formation of food aversions and preferences, we have considered only the sense of taste, with its few basic tastes. The complex impression of taste that we perceive when we have food in our mouths, however, can also be linked to other sensory impressions. The sense of smell is, of course, one of them. Whenever we eat, but especially when swallowing, volatile substances travel from the mouth to the nose. So we also smell what is in our mouths. Moreover, temperature (warm, cold) and composition (crispy, soft, mushy, tough) of food and the chemical stimulants they contain (pungency from pepper or mustard) play important roles, for which the somatosensory nerve system is responsible. These two sensory impressions together with the impressions of taste produce a complex mouth feel that we sense when eating and which is characteristic of different dishes and foods. Although the sensory cells, the involved nerves, and the associated regions of the brain differ for all of these senses, the basic principles of their function described above are the same. This article is too short to consider these differences, but that does not make them any less important, and they deserve separate consideration.

**1** See Inglis J. Miller, "Anatomy of the Peripheral Taste System," in *Handbook of Olfaction and Gustation*, ed. Richard L. Doty (New York, 1995), pp. 521–47.
**2** See Bernd Lindemann, "Taste Reception," *Physiological Reviews* 76, no. 3 (1996), pp. 718–66.
**3** See ibid.
**4** See Jayaram Chandrashekar et al., "The Receptors and Cells for Mammalian Taste," *Nature* 444, no. 7117 (2006), pp. 288–94.
**5** See Christina Kuhn et al., "Bitter Taste Receptors for Saccharin and Acesulfame K," *Journal of Neuroscience* 24, no. 45 (2004), pp. 10260–65.
**6** See Nirupa Chaudhari and Stephen D. Roper, "The Cell Biology of Taste," *Journal of Cell Biology* 190, no. 3 (2010), pp. 285–96.
**7** See Edmund T. Rolls, "Smell, Taste, Texture, and Temperature: Multimodal Representations in the Brain, and Their Relevance to the Control of Appetite," *Nutrition Reviews* 62, no. 3 (2004), pp. 193–204; Dana M. Small, "Central Gustatory Processing in Humans," *Advances in Oto-Rhino-Laryngology* 63 (2006), pp. 191–220.
**8** See Rolls 2004 (see note 7); Small 2006 (see note 7).
**9** See Jacob E. Steiner, "The Gustofacial Response: Observation on Normal and Anencephalic Newborn Infants," *Symposium on Oral Sensation and Perception* 4 (1973), pp. 254–78.
**10** See ibid.
**11** See Ralph Adolphs et al., "Preferring One Taste over Another without Recognizing Either," *Nature Neuroscience* 8, no. 7 (2005), pp. 860–61.
**12** See Sandra Hübner, Jonas Töle, and Wolfgang Meyerhof, "Taste and Nutrition, Part 3," *Ernaehrungs Umschau international* 60, no. 12 (2013), pp. 222–27; Anthony Sclafani, "How Food Preferences Are Learned: Laboratory Animal Models," *Proceedings of Nutrition Society* 54, no. 2 (1995), pp. 419–27.
**13** See Federico Bermúdez-Rattoni, "Molecular Mechanisms of Taste-Recognition Memory," *Nature Reviews Neuroscience* 5, no. 3 (2004), pp. 209–17.
**14** See Gary K. Beauchamp and Julie A. Mennella, "Early Flavor Learning and Its Impact on Later Feeding Behavior," *Journal of Pediatric Gastroenterology and Nutrition* 48, suppl. 1 (2009), pp. 25–30; Leann L. Birch, "Development of Food Preferences," *Annual Review of Nutrition* 19 (1999), pp. 41–62.

# Black, White, and Clear: On the Semantic and Symbolic Meanings Associated with the Absence of Color in Food

Charles Spence

It has long been suggested that we eat first with our eyes.[1] Indeed, of all the visual cues that are available, it is the color of food and its packaging that seem to capture our attention first, and hence drive a majority of our food choices.[2] The research shows that we all tend to associate colors with basic tastes,[3] with aromas/flavors,[4] and even with piquancy.[5]

Although marketers have long argued that the meaning of color may, in some cases at least, be culture-dependent,[6] when it comes to matters of taste, there would appear to be consensus as far as the taste expectations associated with specific colors are concerned. For instance, the majority of the more than 5,000 people from every continent whom we tested at the Science Museum in London a few years ago chose the same pinkish-red colored drink as the sweetest-looking of six beverages.[7] Furthermore, when asked more abstractly about the tastes that they associated with different colors, the majority of people associated pink and red with sweetness, yellow and green with sour, white with salty, and browny-black with bitter-tasting foods [**see fig. 1**].[8] When probed as to *why* they chose a particular color for a given taste, people often report picking the colors of those foods that they happen to associate with that taste, that is, they base their decision on their prior experience.[9]

While colors are typically taken to signify something about the taste (or, better said, the flavor) of food and drink, unusual food colors (e.g., blue) have sometimes been introduced in order to capture people's attention, and/or to discombobulate diners instead.[10] As far as clear and white products are concerned, they tend to be associated with purity. However, when it comes to foods, these colors tend not to be associated with especially positive taste expectations.[11] Below, I take a closer look at some of the ways in which artists (or perhaps better said, artistic types), chefs, and thereafter marketers have explored the symbolic meaning of color, or rather its absence (as in the case of black, white, and clear food and drink).

### Artists

In the context of food, black is associated with bitterness, while, more generally, with mourning. It should perhaps come as no surprise, therefore, to find Jean Des Esseintes, the fictional character in Huysmans's novel *À rebours* (translated as *Against Nature*, 1884), taking the latter association to extreme lengths, serving an entirely black meal on a black tablecloth in a dining room draped in black fabric, while listening to a hidden orchestra playing funeral marches. Notice how the visual appearance, in this case, has a primarily symbolic meaning.

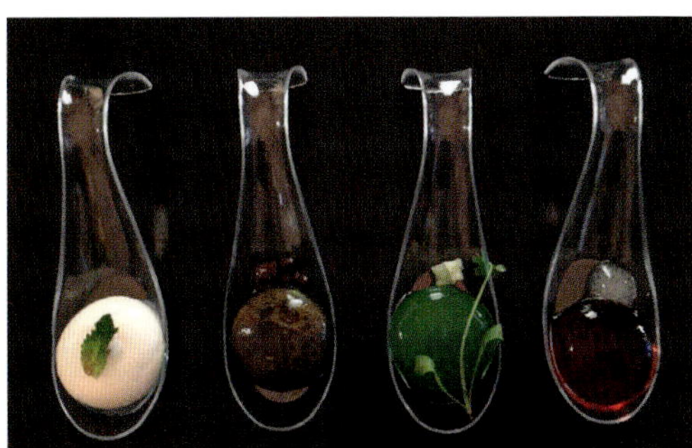

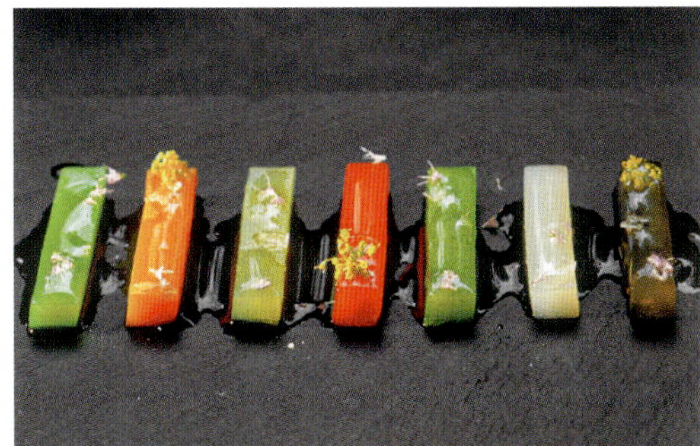

**Fig. 1** a) *The Four Tastes*, amuse-bouche, as served by chef Jozef Youssef of Kitchen Theory. In the restaurant, the spoons were randomly placed down in front of diners, who were asked to arrange them in order, salty on the left, then bitter, sour, and sweet on the right, before eating them.

The chef, in other words, is here explicitly playing with his guests' color-based expectations.

b) The vegetable strips with charcoal oil dish served at elBulli, ca. 2001. The clear charcoal oil is, I think, an intriguing addition to the dish.

"Dining off black-bordered plates, the company had enjoyed turtle soup, Russian rye bread, ripe olives from Turkey, caviar, mullet botargo, black puddings from Frankfurt, game served in sauces the colour of licorice and boot-polish, truffle jellies, chocolate creams, plum puddings, nectarines, pears in grapefruit syrup, mulberries, and black-heart cherries. From dark-tinted glasses they had drunk the wines of Limagne and Roussillon, of Tenedos, Valdepeñas, and Oporto. And after coffee and walnut cordial, they had rounded off the evening with kvass, porter, and stout."[12]

This fictional all-black funeral meal is certainly a long way from the all-white foods once enjoyed by French composer Erik Satie. He once said that: "I eat only white foodstuffs: eggs, sugar, scraped bones; fat from dead animals; veal, salt coconuts, chicken cooked in white water; mouldy fruit, rice, turnips; camphorated sausages, things like spaghetti, cheese (white), cotton salad and certain fish (minus their skins)."[13] The famous French designer Yves Saint Laurent also had a fondness for white foods,[14] as did the Hollywood movie producer Leland Hayward, the latter apparently never eating anything that was not white.[15] Hayward's diet would include scrambled eggs, custard, vanilla ice cream, and chicken hash (though, not all at the same time, one hopes). Meanwhile, in his later years, the Swiss sculptor Alberto Giacometti would only eat boiled eggs (again white), just before midnight. Here, it is interesting to consider why it is that so many of those artists who have chosen to restrict themselves to eating foods of just a single color have gone for white. I, for one, am not aware of anyone who has restricted themselves solely to eating blue foods, say, or just to orange dishes. One of key reasons for choosing white, presumably, is its more symbolic association with purity.[16] Of course, for the vain, white foods also have the advantage that they are less likely to stain one's teeth (or, for that matter, the white carpet). Intriguingly, Marisa Benjamim, one of the speakers at the *Amuse-bouche* symposium at Museum Tinguely in Basel, suggested that the only color that diners simply would not eat was black. Black, she suggested, somehow just seemed to engender a qualitatively different response in her guests than did any other color when she cycled through a series of meals made up entirely of just one color. And for those, Like Benjamim's guests who do not like the idea of a black meal, food artist Marije Vogelzang[17] has subverted the funereal association with black in one of her works. In her *White funeral* dish, she serves a meal made up entirely of white foods [see fig. 2a].

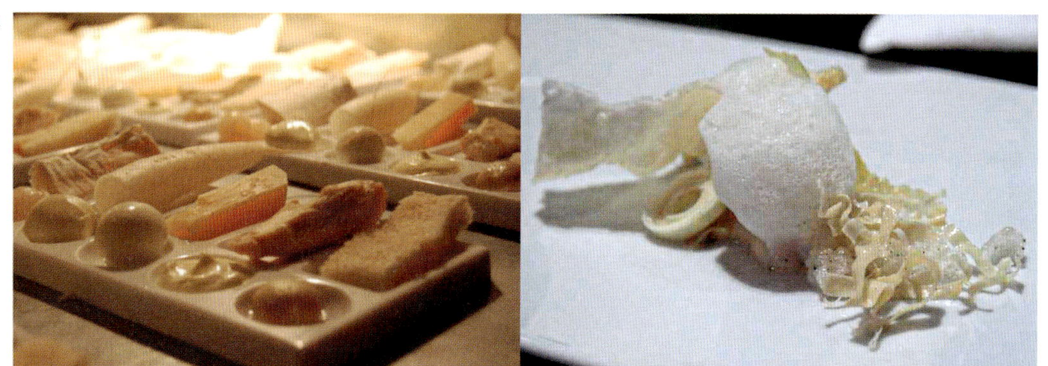

A B

Fig. 2 a) Detail of one of Marije Vogelzang's *White funeral* meals.

b) *Halibut. Black pepper, coffee, lemon* served by Grant Achatz in his restaurant Alinea.

Note that all of the black food elements are presented in white form.

     Charles Spence

Meanwhile, in 2014, an experimental art company based in Birmingham, England, explored the link between synaesthesia, art, and creativity in a unique dining event. Siân Tonkin and Kaye Winwood were the artists behind the *Scintillating Synaesthetic Supper*, an immersive multisensory experience: "If you've ever wondered what the colour white might taste like, the Synaesthetic Supper's coconut meringue, parsnip panna cotta purée, cauliflower crisps and almond milk may have held the answer. And what other colour could be evoked by Oreo crumbs, coffee mousse, cherry gel, rose petals and strong Vietnamese coffee than black? … The five-course supper aimed to demonstrate what it might be like to hear and taste colour in the context of experimental cinema."[18]

### Chefs

A number of famous chefs have made a point of deliberately serving dishes that are either all white or else all black. Think here only of Jordi Roca's white chocolate sorbet that while looking bland certainly packs an intense flavor punch. Meanwhile, a few years ago, Michelin-starred North American chef Grant Achatz served a dish called *Halibut. Black pepper, coffee, lemon* in a white monochromatic presentation [**see fig. 2b**]. The most surprising aspect of the dish is that the majority of the elements are naturally black (coffee, black pepper, black licorice, vanilla) but are served in a white form. The British chef Heston Blumenthal also attempted to develop a white-on-white dish, though it never made it to the table.[19] A conceptually similar dish, and at the same time also a classic of the fine dining repertoire, *White Tomato (soup, sauce, and foam)* is based on a simple but convincing technique, namely, pureed tomatoes sieved through linen.[20]

While white is often associated with a salty taste,[21] this connection may easily be subverted by the form in which a food appears [**see fig. 3**]. However, whatever the expectation people have when looking at white foods, there is apparently a sense in which the plain appearance does not commit them to a particular taste/flavor in quite the same way that colored foods do. In other words, the spectrum of white, like black, can be taken literally in terms of the taste expectations that are associated with it, or else, more symbolically, in a way that the real colors (strictly defined) cannot so easily do. In the latter case, any mismatch that is detected between the expected taste/flavor (based on color) and the actual perceived taste/flavor is likely to be treated as incongruous by the diner. That is, it is less likely that the incongruence will be read as a cue to search for a different meaning in the visual appearance of the food itself, perhaps shifting from the semantic to a more symbolic level of meaning.[22]

Of course, sometimes when food and drink appear to lack any color, it may simply be because we are looking at a black-and-white image. Should that be the case, then there is often a temptation to try and infer the absent colors/flavors of the foods that we can see.[23] Such inferences are, however, not always possible. Just take the unfortunate individual described by the famous writer and neurologist Oliver Sacks in his book *An Anthropologist on Mars* (1995). In this case, the painter in question, Jonathan I., had suddenly lost the ability to see color following brain damage and, as a result, was driven to eat only black and white foods since everything else looked unappealing. Take the following quote to get an idea of what it was like:

"The 'wrongness' of everything was disturbing, even disgusting, and applied to every circumstance of daily life. He found foods disgusting due to their greyish, dead appearance and had to close his eyes to eat. But this did not help very much, for the mental image of a tomato was as black as its appearance. Thus, unable to rectify even the inner image, the idea, of various foods, he turned increasingly to black and white foods—to black olives and white rice, black coffee and yoghurt. These at least appeared relatively normal, whereas most foods,

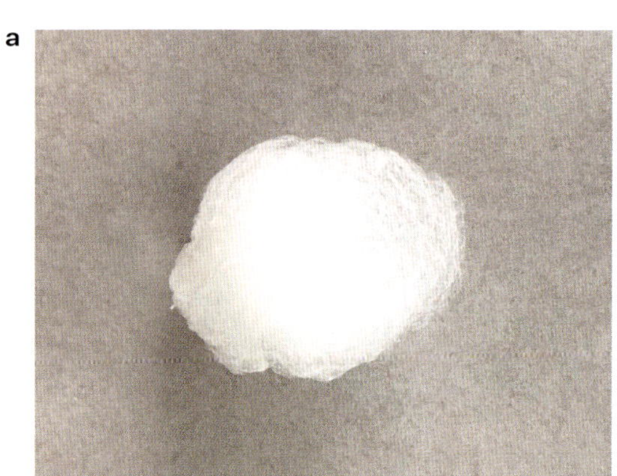

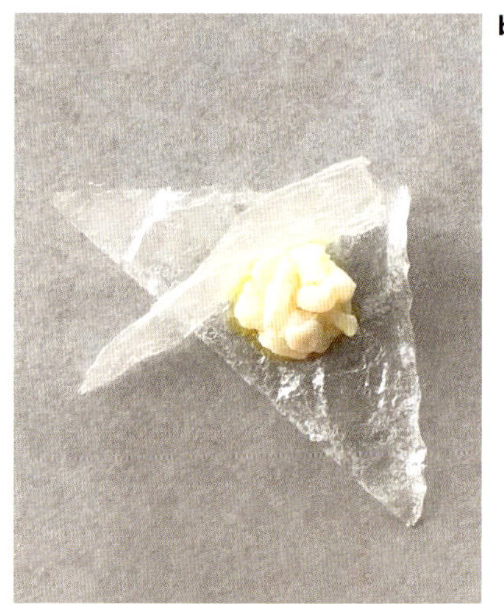

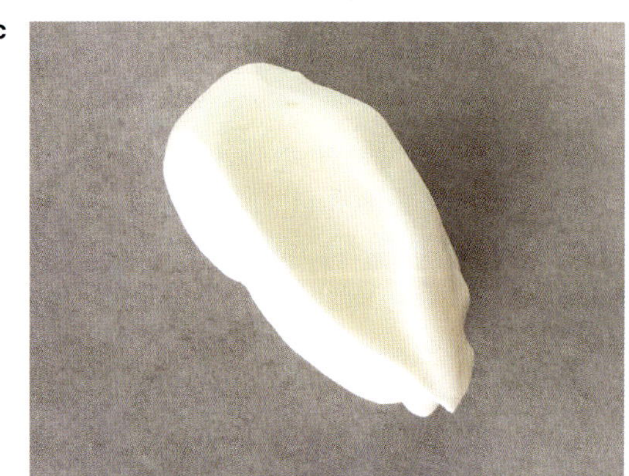

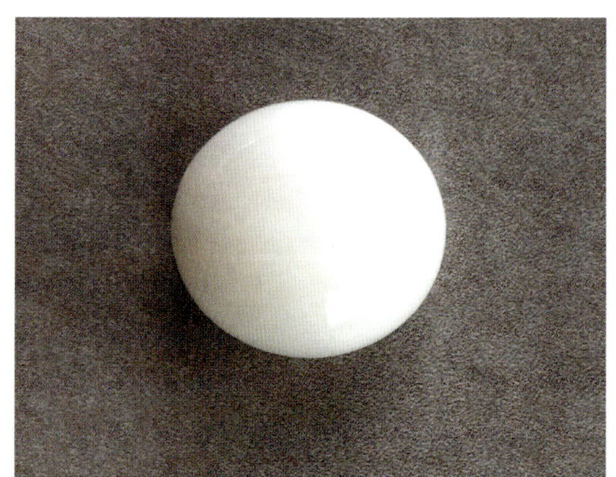

**Fig. 3** Close-up shots of each of the elements in the *Study in White* amuse-bouche dish served by chef Jozef Youssef, from Kitchen Theory, to diners at the Andaz Hotel in London. a) Sweet; b) Sour; c) Bitter; and d) Salty. These forms were also shown to participants in an online study. Intriguingly, while white is normally associated with salty, the candy floss shown in panel a) elicits strong associations with sweetness, thus suggesting that form can override color when people interpret a dish.

                    **Charles Spence**

normally coloured, now appeared horribly abnormal."[24]

At this point, one might also consider the blackness of the food experience associated with the popular dine-in-the-dark restaurant concept. In total darkness, the food (in some sense at least) appears black, and yet we know that it would look different were the lights to be turned on. It is, though, hard to find anyone who believes that the food tastes especially good.[25] Given that we really do eat first with our eyes,[26] I would argue that dining-in-the-dark is more about the total experience, and not the flavor of the food itself.

I was recently lucky enough to dine at Jordan Kahn's Vespertine in LA.[27] Many of the dishes on the tasting menu were served from a range of black, lavastone-esque, artist-designed plateware.[28] Hence, when I was presented with the dish that is shown in figure 4, as was typical of many of the dishes, without any name or explanation,[29] I really had no idea of what to expect. In this case, it appeared as if a familiar food, namely, white merengue, had been made unrecognizable by the addition of what I presume was squid ink. Blitzing in a blender had then eliminated any meaningful form or texture cues.[30] As such, one was left looking at an ethereal, glistening, gritty, black surface that appeared visually as much like a loudspeaker cover as anything else. At the same time, it was both visually captivating and also intimidating. It was, in a very real sense, a blank canvas, at least as far as my flavor expectations were concerned. And, hidden underneath that intimidating and unreadable glistening black surface, hirame (a white fish) and teff (the latter, a tiny ancient grain, apparently packed with nutrition).

Chef Jozef Youssef of Kitchen Theory in London[31] currently serves a dramatic dish called *Scriptura Vitae* consisting of a jet-black squid ink risotto on a white surface. A video, documenting the work of the award-winning designer and calligrapher Aerosyn-Lex Mestrovic, is projected over the tabletop and food.[32] Once again, the visual impres-

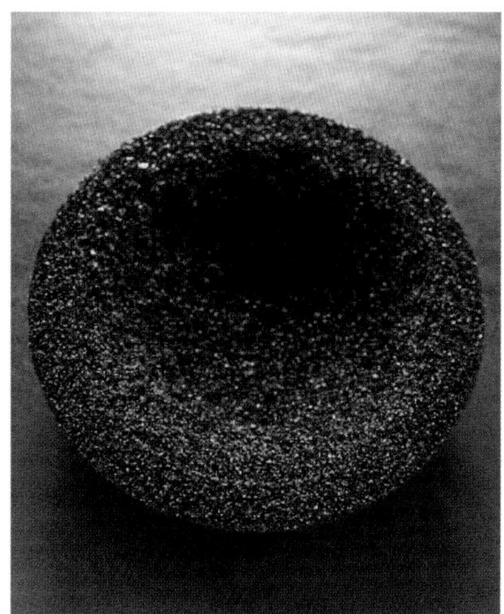

**Fig. 4** One of the most dramatic dishes served recently at Jordan Kahn's Vespertine restaurant in Culver City, Los Angeles. Just what flavor would you expect this dish to have? The dish contains hirame, teff, and burnt onion.

sion is most definitely striking. In this case, though, it is the blackness of the diesel oil swirling hypnotically across the table (the work in question is titled *Diesel oil and ink*) as one eats that makes the jet-black risotto just that little bit harder to swallow. "What exactly am I putting in my mouth?"—this is the thought that likely goes through many a diner's mind. In this case, though, the name of the dish is provided to the diner in advance.

Intriguingly, at the start of the Gastrophysics Chef's Table that is running currently, Youssef serves a black tomato jelly square to diners to illustrate how difficult it is to recognize familiar flavors when the commonly associated color cues are removed. Kahn and Youssef, then, are modernist chefs linked by their fascination for the meanings/associations with black, and with their attempts to subvert the normal color-taste associations/expectations that their diners have.

**Marketing**

Given black's negative association (i.e., with mourning), one might not have expected it to be popular amongst consumers. Certainly, according to John Wheatley, it was a brave move for Alpen, the muesli brand, to go for primarily black packaging (despite the fact that it would stand out from the competition).[33] At the same time, however, black is also associated with exclusivity/premium too.[34] This association between black and premiumness is captured in Peter Greenaway's film *The Cook, the Thief, His Wife and Her Lover*, when the cook, on being asked about the menu pricing at Le Hollandais restaurant, responds: "I charge a lot for anything black. Grapes, olives, blackcurrants … Black truffles are the most expensive. And caviar … Don't you think it's appropriate that the most expensive items are black?"[35]

In terms of the growing popularity of black foods in recent years, first came black garlic (see note 39). Then there was the black squid-ink burger colored with charcoal.[36] Morgenstern's offered a black ice cream, and the Little Damage parlor in Los Angeles apparently created quite a sensation with their charcoal-black ice cream served in a black cone.[37] Meanwhile, a few years ago, Jozef Youssef and I served the passengers on Monarch Airlines flights with a jet-black echinacea and licorice ice cream [see fig. 5]. The idea was to surprise the passengers at the start of their holiday. The ice cream was served as part of an experimental lunchbox delivered to a select group of passengers as part of a promotion around the reimagining of what airline food might be.[38]

"'People do baulk at the colour, but black food is more familiar now thanks to truffles and the popularity of olives … In most cases, we've found the novelty of its look persuades people to try it. Though, intriguingly, because we tend to taste with our eyes, some claim at first they think it tastes like liquorice—which it doesn't.' Using colour to subvert consumers' expectations has proven a successful tactic for many. Rachel's Organic, for example, used black packaging to create associations with premium qualities—an unprecedented step in the dairy sector, where products tend to be yellow or cream."[39]

In recent years, consumers have started to associate black with activated charcoal, which, in turn, is associated with notions of purifying/good/virtuous.[40] That said, as far as I am aware, the actual health claims are largely unsupported. Coco Pops, the popular breakfast cereal, too, has recently come out with a white chocolate version. Customers, at least according to some press headlines, have been overjoyed by this simple transformation from darkness (of chocolate-tainted brown milk) to a bowl of pure white cereal with milk.[41]

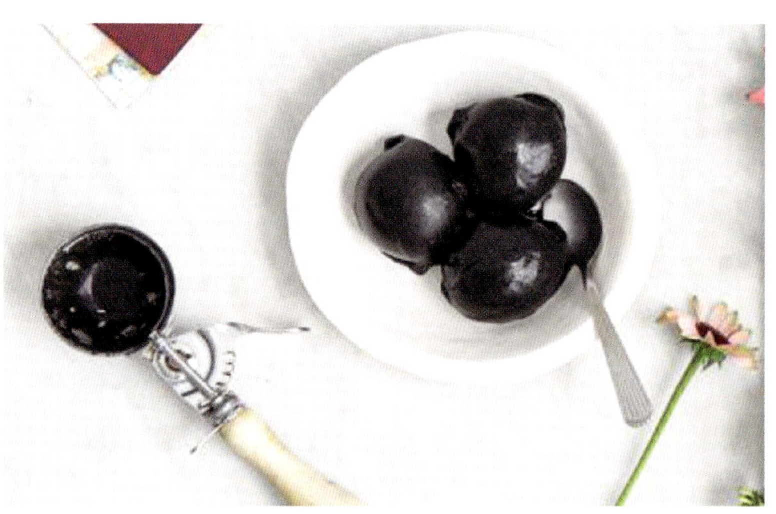

**Fig. 5** The jet-black echinacea and licorice ice cream, created by Jozef Youssef as part of a test lunchbox, was served to passengers on a special reimagining of the food menu for Monarch Airlines.

### Amuse-bouche

At the *Amuse-bouche* symposium held at Museum Tinguely in Basel, the attendees were served a four-course tasting menu consisting of a series of flavored opaque black pyramids designed by Daniel Spoerri. Perhaps unsurprisingly, given the importance of color to setting our flavor expectations, most people struggled to identify from memory the largely familiar flavors that they were, in fact, tasting—including tomato, peppers, potato, chocolate, and orange. The task in this case had deliberately been made all the more difficult because of the absence of any texture or shape cues. Contextualizing this performance/tasting event requires one to consider the long history of interest in the visual appearance of food, amongst artists, chefs, and, more recently, marketers.

In conclusion, color is unquestionably fundamental to many of the decisions we make, and perhaps nowhere more so than in the world of food and drink. That said, there appears to be special symbolic meaning attached to the absence of color, be it in the case of white and clear foods (linked to purity) or in the case of black foods again positively linked to purity/goodness (through a recent association with activated charcoal), but also to mourning and to premiumness.[42] Ultimately, therefore, while black, white, and clear are not, technically speaking, colors, they are nevertheless rich in meaning, both semantic and symbolic. No wonder, then, that such colorless foods have intrigued artists, chefs, and, increasingly, the marketers. Which of the various associations with visual appearance of colorless foods one might trigger in any given situation is presumably largely dependent on context.[43] At the same, time, however, the challenge for some is to access one meaning without the other, possibly unwanted, associations also being primed. The ubiquitous use of black in Kahn's Vespertine restaurant (associated as it is both with premiumness and with mourning) is presumably responsible for headings like the following: "Edible Doom and Gloom: L.A.'s Most Expensive New Restaurant Wants to Depress You for Dinner."[44]

**1** Charles Spence, Katsunori Okajima, Adrian David Cheok, Olivia Petit, and Charles Michel, "Eating with Our Eyes: From Visual Hunger to Digital Satiation," *Brain & Cognition* 110 (2016), pp. 53–63.

**2** Carlos Velasco and Charles Spence, eds., *Multisensory Packaging: Designing New Product Experiences* (Cham, 2019).

**3** For a review, see Charles Spence, Xiaoang Wan, Andy Woods, Carlos Velasco, Jialin Deng, Jozef Youssef, and Ophelia Deroy, "On Tasty Colours and Colourful Tastes? Assessing, Explaining, and Utilizing Crossmodal Correspondences between Colours and Basic Tastes," *Flavour* 4, no. 23 (2015), p. 23.

**4** For instance Charles Spence, "On the Relationship(s) between Colour and Taste," *Experimental Psychology* 66 (2019), pp. 99–111.

**5** Devin Z. Shermer and Carmel A. Levitan, "Red Hot: The Crossmodal Effect of Color Intensity on Piquancy," *Multisensory Research* 27 (2014), pp. 207–23; Charles Spence, "Crossmodal Contributions to the Perception of Piquancy/Spiciness," *Journal of Sensory Studies* 34, no. 1 (2018).

**6** For instance John Wheatley, "Putting Colour into Marketing," *Marketing* 10 (1973), pp. 24–29 and 67.

**7** Carlos Velasco, Charles Michel, Jozef Youssef, Xavier Gamez, Adrian David Cheok, and Charles Spence, "Colour-Taste Correspondences: Designing Food Experiences to Meet Expectations or to Surprise," *International Journal of Food Design* 1 (2016), pp. 83–102.

**8** For a review, see Spence et al. 2015 (see note 3).

**9** See Supreet Saluja and Richard J. Stevenson, "Cross-Modal Associations between Real Tastes and Colors," *Chemical Senses* 43, no. 7 (2018), pp. 475–80; Spence 2019 (see note 4).

**10** For a review, see Charles Spence, "What Is So Unappealing about Blue Food and Drink?," *International Journal of Gastronomy & Food Science* 14 (2018), pp. 1–8.

**11** See Gardiner Harris, "Colorless Food? We Blanch," *The New York Times*, April 2, 2011, p. 3, https://www.nytimes.com/2011/04/03/weekinreview/03harris.html (all URLs accessed in July 2019); Charles Spence, "What Exactly Do Consumers See in Clear Drinks?," *LS:N Global,* July 17, 2018, pp. 1–2.

**12** Joris-Karl Huysmans, *À rebours* (1884; repr., Paris, 1926), p. 13.

**13** As quoted in Robert Orledge, *Satie Remembered* (London, 1995).

**14** Bunny Crumpacker, *The Sex Life of Food: When Body and Soul Meet to Eat* (New York, 2006), p. 113.

**15** See Brooke Hayward, *Haywire* (1977; repr., New York, 2011), pp. 28–29.

**16** Orledge 1995 (see note 13); Oliver Strunk, *Source Readings in Music History* (London, 1998).

**17** http://www.marije vogelzang.nl; Marije Vogelzang, *TEDxMunich—Marije Vogelzang—Food Love* (2010), http://www.youtube.com/watch?v=1WZv459bOCQ.

**18** James Brennan, "What's the taste of colours? Food and synaesthesia," *Fine Dining Lovers*, June 3, 2014, https://www.finedininglovers.com/stories/synaesthesia-food-event/.

**19** See Charles Spence and Betina Piqueras-Fizman, *The Perfect Meal: The Multisensory Science of Food and Dining* (Oxford, 2014).

**20** See Sam Linsell, "White Tomato Essence Soup," *Drizzle & Dip*, May 28, 2012, https://drizzleanddip.com/2012/05/28/

white-tomato-essence-soup/.

**21** See Spence et al. 2015 (see note 3).

**22** See Betina Piqueras-Fiszman and Charles Spence, "Sensory Incongruity in the Food and Beverage Sector: Art, Science, and Commercialization," *Petits Propos Culinaires* 95 (2012), pp. 74–118; Velasco et al. 2016 (see note 7).

**23** On the various meanings that people associate with black-and-white imagery, see Eric A. Greenleaf, "Does Everything Look Worse in Black and White? The Role of Monochrome Images in Consumer Behavior," in *Sensory Marketing: Research on the Sensuality of Products*, ed. Aradhna Krishna (New York, 2010), pp. 241–58, and Hyojin Lee, Xiaoyan Deng, H. Rao Unnava, and Kentaro Fujita, "Monochrome Forests and Colorful Trees: The Effect of Black-and-White versus Color Imagery on Construal Level," *Journal of Consumer Research* 41, no. 4 (2014), pp. 1015–32.

**24** Oliver Sacks, *An Anthropologist on Mars* (London, 1995), p. 5.

**25** For reviews, see Charles Spence and Betina Piqueras-Fiszman, "Dining in the Dark: Why, Exactly, Is the Experience So Popular?," *The Psychologist* 25 (2012), pp. 888–91, and Spence/Piqueras-Fiszman 2014 (see note 19).

**26** Spence et al. 2016 (see note 1).

**27** http://vespertine.la/

**28** Amy Scattergood, "Chef Jordan Kahn's Weird, Expectation-Defying, Silly Ambitious Culinary Dream," *The LA Times*, October 27, 2017, https://www.latimes.com/food/dailydish/la-fo-jordan-kahn-vespertine-20171018-story.html.

**29** Alison Pearlman, "This Hidden Place," *The Eye in Dining*, August 17, 2017, http://theeyeindining.blogspot.com/2017/08/this-hidden-place.html.

**30** See Charles Spence, Arume Corujo, and Jozef Youssef, "Cotton Candy: A Gastrophysical Investigation," *International Journal of Gastronomy & Food Science* 16 (2019).

**31** https://www.kitchen-theory.com

**32** https://www.kitchen-theory.com/aerosyn-lex-mestrovic/

**33** Wheatley 1973 (see note 6).

**34** See Velasco/Spence 2019 (see note 2).

**35** Peter Greenaway, *The Cook, the Thief, His Wife and Her Lover* (NL/GB/FR, 1989), 124 min.

**36** William Cook, "Would You Eat a 'Gourmet' Burger Made with Charred Bamboo and Squid Ink?," *Daily Mail Online*, September 25, 2012, http://www.dailymail.co.uk/news/article-2208321/Burger-King-black-burger-Japan-bamboo-charcoal-squid-ink.html; WSJ Staff, "Burger King Japan to Sell 'Red' Burgers," *The Wall Street Journal*, June 17, 2015, https://blogs.wsj.com/japanrealtime/2015/06/17/burger-king-japan-to-sell-red-burgers/.

**37** Rebecca Nicholson and Morwenna Ferrier, "It's in Smoothies, Toothpaste and Pizza—Is Charcoal the New Black?," *The Guardian*, June 28, 2017, https://www.theguardian.com/lifeandstyle/2017/jun/28/charcoal-black-food-beauty-fad-instagram-health-claims.

**38** Julie Delahaye, "Monarch Airlines May Have Unlocked the Secret to Helping You Relax on a Flight so You Can Avoid 'Air Rage'," *The Daily Mirror*, August 23, 2017, http://www.mirror.co.uk/lifestyle/travel/monarch-airlines-food-box-menu-11038358.

**39** Meg Carter, "All Things Bright and Edible: Fancy Some Black Garlic, Blue Potatoes or Red Cake?," *The Independent*, April 21, 2011, http://www.independent.co.uk/life-style/food-and-drink/features/all-things-bright-and-edible-fancy-some-black-garlic-blue-potatoes-or-red-cake-2270564.html.

**40** Nicholson/Ferrier 2017 (see note 37).

**41** Bryony Jewell, "Shoppers Are Going Wild for Kellogg's' New White Choc Coco Pops—Calling the Cereal a 'Game Changer' and the 'Best Thing since Sliced Bread'," *Daily Mail Online*, June 17, 2019, https://www.dailymail.co.uk/femail/article-7151505/Shoppers-wild-new-White-Choc-Coco-Pops-saying-cereal-going-game-changer.html.

**42** See Velasco/Spence 2019 (see note 2).

**43** On "color-in-context" theory, see Andrew J. Elliot and Markus A. Maier, "Chapter Two: Color-in-Context Theory," *Advances in Experimental Social Psychology* 45 (2012), pp. 61–125.

**44** Gary Baum, "Edible Doom and Gloom: L.A.'s Most Expensive New Restaurant Wants to Depress You for Dinner," *Hollywood Reporter*, July 17, 2017, https://www.hollywoodreporter.com/features/vespertine-restaurant-review-depressing-expensive-dining-1021469.

# Sensory Language in Perspective: An Interdisciplinary Exchange on Taste Descriptions

Jeannette Nuessli Guth & Maren Runte

*De gustibus non est disputandum.*
(There is no disputing about taste.)

Proverb

Eating and drinking are central to life, because we need energy and nutrients to survive. It is equally important that eating food contributes a great deal to joie de vivre. It is therefore hardly surprising that exchange over the taste of our food has occupied humans since time immemorial, whether in verbal or nonverbal form. This suggests that we should have a closer look at the sensory language of eating and drinking—in other words, of taste.

The famous phrase "De gustibus non est disputandum" offers a nice hook for shedding light on these themes from two angles. From a linguistics and sensory science perpective, this succinctly formulated statement can be both affirmed and denied: it is necessary to deny it if one takes into consideration, when talking about taste, individual variations in perception, differences in cultural influence and personal experience, and the ability of individuals to verbalize their perceptions. For just as many reasons, however, one can agree with the statement: If perception and its description are individual, then why should one argue about them? Especially as it is not necessary in normal, everyday situations of talking about eating. Usually it is enough to offer a subjective judgment about taste: "delicious" or "I don't care for it." And if it should happen that the parties to the conversation do not agree, then the exchange will end at some point without resolution, since a person's perception cannot easily be tested under ordinary circumstances.

The discussion of eating is omnipresent in today's media—especially in social media. How we perceive and describe our food is, however, an important subject not just for our personal environment but also for the food industry. We can talk about taste in everyday language, in the language of consumers, or in the language of experts. The technical language used in sensory science is employed in industry and research to describe the products as objectively as possible. Over the course of globalization, understanding the language of the senses in general has become more important as a result of an exchange on taste experience across linguistic and cultural borders.

**Taste from a Sensory Perspective**
Based on physiological facts, we distinguish between five so-called basic tastes: "sweet," "salty," "sour," "bitter," and "umami." The receptors for these different basic tastes are found primarily on the tongue. Taste defined physiologically thus clearly differs from our understanding in everyday language, in which a much broader meaning is attributed to the term "taste."

The first four terms to describe a basic taste—that is, "sweet," "salty," "sour," and "bitter"—are very familiar, since we know "sweet" as the perception of, for example, sugar or honey; "salty" from table salt; "sour" from lemons, unripe fruit, or vinegar; and "bitter" from coffee, beer, or dark chocolate. The term "umami" is less well known. It comes from the Japanese and means, roughly, "delicious." For several years now, this term has been defined in the Duden as follows: "umami: in a direction of taste that is neither sweet nor sour, bitter, or salty."[1] Meat and fish are given as examples. In German, at least, it is not obvious what taste perception is meant. In general, sensory analysis therefore works not only with definitions but also with so-called references. These references can be single substances or concrete products to ensure that people making descriptions know a term and the corresponding perception or can be trained. In the case of "umami," the prototypical substance of reference is monosodium glutamate, which the majority of consumers know as a flavor enhancer. The definition of the adjective "umami" is described much more specifically in English:[2]

"umami (adjective): being, inducing, or marked by one of the five basic taste sensations that is typically induced by several amino acids and nucleotides (such as glutamate and aspartate) and has a rich or meaty flavor characteristic of cheese, cooked meat, mushrooms, soy, and ripe tomatoes."

The following sentence is cited as an example of the term's use: "A crab risotto made from local crabs is powerful with the big *umami* flavor of brown meat." This definition of "umami" in English is more precise from the perspective of sensory analysis and describes the taste perception more clearly by reference to specific substances such as amino acids. In German, "umami" could best be described as "broth-like." Anyone who knows the taste of the typical Swiss seasoning Aromat is also very familiar with the perception of the taste of "umami" without necessarily knowing the technical term for it.

In the literature on sensory science, a comprehensive explanation of the terms to describe products is identified alongside a list of the terminology, definitions, and possible references; for example, the three terms "floral/perfumy," "spicy," and "overall sour" are characterized in simplified form in a publication on the language to describe mangoes [**table 1**].[3]

Specific substances can be named as references. In the case of mangoes, geraniol is employed as a reference for "floral"; it is an aromatic found, for example, in the scent of roses. It is also possible to indicate specific products such as "McCormick ground allspice." For the third term, "overall sour," no reference is given, only a definition. Such definitions and the listing of references are always given for the specified product class; in the case of Table 1, it is the fruit mango. Seen in isolation, the definition of "spicy" would be difficult to understand, since many would sooner expect something "hot" and not primarily the association with cinnamon.

Based on the manner of perception of substances, the first two terms in Table 1 are descriptions of aromas and don't belong to taste in the physiological sense. Because the technical language for describing tastes is limited to five terms, it quickly becomes clear that these terms are not sufficient for a complete description of products. Terms for aromas such as "floral" that in everyday language are categorized as tastes thus rate very highly. In contrast to physiological taste, aromatics are not perceived via the taste buds on the tongue but by corresponding receptors in the nose. The perception of "taste" is thus dependent on the nature of the substance that triggers a sensory perception. This distinction is, however, irrelevant in everyday language, and that can be demonstrated by the way people speak about taste: they seldom distinguish between odor and taste but often speak or write only of taste.[4]

The need for lists of terms with definitions is evident in the professional world from the existence of so-called aroma wheels for many products and from their publication in product-specific lexica in scientific literature. There is also a standard for the description of sensory impressions that lists the terms in various languages.[5] The first aroma wheel was published in modified form for wines by Ann C. Noble in 1987.[6] Aroma wheels are also very interesting to consumers. These lists enable consumers to use "florid" language even when specific expressions are not necessarily understood by everyone in the same way. In sensory analysis, a suitable use of descriptions is often not possible without special training. It would be desirable, in any case, to be more aware in our approach to food. As Ernest Hemingway made clear using the example of wine, sensory training can help perceive products more consciously and increase enjoyment when consuming them: "a person with increasing knowledge and sensory education may derive infinite enjoyment from wine."[7]

In addition to monolingual word lists, in a global world translations need to be critically evaluated. In some cases, international companies use English to describe products in all locations, which can result in challenges. Even the simplest terms for tastes cannot always be translated unproblematically. The German term *sauer* can be cited as an example here. In German, there is just one concept, but in other European languages, such as English, French, and Spanish, this concept is subdivided into different terms, for example, "acid" and "sour" in English.[8]

  Jeannette Nuessli Guth & Maren Runte

**Table 1:** Selected adjectives and definitions to describe mangoes
See Suwonsichon et al. 2012 (see note 3).

| Descriptor | Definition | References |
|---|---|---|
| Floral/perfumy | a sweet, heavy aromatics blend of a combination of flowers which can be somewhat chemical and perfume-like | Geraniol |
| Spicy | a sweet brown, slightly musty aromatics reminiscent of cinnamon | McCormick ground allspice |
| Overall sour | aromatics and flavor notes associated with the impression of all sour substances | |

Even in the multilingual version of the norm DIN ISO 5492, which lists technical terms for sensory analysis in various languages with a word-for-word translation, an awareness of problems that result from multilingualism is evident only to a limited extent.

In practical applications when cooking or producing foods, knowledge of the description and effect of the interplay of sensory impressions helps to create interesting sensory experiences for the consumer: "A little ketchup—and the umami it offers—makes things taste inexplicably more delicious."[9]

**Taste from a Linguistic Perspective**

From a linguistic perspective, taste perceptions can be generally described in one of two ways: first, the speakers can select a single taste term to verbalize their perceptions; second, for lack of a suitable term, they can make use of other strategies to describe sensory impressions to others. Both possibilities of describing taste are presented in what follows and are illustrated with examples.

Various methods are available to collect the vocabulary of taste in a language:[10] one can consult dictionaries, interview native speakers of a language, or collect texts (corpora) and systematically evaluate them. These methods are variously successful. Starting with the example of German vocabulary for tastes, around 20 percent of the 1,000 terms for taste in German have a corresponding semantic description in the large dictionaries of the German language. Dictionaries, however, are a codified part of the language; spontaneously used descriptions of taste cannot be collected in this way.

A larger vocabulary of taste can be collected by evaluating the actual use of language. This takes the form of large collections of texts (corpora) containing spoken (rarely) or written statements. With the aid of linguistic annotations—that is, the enriching of data on language with linguistic information (e.g., word classes), such corpora can be searched and, for example, adjectives found used together with the noun or verb "taste." The vocabulary recorded in dictionaries can be, on the one hand, confirmed by linguistic evaluations of corpora and, on the other hand, considerably enlarged (in German, for example, by an additional 60 percent).

One of the issues that results from the size of the vocabulary of taste is measuring the importance of taste terms by the frequency of their occurrence in written and spoken language. In order to determine the central lexis of the vocabulary of taste, we developed the Basic Taste Term Test (BTTT), which in asking about taste terms takes into account both the speed with which they were written down and their frequency of mention.[11]

Figure 1 shows an illustration of the BTTT for German; the position of the taste terms within the circle is based on the frequency of mention.

The central German vocabulary of taste reveals the following features:
– The most central positions are occupied by the four basic taste qualities *süss* (sweet), *sauer* (sour), *bitter* (bitter), and *salzig* (salty), which in German have to be supplemented by another word: *scharf* (spicy or hot).
– It is striking about this group that the central position is occupied by the term *süss*, which is the most central taste term in the German language because of its early use and based on its frequency.
– By contrast, one basic taste is (still) lacking in everyday language: "umami." The frequency of that term can, however, be observed, and so it is reasonable to expect that "umami" will also enter ordinary language.

The following can be noted about the less central taste terms:
– Positive and negative evaluations of taste descriptions are very important in everyday life: *gut* (good) and *lecker* (delicious) versus *schlecht* (bad) and *eklig* (disgusting) are among the words most commonly used in evaluations.
– Just as important are adjectives that describe an intensity of taste: *würzig* (spicy), *fad(e)* (tasteless), *mild* (mild), *pikant* (piquant), and *geschmacklos* (tasteless).

These results must be put in the context of a European comparison, however: in English, "bitter" is not one of the most central taste terms; its metaphorical use dominates ("bitter pill," etc.). In English, French, and Spanish, as noted above, the German word "sour" can be translated by two words: for example, "acid" and "sour," which can be rendered by the concepts "containing an acid" and "having a sour taste." These differences, even with supposedly easily translatable basic taste qualities, make it clear how important it is to take care when translating terms for the sensory analysis of food.[12]

Even though the various possibilities for forming words in German make for a very large vocabulary of tastes in German—thanks to compounds such as *himbeerartig* (raspberry-like), *bananig* (banana-ish), *süsslich* (sweetish)—numerous other possibilities of linguistic expression and strategies for describing taste impressions can be shown. In what follows, we list and discuss selected strategies[13] that we collected either during focus group discussions of taste terms or based on tastings of basic foods (bread, coffee, yogurt, etc.). We made audiovisual recordings of the focus group discussions then transcribed them to permit a precise analysis of the data.

**– Discussion of term fields:** To make descriptions of taste as precise as possible, focus groups may be observed in which the speakers introduce semantically very similar terms—*knackig* (crunchy), *trocken* (dry), *kross* (crispy), etc.—and try to distinguish their meanings to arrive at the most suitable expression for the sensory perception.

**– Identifying prototypical references:** In order to describe the taste of products more precisely, the speakers often name prototypical foods, the tastes of which they then describe more clearly ("it tastes like …").

**– Images and scenes:** Precisely when the speakers do not succeed in making the description of taste more precise by other meanings (naming a taste term or prototypical references), they fall back on theatrical or visual illustrations. In the following example, the speaker relies on the picturesque image of tree mushrooms in the forest to describe the taste of a certain loaf of bread.

Example: Focus group of women on bread (recorded November 5, 2009):

**Ida:** … I was trying the WHOLE time before to SEARCH for something; but how that (.)

**Fig. 1:** The thirty central taste terms in the German language
Nuessli Guth and Runte 2017 (see note 4).

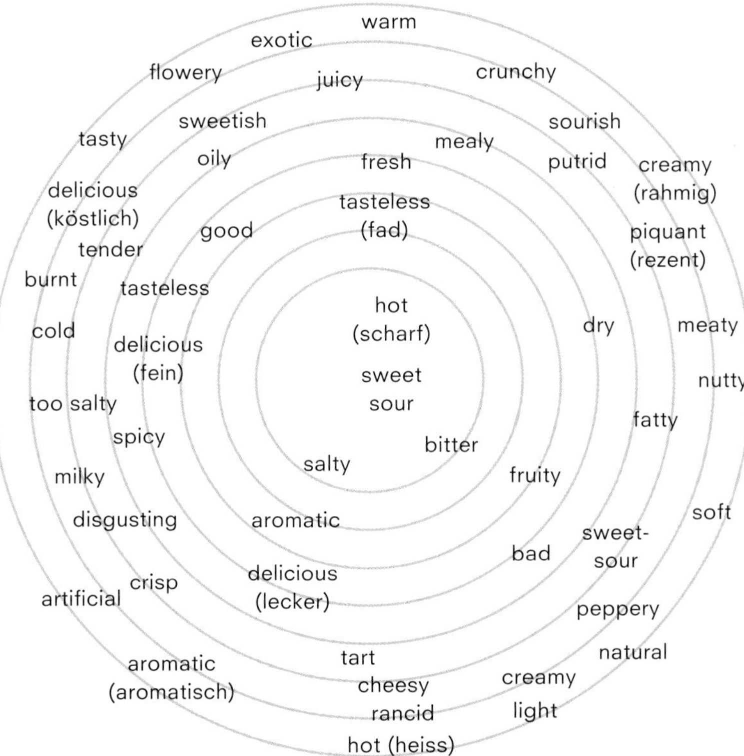

in order to describe the BREAD, its TASTE,
somehow; and then I just (-)- now thought
of TREE mushrooms, when you go into the
FOREST ... <<indicating mushrooms with
her hands>> everywhere—the MUSHrooms
on the TREES>> smell like that (.) that is,
way that SMELLS [the bread TASTES.]
**Liv:** [((laughs))]
**Ida:** so (-) maybe also a little like TRUFfles
or something, but anyone something that
comes out of the GROUND; and from the
FOREST -
**Joy:** EARTHy;
**Ida:** [mhm (.) so erm EXACTLY;]
**Ada:** [EARTHy is good;]

**– Gestures:** In some cases, it does not appear
to be enough to name a single taste term;
to illustrate this better, it is supported by
gestures. We were able to observe, for example, that when describing *fettig* (fatty), which
is associated with *triefend* (dripping), the
movement of a drop was depicted. The term
*knackig* (crunchy), by contrast, was accompanied by a hand gesture intended to depict
the breaking of a fresh vegetable (such as a
carrot or cucumber).

**Perception and Language in Interplay**
The collaboration of linguistics and sensory
science leads to a better understanding of
the importance of attributed language in the
context of coming to an agreement about
sensory impressions from food and beverages. That is true of ordinary language, which
depicts taste within a large spectrum, and
for the sensory language, in which descriptions of products have to be provided that
are as precise as possible in an international,
multilingual context.

The clear differences in the nature of the
description are striking: everyday language,
and hence also the language of consumers,
is not limited just to describing taste in the
physiological sense. Here, in addition to
other types of perception (e.g., consistency,
temperature, smell), subjective impressions
in particular play a big role. Especially for
those who are new to sensory analysis, taste
and smell are often linked to emotions and
memories. In order to understand how we
talk about taste perception in everyday life,
such aspects have to be taken into account
as well.

All of this is also important for sensory
science, however, when the goal is to understand how consumers talk about products.
Awareness of the importance of language
is also relevant in another context: in the
multilingual communications of internation-
ally active companies in the food industry,
since cultural and linguistic differences must
be taken into account in definitions for
sensory experts as well.

**1** Duden, s.v. "umami," https://www.duden.de, accessed November 22, 2019; "in einer Geschmacksrichtung liegend, die weder süß noch sauer, bitter oder salzig ist."

**2** Merriam-Webster, s.v. "umami," https://www.merriam-webster.com, accessed November 22, 2019.

**3** Suntaree Suwonsichon, Edgar Chambers IV, Varapha Kongpensook, and Chintanta Oupadissakoon, "Sensory Lexicon for Mango as Affected by Cultivars and Stages of Ripeness," *Journal of Sensory Studies* 27, no. 3 (2012), pp. 148–60.

**4** See Jeannette Nuessli Guth and Maren Runte, "Odour Descriptions from a Language Perspective," in *Springer Handbook of Odor*, ed. Andrea Buettner (Cham, 2017), pp. 1013–26.

**5** See DIN EN ISO 5492: "Sensory Analysis: Vocabulary," multilingual version, 2009.

**6** Ann C. Noble et al., "Modification of a Standardized System of Wine Aroma Terminology," *American Journal of Enology and Viticulture* 38, no. 2 (1987), pp. 143–46.

**7** Ernest Hemingway, *Death in the Afternoon* (New York, 2002; orig. pub. 1932), p. 18.

**8** See Jeannette Nuessli Guth and Maren Runte, "Is It Just Sour Grapes? A Cross-Language Approach to Understand Taste," 12th Pangborn Sensory Science Symposium, Providence, RI, USA, August 20–24, 2017.

**9** Samin Nosrat, *Salt, Fat, Acid, Heat: Mastering the Elements of Good Cooking* (New York: Simon & Schuster, 2017), p. 124.

**10** The accounts that follow are based in part on the results of the project "Sensory Language and the Semantics of Taste" (see the information at http://www.sensorysemantics.ch).

**11** Nuessli Guth and Runte 2017 (see note 4).

**12** See Jeannette Nuessli Guth and Maren Runte, "How about Hot and Spicy in Sensory and Linguistics: Cross-Cultural Insights and Language Concepts," 11th Pangborn Sensory Science Symposium, Gothenburg, Sweden, August 23–27, 2015.

**13** For a more detailed account, see Larissa Bieler and Maren Runte, "Semantik der Sinne: Die lexikografische Erfassung von Geschmacksadjektiven," *Lexicographica, Series maior* 26 (2010), pp. 109–28.

# A Question of Taste

**Elisabeth Bronfen**

We might ask: Why does one speak of delicate, sure taste when discussing the ability to make an aesthetic value judgment? As the proverb says, you eat with your eyes first, but why should we feel something on the tongue when we see? Moreover, sure taste means much more than the ability to make a judgment about a work of art. It suggests rather an attitude or expresses a behavior toward a thing that is about more than personal preferences. This raises another question: What does the sense of taste have to do with certain aesthetic principles becoming visible that are not only subjective but at the same time concern a certain era or epoch, even characterize it? To claim that one cannot dispute taste implicitly means that there is agreement about certain rules. It means sticking to a common ground—or producing it performatively by this statement—because there is agreement on the aesthetic or moral assessment of a certain thing. We also assert that something violates good taste when we want to reject or condemn certain behaviors or view them as inappropriate.

The semantic mutability associated with the idea of good taste is thus also evident from it being a question of the cultural habitus by which people are accepted in certain circles or remain excluded from them. Then it is important to retain this good taste in order to preserve a certain exclusivity. At the same time, however, we also bring the concept of taste into play when the goal is to discover something new. After all, taste is acquired not only from a thing. If we engage with something for a time, we can also acquire a taste for it. We can, sometimes quite unexpectedly, find taste in something new.

Both the question of habitus as a basic outlook toward an appearance, a behavior, or a stance and the question of slow habituation to something unfamiliar need not, but can be, related to culinary experiences. Things taste good because they are familiar to us or because a happy, pleasing interplay of aromas is achieved with them. A practiced chef does indeed need sure taste in order to season her creations appropriately. At the same time, however, what tastes good to us on the plate often says something about a particular historical period as well. With his spices and other products from the Middle East, the British cult chef Yotam Ottolenghi personifies the 2010s just as much as the American television chef Julia Child's fondness for butter and meat exemplifies the prosperity of the 1960s. Whereas habitus is expressed in a feeling of belonging to a group because one likes to eat the same foods, one might also note by contrast: certain dishes that once set the tone—sauces with lots of butter and those based on roux—have become a taste that needs to be reacquired. Remember, moreover, that in the 1980s the idea of eating raw slices of fish on balls of rice still took some getting used to, so we can also predict the following for our future: we will slowly develop the taste to enjoy a meal rich in insects.

The question of what the idea of good taste entails becomes even more complicated if one considers the Swiss German meaning of the word *schmöcke* ("to smell," but more recently also "to taste," whereas its standard German equivalent *schmecken* only means "to taste"). The language makes no clear distinction between the taste we sense on the tongue and the aroma we discover with the nose. In fact, these two senses are always found together when eating. The aroma of a good meal challenges the sense of taste in a variety of ways: it gives it now a more intense, now a stronger, now a denser note. At the same time, however, distinguishing between aroma and taste is important, as thousands of different aromas can be compiled but there are only five basic tastes: salty, sweet, sour, bitter, and the term we have borrowed from Asian cuisine in the sense of "savory," namely, umami. Proper seasoning, in turn, means finding a happy balance such that the aromatic possibilities of the natural taste of the ingredients used are fully utilized, heightened, and rounded off without covering it up—as often happens today when dishes are very heavily seasoned. Such heavy seasoning may improve products with little taste of their own; the consequence of our current penchant for spice mixes that combine a large number of spices, bringing us back to the question of habitus, is that we are no longer accustomed to detecting—that is, enjoying—a subtler, more natural taste.

The following assertion therefore goes without saying: in my view, nothing is so crucial when cooking as the ability to season to taste. One does need a good hand on which one can rely spontaneously. Intuition plays a big role here. Seasoning, however, is also a skill that can be acquired by systematically trying out, experimenting, and analyzing. That, in turn, means that you have to be conscious of the properties of the five basic tastes, to imagine their interplay. But you also must be able to rely on your own experience, on memories of successful—and unsuccessful—aromatic combinations. So seasoning is in fact also related to a kind of seeing: to the images the mind's eye forms with one's own imagination.

It pays, therefore, to call to mind again briefly the effect of the five basic tastes. Here, too, as was already suggested when discussing the question of taste, proverbs are revealing. Salt turns out to be crucial to the question raised here. Because it teases out the taste of food in the first place, we speak of the "Salz in der Suppe" (salt in the soup) to refer to what is truly interesting about something. If you really dislike someone, by contrast, you say: "Dem gönne ich das Salz in der Suppe nicht" (I begrudge him the salt in his soup). If you want to praise a modest life, the proverb visually evokes a scene in which one is content with or prepared to put up with salted bread alone.

What these proverbs illustrate is how essential salt is as a component of nearly all dishes. It is probably the most important ingredient in the kitchen, because it emphasizes and heightens all of the other tastes of the ingredients used, and, one could even say, causes them to shine. Its essentialness is also revealed by the fact that, if dosed properly, the salt will always remain in the background. It should act like a secret stage director of a scene: someone who has everything completely under control but does not enter the limelight. If you perceive salt as a separate taste in a dish, then you have added too much, and the dish is said to be oversalted. This, too, reveals another aspect associated with salt. While it defines everything else in its interplay, because it allows it to develop, salt cannot itself stand out. The power of salt lies in the unspoken. The question of balance, of interplay, is, however, also revealed by the fact that salt intensifies not only the savory but also the sweet and the sour, even while it moderates a bitter taste.

But what about the sweetness we associate with sugar, molasses, syrup, honey, and fruit but also milk? It is understood as an energy source that at the same time has the effect of producing something delightful. Work and variety make life sweet, just as sweetness is added to correct the unpleasant or boring. The bitter pill of duty can be sweetened; a sad day can be made sweet by unexpected joy. So it is scarcely surprising that even revenge is sweet for some. The cherries in the neighbor's garden always taste better because they are forbidden or inaccessible. Proverbs also evoke a scene that operates with this taste and thus fosters a feeling of excited happiness, since it makes one feel like a kid in a candy store. These ideas handed down by cultural knowledge are also related to culinary realities. Sweetness can either balance out or refresh the aroma of a dish—above all, a tomato, which, when grown in northern, colder climates, can often taste bland, so that its own sweetness sometimes needs assistance.

Proverbs usually think of sour as the opposite of sweet. One has a sour face when dissatisfied. Having to do something you don't want to do is called "In den sauren Apfel beissen müssen" (Having to bite into the sour apple). A bad mood in general is regarded as sour. Yet sour actually has a positive quality on the tongue: the mucous membranes contract and stimulate the flow of saliva, which has the effect that

　　　　　　　　　　　　　　　　　　　　**Elisabeth Bronfen**

one is better prepared to absorb food. That is why a dish that is slightly sour is called "mouthwatering." As with salt, however, the sour, too, should recede to the background in a successful seasoning. The sour should support the appropriate mix of different ingredients without drawing attention to itself. Because sourness stimulates the flow of saliva, it should not be surprising that this quality of taste can be employed as a corrective to balance higher fat content or intense sweetness. A small shot of sourness protects against feeling full, making the mouth water again. That is not only why a glass of red wine complements the food, but also why its tannins have a souring effect in a stew that stimulates appetite.

Bitter taste is, by contrast, particularly tricky, since it can even become unpleasant, as it serves as a warning sign that something could be poisonous. It is therefore not surprising how often bitterness is used in figures of speech. We must hold out until the bitter end, are bitterly disappointed, bitterly regret an act. An unpleasant event leaves a bitter taste in one's mouth; we endure bitter times or a bitter fate, and we strike a bitter tone when something does not suit us. In superstitions, moreover, there is a physical correspondence to this taste that is usually perceived as unpleasant. The gall bladder has, since time immemorial, been thought of as an organ that produces a bitter fluid, the overproduction of which leads to an affective flooding of the body that results in irritation, anger, and surfeit. Yet an opposite movement is also heralded in the concept of the bitter. We call an unpleasant medicine that we cannot refuse a bitter pill we have to swallow, and often use this in a metaphorical sense. This suggests that this taste in particular functions like the pharmakon in Plato's dialogue between Phaedrus and Socrates, in which everything depends on the correct dose. If one takes too much bitter, it becomes a dangerous poison; if one takes the right amount, it comes a pleasant medicine. Coffee stimulates our nervous system. Tonic water, in turn, belonged to the standard equipment of the British colonial army, because the quinine it contains was used to combat malaria. We know this remedy today as a gin and tonic: the perfect balance of sweet and bitter on a hot summer afternoon.

The fifth and final quality of taste is the note known by the term "umami," which is perceived as piquant or intensely savory and, although it has been around for more than a century, typifies the culinary taste of our time, since green tea, miso, soy sauce, and fish sauces have become as ordinary in our world of "fusion cooking" as the anchovies, olives, and aged parmesan of the 1970s. Like sourness, this quality of taste does more than freshen up a dish. Umami gives it intensity and density, especially when several ingredients that lend this taste are combined. That is why one grates parmesan over spaghetti with tomato sauce, but also why one serves a burger with ketchup. Like salt, umami makes the savory quality of the main ingredient shine. My particular penchant for this taste, and the fact that umami corrects the richness of cream, has moved me to combine soy sauce with more than just peanut sauce, as is familiar from Asian cuisine. The combination of soy sauce and cream is a match made in heaven. Once you have accepted the idea, you quickly develop a taste for this unorthodox mixture.

The issue of imagination already mentioned at the beginning now comes into play in that seasoning means not only mastering these five tastes. It is also necessary to imagine the immense diversity of aromas that can lend a dish a very special note. They range from the meaty, the fishy, the spicy, and the nutty by way of the fruity, the flowery, the earthy, the woody, and the smoky to the dark, the deep, the airy, and the velvety. And it has a little to do with magic, since the right combination of aromas intensifies the taste of a dish, brings out different notes in the taste, and at the same time transforms them. In my own cooking practice, I also bring imagination into play because a successful aromatic combination only rarely results by chance. On the one hand, it belongs rather to the learned culinary repertoire that I recall when thinking about dishes and that I have to constantly practice anew. On the other hand, often when planning a menu, and later when buying the ingredients, I am already trying out different combinations of tastes in my head. I think about how what I am imagining could be achieved and adapt the cooking process to those ideas. Then when eating I analyze the interplay of the resulting aromas. I ask myself how they influence one another and imagine once more what nuances could have been combined differently. What effects have been achieved, and what else could have been attained by slightly varying the seasoning? Where would it pay to experiment more?

Because, moreover, memory plays a considerably important role in the imagination, I recommend that everyone keep a personal archive of aromas, both on paper and in your head. Much like when playing chess, with every new hand movement, adding new aromatic ingredients to a dish, one should remember past strategies. When taking notes—I have an elegant black notebook for the purpose—it pays to have a category for failed experiments. It is also important to remember what did not work, for failure actually does offer new possibilities to try out as well. It is also useful when compiling a personal archive of aromas to note the flavor combinations that complement each other perfectly and bring the taste of the ingredients used into a harmonious whole: such as squash and vanilla, apricot and rosemary, beet and coriander. But it also makes sense to record combinations that are about an aromatic contrast, in terms of both taste and texture: the savory crust of cheese on a creamy-soft macaroni and cheese, grated apples in the velvety purée of a vegetable soup, a garlicky, nutty crunch on al dente spaghetti. Finally, one should note aromatic combinations that offer taste inspirations. When you bite into a piece of preserved lemon—which I like to put both on salads and in stews—the intense citrus taste explodes in your mouth. The same happens with fish roe folded into a fish tartar. When you bite into them, these crunchy pearls release another small spray of umami in your mouth.

In addition to a trained imagination, the rich experience already acquired from combining spices, herbs, and ingredients plays a role. Because it is also about achieving an aromatic balance, adapting the taste of a dish according to the ingredients as you cook. This requires more than the supplies of herbs and spices stored in your kitchen. It also comes down to a catalogue of questions that are called to mind when adjusting the seasoning. Would more salt underscore the taste? Would lemon juice or vinegar liven up the dish? Would a little sweetness bring out the other aromas more? Would a little more hotness provide the desired bite? Does one taste dominate too much, so that it should be moderated? Does the dish have the right dose of umami? Have the desired aromas unfolded, or did they disappear, so that they need to be refreshed? In that case, does the aroma need more of the spices already used or an ingredient to complement their taste, such as butter or cream, to be whisked in or herbs or nuts to garnish it? It is not enough to reach for these ingredients, but it is necessary to imagine ahead of time what they will do. Precisely for this reason, it is necessary to have your archive of aromas in your head as well. For the question of taste turns out to be an astonishing source of discoveries. Or it shows us the way back to something very familiar.



Elisabeth Bronfen

More thoughts about eating, cooking, and recipes
from Elisabeth Bronfen's cosmopolitan everyday
cuisine can be found in her book *Obsessed:
The Cultural Critic's Life in the Kitchen*, published
by Rutgers University Press in 2019.

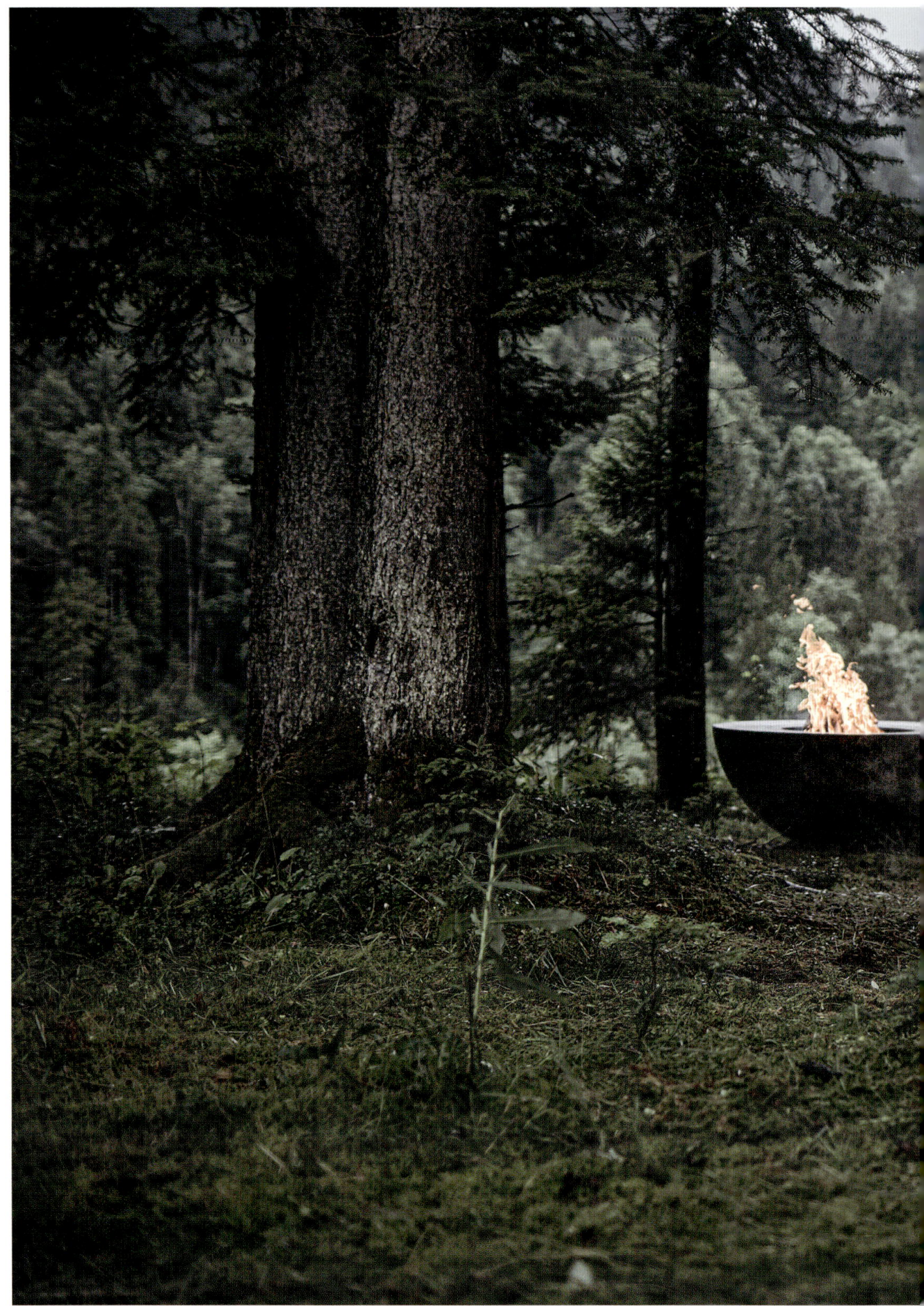

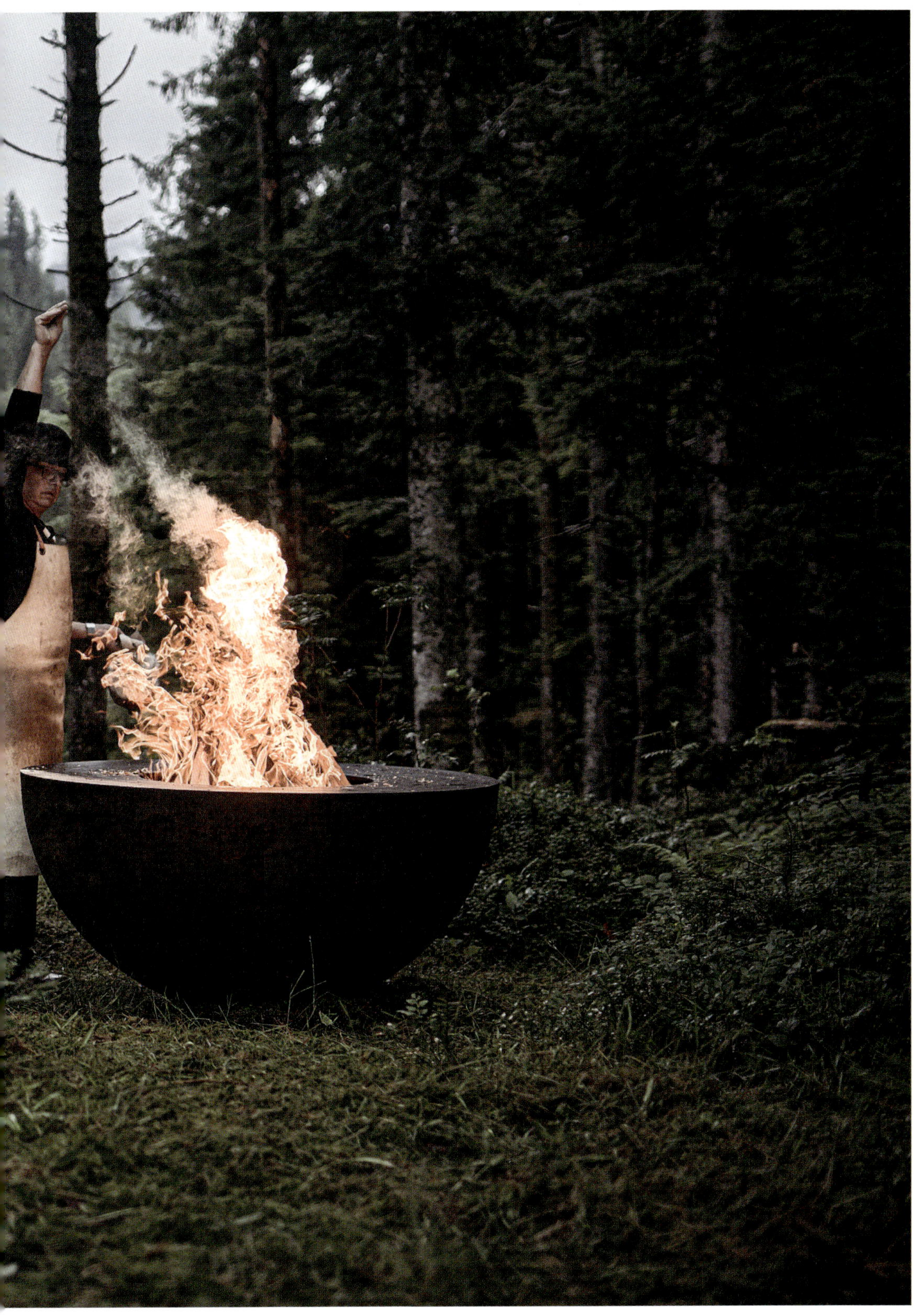

# Cooking with Stones

**Stefan Wiesner in Conversation
with Annja Müller-Alsbach**

Annja Müller-Alsbach: **Stefan, you're the chef at your Gasthaus Rössli in Escholzmatt in the Entlebuch district, between Lucerne and Bern, with a Michelin star and seventeen points in Gault & Millau. You're also a guest lecturer in the Institute of Aesthetic Practice at the University of Applied Sciences and Arts Northwestern Switzerland (FHNW) in Basel and the author of several cookbooks. You cook with rather unfamiliar ingredients, such as wood and stones, and pursue a specific philosophy in your work. What would you call your job?**

**Stefan Wiesner:** It's more than just a job; it's a vocation. It's a way of life, a constant process I find myself involved in. I have always been a very weak student. So long as I did not know why something is the way it is, I didn't understand it. I am dyslexic and still have problems with certain letters, with commas and periods, because I do not find them logical. It was like that during my training as a cook. In the beginning I thought I had to understand everything— why dishes are called, for example, Pêche Melba or Poire Belle Hélène. Suddenly I understood that they're fantasy names. I understood that Poire Belle Hélène is dedicated to a woman, and that Rossini is a composer and "à la Rossini" in itself has nothing to do with truffles. And I understood that I, too—that I myself—could give a dish a name. Once I had understood this inhibition threshold, then I also realized that I could perfectly well make a classic hollandaise a different way.

AMA: **Where did you do your apprenticeship?**

SW: I did my apprenticeship at the Château Gütsch in Lucerne, under Herr Häfliger, who cooked "freestyle" back then. He invented some things, gave dishes new names (at the time he was one of the few in Lucerne who cooked that way). After my apprenticeship, I went home to my parents' Gasthaus Rössli in Escholzmatt, and after that I worked in

various other restaurants. Finally, I worked at Le Manoir in Lucerne. In my opinion Herr Stübiger, the head of the kitchen there, was the best chef by miles at the time. He was honored for his poultry cuisine—duck, wild duck, geese, quail. He cooked nouvelle cuisine. There I learned that you do not use flour for binding sauces (you reduce them), and that you make pure stock to cook sauces. That was a revelation to me.

AMA: **Then you came from this nouvelle cuisine to Escholzmatt, to the Rössli, with high expectations of your ingredients?**

SW: Not to start with. Initially, I even cooked with convenience products in the Rössli. At that time, I had actually already started working out my own philosophy as a chef. But I was always struggling. On the one hand, I wanted to satisfy the local guests, but, on the other, to cook with good raw materials in unusual ways. So I found my head spinning, and I asked myself: What can I serve to whom, and at what price? Who am I catering to with my cuisine? That was a trying time.

AMA: **But today, many years later, things look a bit different. Now you're a star chef and have become known as Wiesner the Wizard. And your cooking is described as "alchemical natural cuisine." Can you explain how this came about and how you see it today?**

SW: For that I have to go back again to the past, to when I started as a chef at the Rössli. My cuisine developed as a result of financial pressure after the purchase from my parents. Of course, I wanted to cook with high-quality Balik smoked salmon that was expensive, but then I realized that it was not possible for financial reasons. So that was why, inspired by my childhood, I started looking for my raw materials just outside the door, in the nearby woods and pastures: I did not have to buy them; they were just there, freely available.

AMA: **So, today, you collect most of your ingredients from your immediate surroundings in the Entlebuch?**

SW: Yes. I don't cost in my foraging hours, so these natural products are to all intents and purposes free. My cuisine is largely based on unusual ingredients, because of my passion for nature. To begin with, this was out of necessity, but later it was more and more for artistic reasons. We sometimes use very simple ingredients and make quality dishes from them via a very elaborate process.

AMA: **So over time, you've learned to cook with ingredients not normally used in the kitchen—such as wood, stones, hay—and turn them into tasty dishes?**

SW: Yes, that's exactly what I mean by alchemical natural cuisine.

AMA: **Isn't this something akin to an avant-garde artist working with new materials, rather than traditional artistic mediums like paint, marble, and metal?**

SW: Yes, I can certainly see a similarity between my philosophy and working method and those of some of today's artists. But unlike a painter, for example, there is a lot more that I can incorporate into my work as a chef: for example, the world of scent, or by bringing in music. My first book, in 2003, *Gold, Holz, Stein: Sinnliche Sensationen aus Wiesners alchemistischer Naturküche* (Gold, Wood, Stone: Sensual Sensations from Wiesner's Alchemical Natural Cuisine) set out who I am and what I do. When it appeared, and I was referred to in the press as the "Paracelsus of the kitchen," or described as "cooking with the forest," I began to find out who this Paracelsus was. Actually, I acquired a modicum of artistic education by evolving my own menu ideas. For example, my menu to Alexander Scriabin, in which I addressed his "keyboard with lights" (with notes corresponding to colors) and "mystical

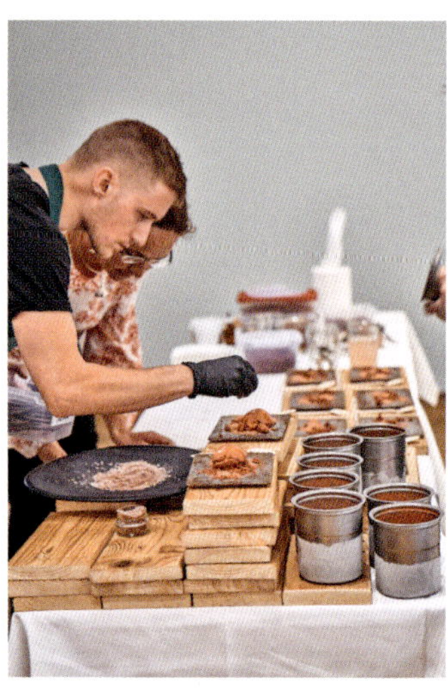

Preparation of Stefan Wiesner's iron-ore ice cream called *Flint* at the *Amuse-bouche* symposium, April 5, 2019

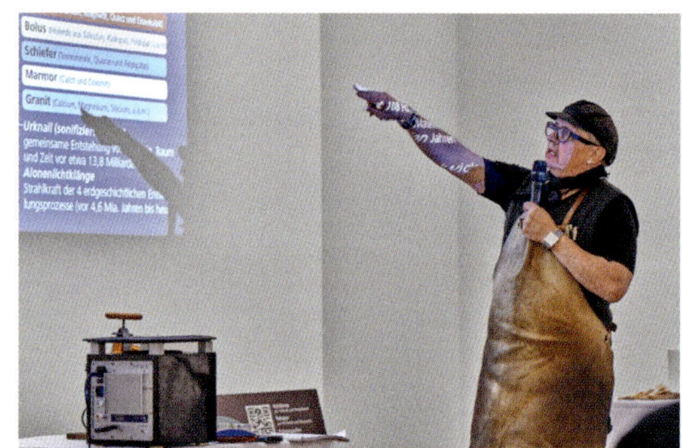

Stefan Wiesner at the *Amuse-bouche* symposium, April 5, 2019

          **Stefan Wiesner, Annja Müller-Alsbach**

chord," or the menus to Joseph Beuys, to Futurism or Dada, the menus *Nature Speaks*, and then simply *Paracelsus*. And so my menus switch to and fro between themes from modern art and ancient knowledge.

AMA: **I came to you in March and ate your *Fire and Flame* menu. Everything was about cooking on the fire. Can you explain how you build such a menu?**

SW: First and foremost, there is my curiosity to find out about something new. Who is Alexander Scriabin, for example? What does he do? His composition *Prometheus: The Poem of Fire* is a modern piece of music that is not easily accessible even today. Artists like him are the ones who have influenced me a lot. He wanted to build a semisphere in India—for him the most sensuous land, or so he claimed—in which he aimed to address all the senses in one gigantic multimedia production, which sought to combine taste, smell, color, sound, dance, and interior design with music …

AMA: **… to realize a total work of art.**

SW: Yes, exactly! That's my big role model. I started with Scriabin, and then came the second book in 2011—*Avantgardistische Naturküche: Mit Lexikon der Geschmackskombinationen* (Avant-Garde Natural Cuisine, with a Lexicon of Taste Combinations), which is about so-called taste families and modifiers. Some of my menus are based on perfumes; I've hidden certain fragrances in them—by Nino Cerruti, Hugo Boss, or Jil Sander, for example. When a perfumer reads the ingredients of the menus listed in *Avantgardistische Naturküche*, he knows that it is this or that fragrance, or this or that perfume. And here, too, I have been intensively preoccupied with perfume. Patrick Süskind's 1985 novel *Das Parfum* (translated as *Perfume: The Story of a Murderer*) and Alexander Scriabin were crucial to my development.

 After my second cookbook, I started to work on my philosophy, and this led to various so-called Wiesner Keys. One of them is founded on the cosmic Big Bang. Based on this key [**fig. 1**], I explain in lectures why (and the basis on which) I cook with stones.

AMA: **The book *Avantgardistische Naturküche* is about taste families and fragrance families, and the topic of modifiers.[1] Where did these taste and fragrance families come from? Did a list of them already exist?**

SW: No, there wasn't one like this before. The lexicon in the appendix is very largely the work of the perfumer Jimmy Studer; it is based on his experiences and our common work. Before we published this book, I already knew the basics of taste families from my everyday life as a chef, but not in this theoretical form of an exact listing. And I was unlucky—I published the book too late and it appeared at the same time that "food pairing" came up, which works similarly. Food pairing is scientific, has to do with basic molecules, and asks which tastes best complement each other. Mandarin oranges, for example, have not only a citrus note but a tart note as well, and the latter is identical to thyme: so you can successfully pair thyme with mandarins. However, as I said, the chapter on modifiers in the book is the work of a perfumer, and perfumers go further than the normal food pairing—they build up a fragrance or even a taste composition. For example, you can tell a perfumer, "Make me a tobacco taste!" He then picks apricots and raspberries and other ingredients, and in the end he has built a tobacco flavor. Also, food pairing does not make use of resins… all of this can be found in our dictionary.

AMA: **As part of our symposium, you served an iron-ore ice cream that carries the title *Flint* [fig. 2] in the *Fire and Flame* menu. I know from your books that you first cook in your head and then record the details of the dishes in drawings and sketches. How does a dessert like this come about?**

SW: My train of thought with this dessert [**fig. 3**] began with iron: iron is red for me (in my mind, red signifies fire), and for me the two together mean flint. My approach to cooking with iron itself goes back a long time. To start with, I cooked with iron nails by decoction, and I had already made some ice cream this way. Iron oxide is very good and easy for the body to absorb, for example as rust in combination with acid. In the past, people used to deliberately stick nails into apples and then eat the apples that had been stained with rust, thus transporting the rust, the iron, into the body. My logical conclusion was to mix the nails with yoghurt. Yoghurt is acid that transports the iron into the body. And only when I met the painter Urs Furrer …

AMA: … **who supplies you with the finely ground stone pigments that he uses in his own paintings.**

SW: Yes, exactly. Now that I can cook with his stone pigments, a huge, coherent world has opened up for me. Based on the Big Bang and the four primal forces, my Wiesner Key graphically depicts how minerals and the various natural life forms are interconnected as elements of a cycle [**fig. 1**]. Now it all adds up for me. As a result, my cooking philosophy has changed a bit: it has become more concentrated, focusing on just one ingredient per course. In my current menu *Jeremias Gotthelf*, for example, I deal only with potato in one course, or only with lettuce in another.

AMA: **Your contribution to the symposium was called *Cooking with Stones*. Which stone exactly did you use for your dessert *Flint*?**

SW: Iron ore from Gonzen, a town in the canton of St. Gallen. In Scuol, which is in the canton of Graubünden, you can taste the different flavors of water in the local spa at a water bar: one tastes sulfurous, one is milky, and so on. Of course, it is also the stones, the minerals, that give the waters their unique tastes. If you focused your sensory faculties on rocks for a long while, then with time you could better taste the differences.

AMA: **At the symposium you showed how to distill this finely ground stone pigment.**

SW: Distilling stones is theoretically not possible, because stones per se are bone dry. But in the process of grinding them into fine pigment powder, water is absorbed from the air, and I can distill this out again. Once you have understood that, then you can add a little water to the stone meal, combine it into a mixture, and let it rest for a while.

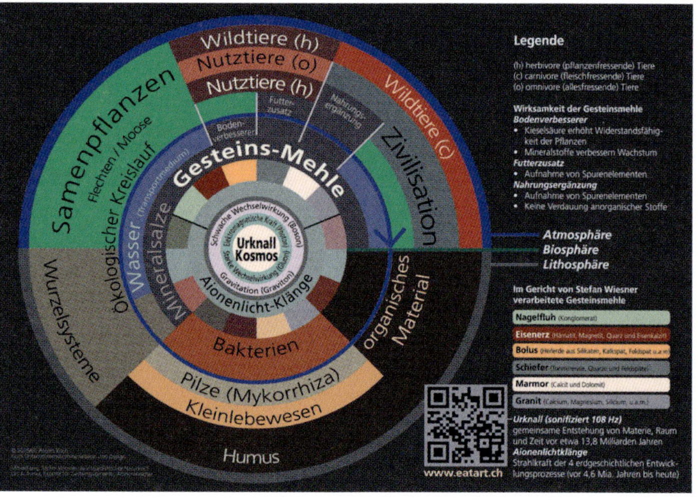


Fig. 1 The Wiesner Key for cooking with different kinds of stone meal, designed by Robert Koch in collaboration with Stefan Wiesner, advant-garde nature chef, and Urs A. Furrer, expert on stone pigments



Stefan Wiesner, Annja Müller-Alsbach

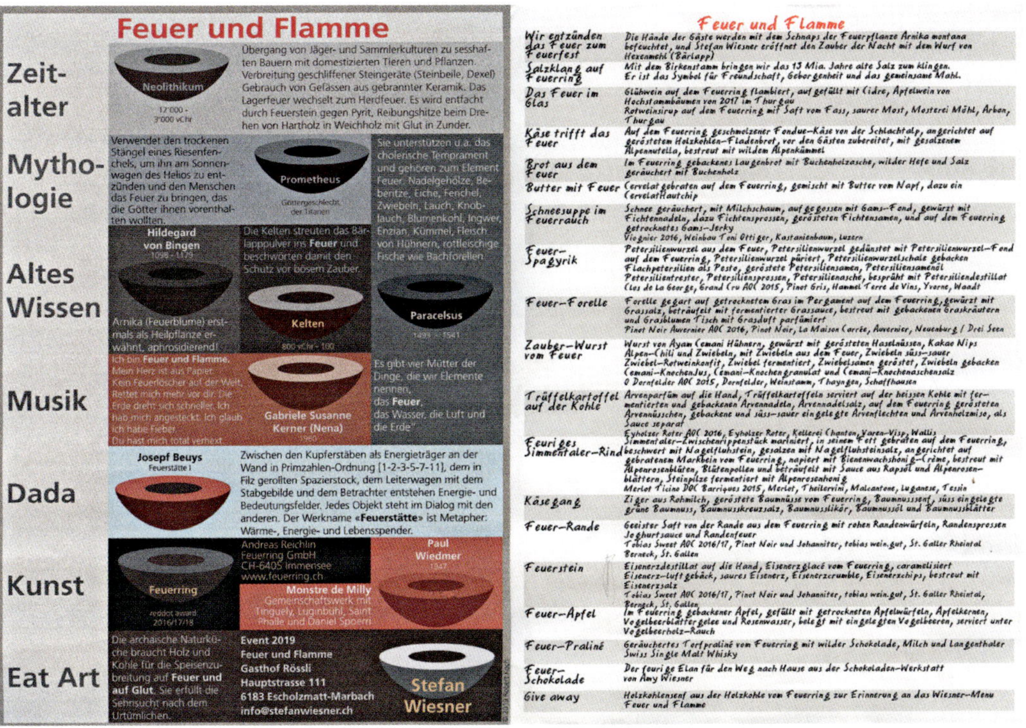


**Fig. 2** Stefan Wiesner, menu for *Fire and Flame*, 2019

Then I can withdraw the water by distilling it, drawing the taste of the stone meal out.

AMA: **But of course a very good dish is not just about taste; it's also about textures, the sense of touch, the sense of smell, the visual aspect—everything works together.**

SW: I start with chords, like a musician. These chords are composed of flavors and textures. The *Flint* dessert has a first note: the distillate. The ice cream is the second, the biscuit the third, and acidic iron is number four. Iron-ore crumble is the fifth note, followed by iron-ore chips, and the iron-ore salt sprinkled over the dish provides the last note. So *Flint* has a total of seven notes. The more I use in a dish, the more intensely I play with you. If you have a course of seven or even ten notes, then with each forkful, each spoonful, something is happening to you: "Sweet … ah, sour … ah, crispy … ah, it's hot here … and it's cold there!" You focus on the dish. This is more than food intake: as a chef, I capture your olfactory sense, your visual sense, your whole body.

AMA: **Your drawing for this dessert** [fig. 3] **is your first concept, before trying out the dish. Do flavor combinations exist in your head beforehand?**

SW: Yes. The important starting point for this menu is what fire thematically contains. What does fire involve? What does it mean to cook on a fire? What do my mental images of fire look like, and what is the story of fire? There are different approaches for me: if I prepare the dish directly on the fire, then it is the direct material connection with fire, or it may be only a visual cue, the image of the fire flower [fireball lily], for example. And the season when I cook a certain menu is always very important.

AMA: **You wrote in one of your books that a good cook always has to know what tastes best when.**

SW: Yes, theoretically that's true. But at the same time, I also have to differ. An exponent of haute cuisine, for example, will say: at this precise moment this particular strawberry variety from that producer tastes the best. That may be true. But I say that even an immature, bright-green strawberry can taste very good. I can explain this with another example. You want to prepare a great strawberry dessert for Mother's Day. So you buy strawberries in the supermarket, try them, and find that they taste like cucumbers. A good cook should then reason like this: "Cucumber … aha—I'll make the dish with vinegar, oil, and dill!"

AMA: **In addition to distillation, are there any other cooking techniques you know that produce interesting and unexpected flavor changes in an ingredient?**

SW: Yes. Working with ants, for example. Last fall we put a pumpkin on an anthill. Within a week the ants had transformed it with their formic acid. Then we cooked the pumpkin sous vide and puréed it. The formic acid was in the pumpkin; normally a pumpkin is not acidic, but through this process it became so. Or else you can take an egg to the ants for flavoring—eggs are known to have a porous shell and absorb odors and flavors from the environment very quickly— that's wonderful! One can change the taste of an egg very quickly: for example, when I put a truffle alongside an egg, the egg quite soon tastes of truffle.

AMA: **So you do not have to use the well-known classic cooking techniques. Your cuisine goes much further, leaving these transformation processes to nature.**

SW: Yes. For example, you can bury something in the ground for a long time. For my *Jeremias Gotthelf* menu, we are now cooking potatoes directly in the soil in which they grew. We make this earth edible again, turning it into a crumble, chocolate sauce …

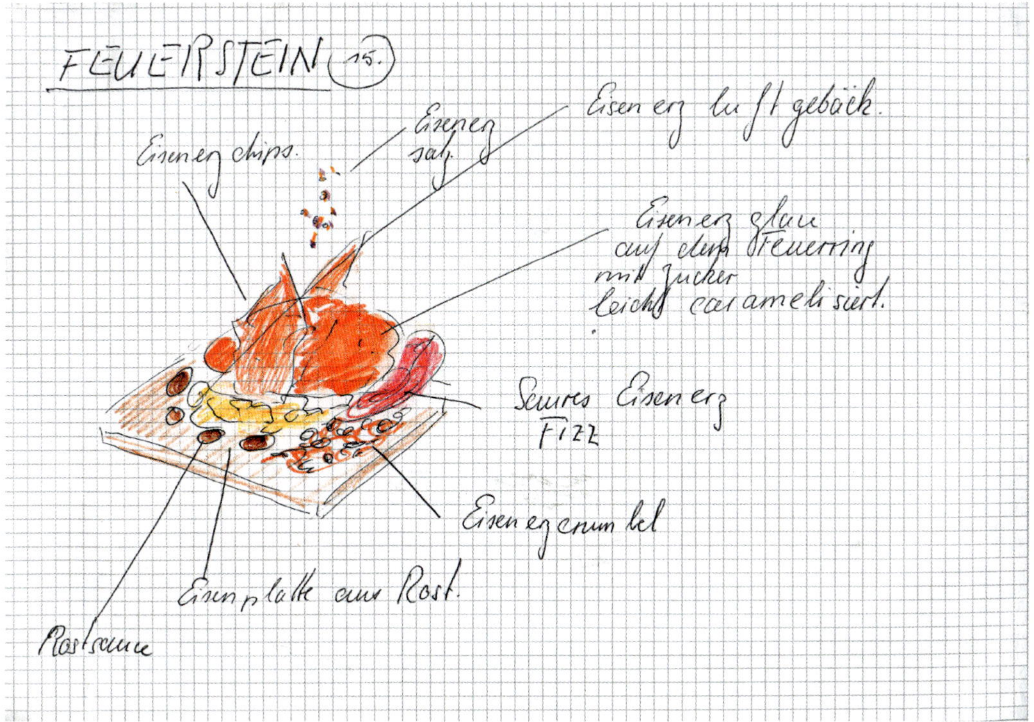


**Fig. 3** Stefan Wiesner,
sketch of the dessert
*Flint* from the menu
*Fire and Flame*, 2019

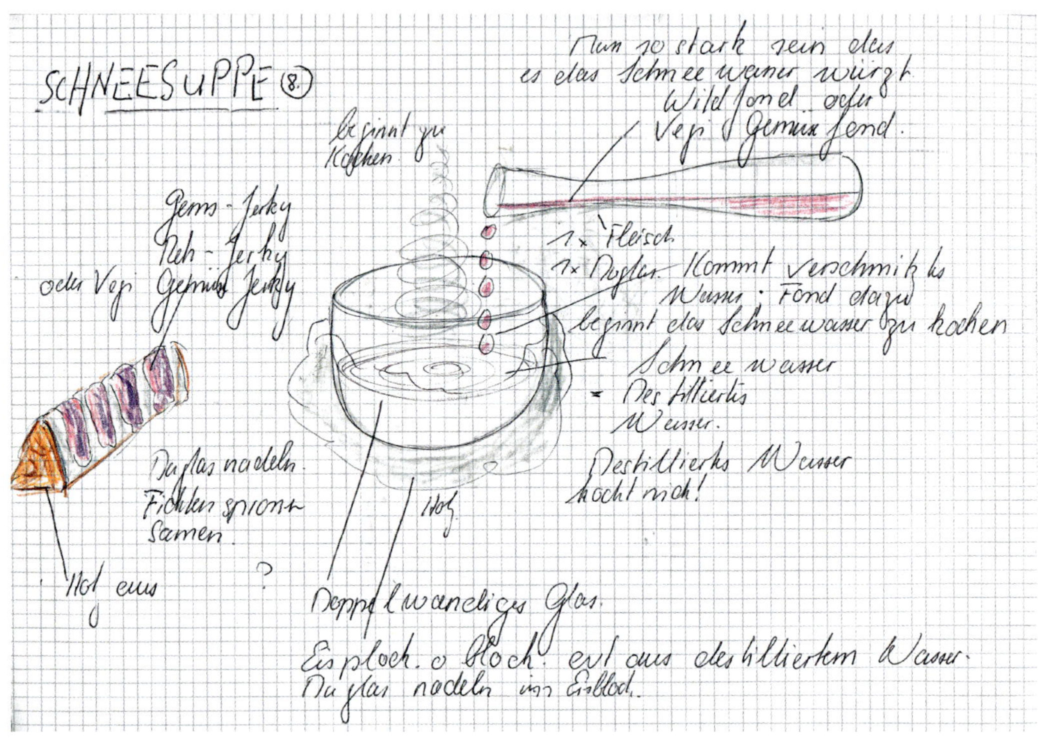


Stefan Wiesner, sketch
of the dish *Snow Soup
in Fire Smoke* from the
menu *Fire and Flame*,
2019

     **Stefan Wiesner, Annja Müller-Alsbach**

We cook everything that has to do with the potato, even its roots, which are said to be poisonous. We pickle them and we use the potato peel. This is fascinating, although it is actually no more than a potato that comes from the earth.

**AMA: Is there one of the unusual ingredients that you particularly like working with?**

SW: Yes, wood! The forest, that's the most beautiful and valuable material for me. Trees can communicate with each other. At least for the moment, the subtleties of the forest's flavors are even richer for me than those of stones.

**AMA: How do you see your future should you no longer be working as the chef here at the Rössli?**

SW: I've tried to establish an academy. The problem is that my cooking philosophy is obviously not understood by those in the trade associations who are responsible for the training of cooks. I tried, but it does not work. Therefore, I've been offering courses and workshops for amateur and professional chefs in my own Nature Academy at Gasthaus Rössli for some time now.

**AMA: In addition to your work at Rössli, you are a lecturer at the FHNW in Basel in the aesthetic practice module. How do you approach teaching future visual artists and designers?**

SW: First, I explain my Wiesner Key to them. I want to make them aware that they have to create their own foundation for themselves. They must develop their own philosophy out of knowledge from the past and from the most up-to-date discoveries. I try to teach them to play around with it. Then I explain what materials they can use. I go with them into the forest and show them the beauty of nature, show them that nature is the greatest artist. Then we cook in the forest

using ingredients from nature. And I do a sausage workshop with them. They are given the task of developing a theme that they must then implement in the sausage they produce: for example, a sausage without intestine casing.

**AMA: How does that work, making a sausage with no casing?**

SW: You use a Coca-Cola can, for example, or you fill a brassiere with sausage meat, or you can use stockings. Two students had not prepared their own topic, so I gave them the themes of "green" and "black," and they had to look for edible materials that matched the theme of "green" and "black" in the immediate vicinity—in the shopping center, in the studio. Another student made a heavy metal sausage. She burned drumsticks, put the ashes into the sausage, then sonicated the salt with the music of Iron Maiden and added it to the sausage meat as well. The mixture was then stuffed into iron tubes and grilled in them. She served it to Iron Maiden background music and next to an Iron Maiden T-shirt. That student understood how far you can go. When I teach cooks, they are often biased and hard to convince; art students, on the other hand, often have a greater affinity with my sort of cookery. There is more understanding of my cooking philosophy in the art world.

**AMA: How do you understand your job and philosophy as a chef as compared to the creative work of visual artists? What do you want to give the art students and the participants of the Nature Academy on the way?**

SW: I think that as a cook I can go much further with my art, with my Wiesner philosophy, than a painter or sculptor in the traditional sense can do. My goal is to serve my guests at the Rössli with dishes in such a way as to stimulate all of their senses and at the same time excite their spirit and their imagination. It is essential to this that I still

tell them the stories behind the individual
courses of my menus before serving the
individual dishes: what I call storytelling.
I explain the ingredients and the preparation
methods, their effects, how they interact, and
what my vision is. I deliberately distribute
the menu only at the end. I believe that as
a chef, I can manipulate my guests in some
way. For example, dishes can be erotically
stimulating, or they can trigger positive and
negative emotions and memories. Theoretically, I can influence the health of the guest
with my food. My dishes should appeal
to more senses than just that of taste. For
example, before or during service of a dish,
I spray a natural perfume, I pour a certain
essence on guests' hands, integrate acoustic
stimuli such as music or noises, or I influence
the ambiance of the dining room. I take my
guests on a sensual journey with every bite
they eat. I try to pass on this all-embracing
aesthetic experience of cookery.



Stefan Wiesner, Annja Müller-Alsbach

This interview was conducted
on July 26, 2019, in Escholzmatt,
Switzerland, and appears here in
shortened and revised form.

1 "Modifiers serve
to enhance and/or
supplement a certain
taste or smell. Their
effects ennoble and
harmonize. Vanilla,
banana, and ginger
complement almost
all ingredients."
Stefan Wiesner,
*Avantgardistische
Naturküche: Mit Lexikon
der Geschmacks-
kombinationen*
(Aarau, 2011), p. 222.

# The Still Life as a Feast for the Eyes

Karin Leonhard

Legend has it that Nathaniel Bacon (1585–1627) was very fond of his kitchen maid, and not just as a model. He immortalized her in several of his paintings, but she plays her most prominent role in his kitchen still life from around 1620–25 that is exhibited at the Tate Gallery in London [**fig. 1**]. There she is flanked in a charming way by an enormous offering of fruits and vegetables from Bacon's household, more precisely from his exclusive gardens in Suffolk. Bacon was the scion of a wealthy English family and the nephew of the natural philosopher Francis Bacon (1561–1626). Just like his grandfather, father, and uncle before him, he was also especially interested in growing plants and horticulture. After marrying the wealthy widow Jane Cornwallis (1581–1659), he lived at Culford Hall in southern England. Several of his kitchen and market scenes survive there, for Bacon was active from the early seventeenth century as an extremely talented amateur painter, especially of still lifes and portraits. Scholars suspect that during a lengthy stay on the continent—in the Netherlands, for example—the still recent genre of market and kitchen paintings had come to his attention; this genre had been established by Flemish masters such as Pieter Aertsen (ca. 1509–1575) and Joachim Beuckelaer (ca. 1530–1573/74) and was to substantially influence the still life painting of the time. Such painters were imported to England in the early seventeenth century, but Bacon was the first English painter to turn to such subjects himself and to execute them immediately in large formats.

In his still lifes, therefore, his horticultural and artistic interests converge, which is why they are especially relevant for us. Bacon had, as noted, grown up in a family for which horticulture was a constant topic. His uncle Francis had designed a much praised garden on his estate Old Gorhambury, and in 1625 he also wrote the first essay in English on the art of the garden: "Of Gardens." Nathaniel and his wife, Jane, were also friends with Lucy Harington (1580–1627), Countess of Bedford, whose formal gardens in Twickenham and Moor Park, Hertfordshire, were of exquisite beauty and inspired visitors to true hymns of praise. Letters survive in which the Countess asks Nathaniel for plants from his garden, and the inventory catalog of the English gardener and botanist John Tradescant the Younger (1608–1662) lists "Sir Nathaniel Bacon's great Peare," a variety of pear, as if it were famous. In his *Cookmaid with Still Life of Vegetables and Fruit*, we can see, with extreme foreshortening, parts of his kitchen garden in extreme perspectival reduction, from which many of

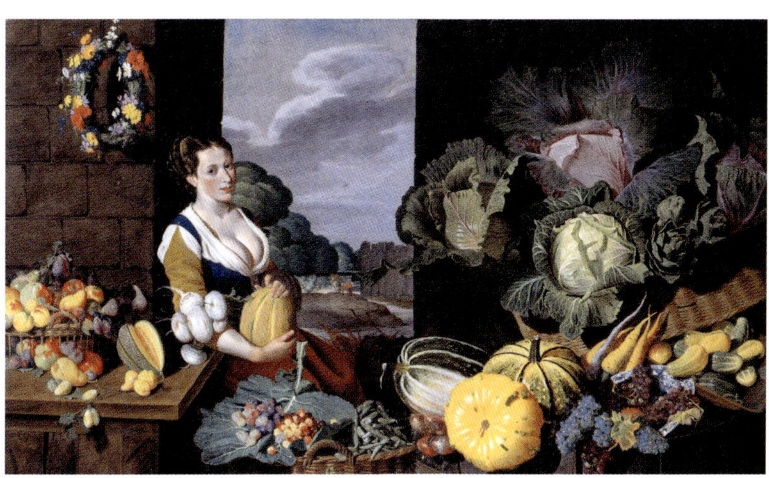

Fig. 1 Nathaniel Bacon
*Cookmaid with Still Life of Vegetables and Fruit*,
ca. 1620–25
Oil on canvas,
151 × 247.5 cm
Tate Britain, London

the abundant vegetables and fruits seen in the foreground of the painting originated. This results in a close connection between the expanding depths of the painting, in which a group of people is seen in miniature and the almost monumental-looking fruit is shown in close-up, whose skins and sheets are so delicately painted that viewers feel as if they could almost grasp them in their hands. Especially the heads of cabbage daringly placed in the right half of the painting, with the tactilely painted leaves with large veins, seem giant in comparison to the small figures in the background, so that the hierarchical relation of human and vegetal existence is reversed here, and an appropriate venue is created for the protruding force of nature: Mother Earth. The buxom kitchen maid, in turn, looks like a suitable representative of this primordial force of growth and nourishment. The impression of fertility that the painting radiates is suggested by the parallelism of the melons on offer and the equally permissively presented and voluptuous décolletage of the girl—and, in the case of the melon already cut open to the right of her, is pointedly illustrated to even the most naive viewer by a repetition of motifs. Abundance and opulence are the main subjects of the painting as a whole, and it becomes clear that this impression is indebted both to the rich natural motif of fruit and flowers and to their artistic rendering: Mother Nature's biotic power to produce a number of varieties, forms, and colors competes with the painter's creative abilities to conjure up such diversity on the canvas with his brush.

Barrie Juniper has shown that Bacon, in his garden in Suffolk, cultivated a wide variety of fruit and vegetables that were still regarded as exotic in the early seventeenth century. Botanical knowledge was spreading in England at the time, and new plants, especially from America, were coming onto the market. In 1621, Henry Danvers (1573–1643) designed the first botanical garden—initially as a physic garden—in order to, as he put it, "promote the furtherance of learning and to glorify nature." In Bacon's kitchen still life, in turn, we see primarily squash-like plants, whose seeds had been imported from the Americas, which were very popular in England from the early sixteenth century onward, not least because they were easy to grow. The aforementioned melons, by contrast, needed to be cultivated carefully in so-called dung beds to ensure the necessary warmth and hence the growth of large, sweet fruit. Not easy to spot at first glance, but emphasized by Juniper as unusual, are the legumes in the basket in the foreground, especially the runner bean, which also originated in the Americas, and the gleaming white turnips, which the maid is proudly holding in her arms, still considered a rarity at the time. Not all of the grape varieties depicted were native, according to Juniper, so that the knowledgeable viewer was clearly shown Bacon's extraordinary cuisine and exquisite taste.[1] It is striking to see how subtly the different qualities of the fruits were worked out: hard and rough peels are placed next to soft and velvety ones; the netlike structure of the cabbage leaves corresponds to the striking surfaces of the squashes, which look smooth or ribbed and sometimes quite warty; the colors of the fruit and vegetables point to varying degrees of ripeness, yet everything appears to be at its peak and it is suggested that the fruits would taste sweet or at least intense. In fact, the painter's palette is playing—in relation to the desired reception by the viewer, that is—an important "preparatory" role here, since the color employed by Bacon is bright and highly saturated. The clothes of the kitchen maid are in the primary colors red, yellow, and blue, and this chromatic composition runs through the entire painting in constantly altered proportionality. Another hint of the coloristic values of the painting is the wreath of braided flowers hanging on the wall, which perhaps is noticed only upon closer inspection. It raises the question as to why someone in the seventeenth century would believe that a still life could function analogously to the sense of taste and hence literally become a feast for the eyes.

      **Karin Leonhard**

### Saturated Colors

Whenever a wreath or garland of flowers appears in a seventeenth-century painting, one is reminded of the anecdote found in Pliny the Elder (ca. 23/24–79) concerning the painter Pausias and the flower girl Glycera. The Dutch painter and writer Karel van Mander (1548–1606) took it up in his *Grondt der edel vry schilder-const* (translated as *The Foundation of the Noble Free Art of Painting*) of 1604, which was intended for apprentice painters but did not offer instructions on the practice of paintings. Instead, it addressed the principles of art on a high literary level—and made it the model of a varied and balanced coloring of paintings: "If we too get this part right, like the girl Glycera from Sicyon, a seller of wreaths of flowers, who knew how to arrange her flowers in 10,000 ways in an uncommonly beautiful fashion and so beautifully especially in the combination of colors that it charmed the painter Pausias and he courted her, then our work will be wonderfully improved. … Let us rend our garments like Pausias when he saw this artful composition, imitating her bouquets and wreaths of flowers, so that he became very artful in these things."[2] Later, in the seventeenth century, Joachim von Sandrart (1606–1688) refers to this same anecdote and to a subgenre of the still life that was emerging in the meanwhile: the still life with flowers.[3] He cites Pausias as a painter who had become famous especially for "his art / to elevate and round off with colors," and Glycera the wreath binder was thus seen as his muse.[4] Van Mander's text was known in England soon after its publication, and it is reasonable to assume that Bacon was familiar with it. The integration of the wreath of flowers into his kitchen scene shows that the painter's colorful palette was understood to be an important tool when rendering the variety of fruit, and not just their forms and surfaces, but also and above all for their different qualities: ripe/unripe, sweet/sour, moist/dry, and so on. Here, too, Bacon could take up a thread in Van Mander, who had asserted in his *Grondt*: "Color lends things

their distinctiveness."[5] The idea that the coloration of things signals individual qualities or, above all, conditions was for a long time a driving force for still-life painting because its theory provided support for the pictures. The work *De groote waereld in't kleen geschildert* of 1692, by Willem Beurs (1656–1700), which addresses both the theory and practice of colors, also belongs to this tradition—the flower painter Beurs understood color to be the criterion that both reveals and orders the diversity of the world. Using the example of grapes, he makes it clear that the differences in ripeness must be differentiated in the coloring and that there are instructions—that is, recipes—for the apprentice painter to do so in the correct way: "One applies these with lake alone or with brownish-red and lake / after they are ripe; or even with some green underneath / when they have to be depicted as somewhat less ripe. The ripe ones have to be painted in the reflection with cinnabar or brownish-red / when, namely, the reflection is all red: but where it is not / some stil de grain yellow should be added under it. The grape on top is yellow as ocher / so it has to be painted there too with ocher and black"[6] **[fig. 2]**. Beurs continues describing the effect of this nuanced application of paint—by means of successful coloration, namely, he says that the painter manages to stimulate both the imagination and the appetite of the viewer: "If someone learns to paint grapes in this way / he will with time learn to make them so natural / that not only birds / but also people can be lured with them / and the womenfolk in their particular estate very easily stimulate their imagination and appetite."[7] According to Beurs, simply looking at fruit and other comestibles arouses the pleasure of taste. Elsewhere, in the discussion of depicting root vegetables and legumes, he begins to describe the viewing of a still life or kitchen painting in general as a culinary event. The emphasis he places on the different elements of such a meal is striking. They correspond, namely, to the different parts of the human body, which, according to Beurs, have to be nourished in different ways: "Just as the fruit / that are eaten either alone or together with others / delight the eyes of he who sees them / and awaken in him a special pleasure / this happens no less in the root vegetables and legumes that are prepared in the kitchen in different ways for eating / so that they nourish the human body / which is composed of many parts / in many ways / and keep its effects fresh and healthy."[8] Beurs goes so far as to propose to painters that they assemble the vegetables and fruit of their still lifes as if preparing a meal in order to stimulate the viewer's appetite, on the one hand, and satisfy it, on the other: "If now someone does not want to know / what he is sometimes eating or is prescribed to eat root vegetables and legumes / that grow in front of kitchens / he will not go wrong / if he seeks out a sensible and practiced painter and has him make a painting of three or four pieces / containing nearly all fruit / and those that belong together / should also be painted together. Then he can always just look at these lists / and that will easily bring something to mind / and awaken his appetite to eat as he pleases."[9] Here the still life functions as a kind of cookbook proposing different combinations of tastes and illustrating the meal in anticipation. Bacon's kitchen still life seems to fulfill just such a task when one considers the demonstrative stance with which the maid spreads out the freshly harvested fruit in order to then turn it into a frugal meal.

## Bitterness and Sweetness

That still lifes can and should stimulate the appetite is repeatedly stated in early modern texts and treatises. They discuss the possibility of conflating the senses of seeing and taste, which were regarded as probable already in antique and medieval theories of perception and even taken as a given in peripatetic writings and commentaries. Aristotle (384–322 BC), namely, discusses the processes of visual perception in connection with other sense impressions, especially smell and taste, and even makes them analogous, because he believes that they are based on two opposed principles, such as black and white or bitterness and sweetness, and so forth: "every sensible object involves contrariety."[10] Thus he can equate white and yellow colors with a sweet taste but black ones with a bitter or harsh taste, and the parallels between the senses of seeing and taste are also made on the secondary level of mixed forms.[11]

But why does the sense of smell correspond with the sense of taste and hence also with that of vision? According to Aristotle, the correspondence is explained by the so-called "variants" in each case, which are emitted by visible, tasteable, smellable

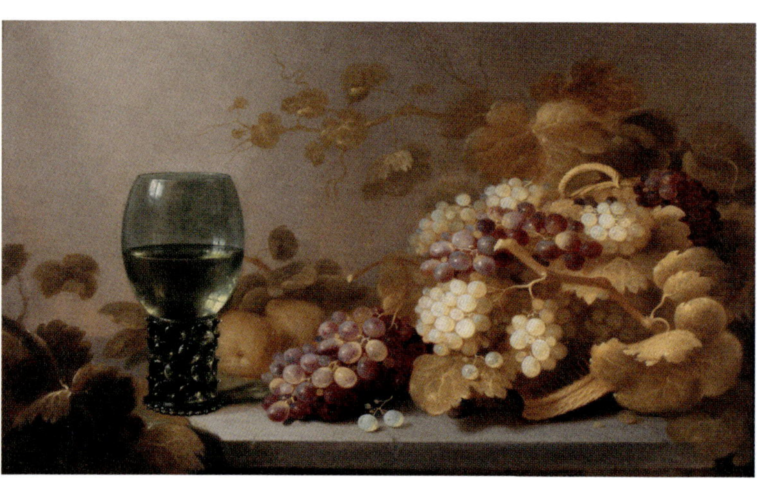

Fig. 2 Roelof Koets and Pieter Claesz
*Still Life with Grapes, Apples, and Rummer*, 1634
Oil on oak, 52.5 × 84 cm
Gift of the Albert Koechlin-Stiftung, 2003, Kunstmuseum St. Gallen



Karin Leonhard

objects and reach the sense organs. When the "variant" of the taste has, for example, the same mixture between sweet and bitter as the "variant" between white and black, then the two can be related and linked to each other as impressions. "As colours come from a mixing of white and black," according to Aristotle in *De sensu*, "so flavours are a mixing of sweet and bitter. And each pair, in some greater or smaller ratio … so do flavours from a mixing of sweet and bitter. The several colours exhibit varying proportions. … Only the flavour of the sweet is rich, and the salt is virtually the same as the bitter; between these extremes lie the harsh, the pungent, the astringent, and the acid. The kinds of flavour are roughly equal in number to those of colours. There are seven of each, if, as is natural, one regards grey as a variety of black (the alternative is to class yellow with white, as rich with sweet); red, purple, green and blue are colours intermediate between white and black, and the rest are combinations of these. And just as black is a privation of white in the transparent, so the salt or bitter is privation of the sweet in nutrient moisture."[12] Several of these mixtures are said to be out of tune, like chords in music, and cause discomfort, whereas others please our senses more. Fundamentally, there are certain colors, scents, and tastes, Aristotle continues, that inherently seem more pleasant to us than others. He cites as an example the scent of flowers, since it is always pleasant.[13]

Such statements were carried over into the early modern period and played a role for the genre of the still life as well. For even if taste and smell cannot be depicted in paintings, they nevertheless constitute one part of the iconography of still lifes. Such works enter into a close alliance with the pictorial motifs, that is, with the fruit and flowers in all states of ripening and withering, respectively, and their color, scent, and taste change in that process. For that reason, one can say that the still life, or part of it, reflects the essence of sensory perception— primarily visual perception, but also smell-ing, tasting, hearing, and touching [**fig. 3**]. And perhaps Justus Juncker (ca. 1701/03– 1767) not only summed up in *Still Life with Pear and Insects*, in a slightly ironic gesture, this tradition of the genre but also brought it to a close: a pear depicted in glowing colors that evoke for a moment the sweetness and juiciness of the ripe fruit contrast with the cold stone plinth on which it was once placed with circumspection. At the moment in which its sensuousness was transformed into a painting, it became a memorial to itself.

The painters of the seventeenth and early eighteen centuries found themselves in a real competition to depict in painting extremes of taste, such as sweetness or bitterness. In *Still Life with Rummer, Lemon, and Oranges* by Willem Kalf (ca. 1619–1693) [**fig. 4**], for example, the sharp edges of the peeled lemon correspond to the effort to make the sharpness of the acid visible in the small, glimmering pearls lining the upper edge of the fruit, which show how juicy it still is. A single seed is lying on the cool stone plinth, as if it had just fallen or been squeezed out of the flesh of the fruit. The rind of the lemon, in turn, stands out as white against the yellow zest along the cuts, which not only emphasizes the pores that make up the zest but also sounds a bright, piercing chord of color that strongly contrasts with the basal, earthy primary shades of the painting. That colors not only have chromatic properties but can evoke gustatory sensations was meticulously summed up once again by Johann Wolfgang von Goethe (1749–1832) with knowledge of and reference to early modern theories of color: "Every color, of whatever kind, can be full of itself, increased, overcrowded, saturated and in that case will seem more or less dark. The ancients then called them suasum πεπεισμενον [saturated], in se consumptum [consumed in itself], plenum [full], saturum κατακορες [sated], meracum ακρατον [unmixed], pressum βαρυ [heavy, pressed], adstrictum [bound together], triste [sad], austerum αυστηρον [dark], amarum πικρον [bitter, unpleasant], nubilum αμαυρον [cloudy, gloomy], profundum βαθυ [deep, vast]. It can, moreover, seem diluted and in a certain pallor; in that case, it is called dilutum [diluted], liquidum, ὑδαρες [watery, bright], pallidum εκλευκον [pale]."[14] The colors of nature can also flow together and unite, transition into one another, mix and separate, as on the painter's palette or the painting's canvas; they can be thinned and thickened; they can coagulate, congeal, darken, and fade. They can be sweet or tart, dry or damp, warm or cold, friendly or gloomy, since at any moment they are beset with qualities and indicate inner "states." Perhaps this explains—that is, the impression of "sweetness" and "bitterness" in the colors and the not just metaphorical use of terms such as "growth," "ripeness," and "decay"— the pulsating power of many a Baroque still life. Perhaps, too, this also begins to sketch the backdrop against which the genre of the still life could be established as a genuine place for color studies and become, as one can later rightly say, self-reflexive.[15]

The still lifes of the German-Dutch painter Abraham Mignon (1640–1679) offer insights into the contemporaneous reception [**figs. 5 and 6**]. Jacob Campo Weyerman (1677–1747), who was himself active as a painter of still lifes, provided extensive information about this in his *Levensbeschryvingen*. He says that each detail in the paintings is precisely worked out and plastically modeled with reflected light and cast shadows. Weyerman cannot resist the pleasure of mimetic detail in these paintings and describes a still life with flowers by Mignon in which the foliage is said to be depicted so naturally and delicately that no greater life (*leeven*) could be achieved with artificial colors. But a painting in the art gallery of the Delft collector Valerius de Reuver (1686–1739) is also said to have been splendidly painted: the peaches are almost melting in their ripeness and reveal nuances of color, conveying a beauty that could not be surpassed by those in nature; the grapes are said to be depicted so transparently that

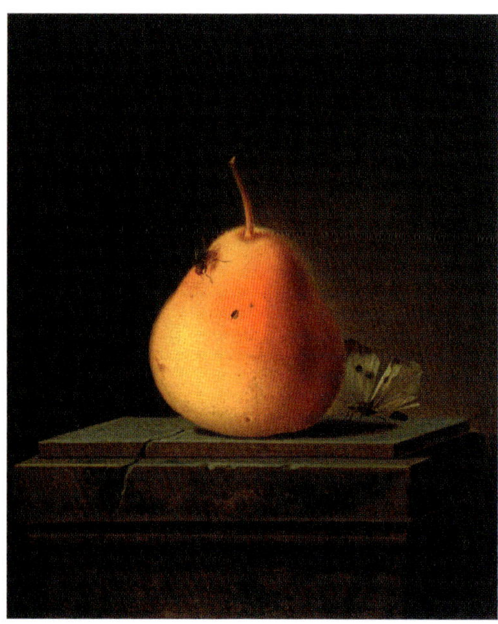

**Fig. 3** Justus Juncker *Still Life with Pear and Insects,* signed and dated "Juncker f. 1765"

Oil on oak, 25.8 × 21.4 cm Städel Museum, Frankfurt am Main

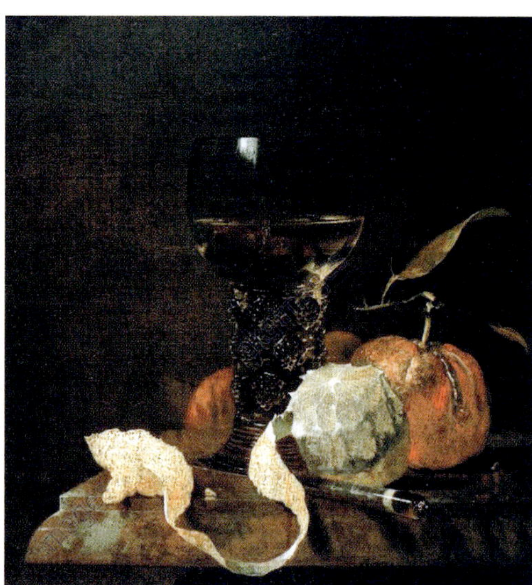

**Fig. 4** Willem Kalf *Still Life with Rummer, Lemon, and Oranges,* ca. 1663–64

Oil on canvas, 36 × 30 cm Staatliche Kunsthalle, Karlsruhe

     **Karin Leonhard**

one thinks one sees their seeds moving in the juice. He writes that it is remarkable how the painter's brush, even in such a trivial subject as the grape, can so artfully assimilate nature through the colors, arrangement, and depiction of different degrees of ripeness, so that one has the sense of facing not a brushstroke or dab of paint but the natural model itself.[16] All of the other fruits are said to be drawn, painted, and modeled with the same skill, as if the painted had covered them with their own skins and peels. The still life with fruit in Cambridge and, above all, the still life with fruit in a private collection, in which the fuzzy skin of a quince and the velvety surfaces of the peach have tiny drops of water, illustrate what Weyerman meant by that remark. Smooth peels with harsh highlights alternate with soft ones whose reflections glimmer gently; sometimes the skins have burst and the moist insides emerge. The pearls seem to be not just drops of dew but the ripeness and sweetness of the fruit's flesh sweating out. Insects are attracted by it, like the birds in Zeuxis's painting. And like Willem Beurs before him, Weyerman, too, testifies in conclusion to the power of still lifes to stir the appetite when he observes "that not just birds / but also people can be enticed by it."[17]

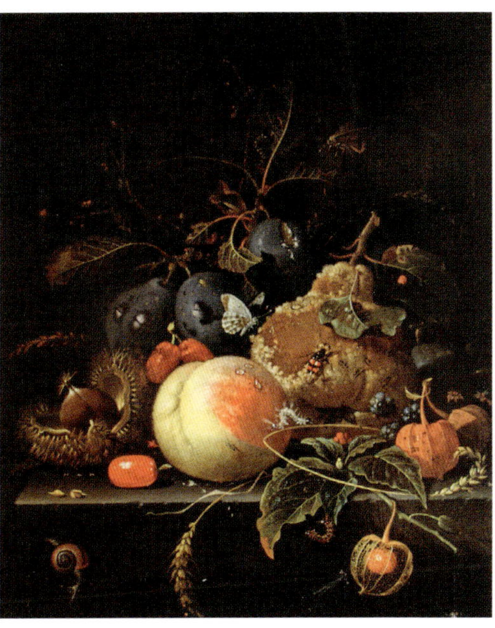

Fig. 5 Abraham Mignon
*Still Life with Rotting Fruit and Nuts on a Stone Ledge,* undated

Oil on panel, 34 × 27 cm
Fitzwilliam Museum, Cambridge

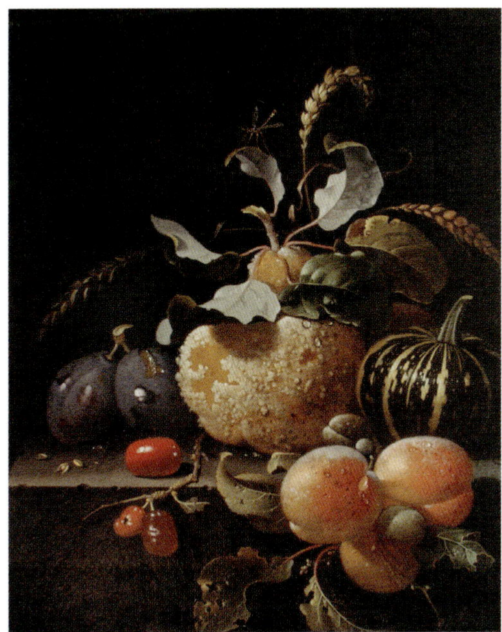

Fig. 6 Abraham Mignon
*Still Life with Fruit,* undated
Signed "A Mignon [with ligature] fe."

Oil on panel, 33 × 26 cm
Private collection

 Karin Leonhard

**1** Barrie Juniper, "Sir Nathaniel Bacon II: The Vegetable World," *British Art Journal* 1, no. 2 (Spring 2000), pp. 16–18.
**2** Rudolf Hoecker, *Das Lehrgedicht des Karel van Mander: Text, Übersetzung und Kommentar nebst Anhang über Manders Geschichtskonstruktion und Kunsttheorie*, vol. 8: *Quellenstudien zur holländischen Kunstgeschichte* (The Hague, 1916), p. 257. Karel van Mander, "Den Grondt der Edel vry Schilder-const: Waer in haer ghestalt, aerdt ende wesen, de leer-lustighe Jeught in verscheyden Deelen in Rijm-dicht wort voor ghedraghen," in *Het schilder-boeck* (Amsterdam, 1604), XI/2–3, 45r–45v: "Indien wy dit deel oock recht treffen conen / T'sal fraeylijck ons werc verschoonen te wonder / Als de Maeght Clycera van Scytionen, Bloem-krans vercoopster / die met onghewonen Aerdighen aerdt / thien duysent voudich onder Een wist te voeghen haer Bloemkens / bysonder Van verwen soo lustich / dat hem verblijde Pausias Schilder / diese daerom vrijde. … Laet ons oock aldus sorteren ons Laken / want Pausias, siende dit constich voegen / want Pausias, siende dit constich voegen / Haer Tuylkens en Hoeykens hy nae ginc maken / En werdt gheheel constich in dese saken."
**3** Joachim von Sandrart, *Teutsche Academie der Edlen Bau-, Bild- und Mahlerey-Künste*, part 1 (Nuremberg, 1675); part 2 (Nuremberg, 1679), vol. II/1, p. 25: "He [Pausias] in his youth courted a flower seller in Sicyon named Glycera, who knew a thousand ways / to bind decoratively bouquets and wreaths of flowers: which he then tried to imitate with the brush. But she knew how to change and arrange the flowers / according to colors / in so many different ways / that he could not keep up: the struggle was a pleasure to see / and he improved greatly in his art as a result."
**4** The Dutch painter and art theorist Samuel van Hoogstraten argued similarly in his *Inleyding tot de hooge schoole der schilderkonst: anders de zichtbaere werelt* (Amsterdam, 1678), comparing the painter's composition with color to arranging flowers, and so he called it, like Van Mander before him, a *tuilkonst* (art of flower arrangement). For more on this, see Paul Taylor, "The Concept of *Houding* in Dutch Art Theory," *Journal of the Warburg and Courtauld Institutes* 55 (1992), pp. 210–32; Paul Taylor, *Dutch Flower Painting, 1600–1720* (New Haven, CT, 1995), esp. pp. 77–114 ("The Flower Piece and Dutch Art Theory").
**5** Hoecker 1916, XIII, 50v (see note 2).
**6** Willem Beurs, *De groote waereld in 't kleen geschildert* (Amsterdam, 1692), pp. 135–36.
**7** Ibid., pp. 136–37.
**8** Ibid., pp. 149–50.
**9** Ibid., pp. 153–54.
**10** Aristotle, "On Sense and Sensible Objects," in *On the Soul; Parva Naturalia; On Breath*, trans. W. S. Hett, rev. ed. (Cambridge, MA, 1957), pp. 207–77, esp. p. 263 (445b25–26).
**11** See ibid., p. 245 (442a17–26).
**12** Ibid., p. 245 (442a13–27).
**13** Ibid., p. 253 (443b28–29). In his *Philebos* (51a–e), Plato expressed himself very similarly, describing the scent of flowers as a true pleasure, a blessing.
**14** Johann Wolfgang von Goethe, "Zur Farbenlehre," in *Gedenkausgabe der Werke, Briefe und Gespräche*, vol. 16: *Naturwissenschaftliche Schriften I* (Zurich, 1961), p. 288.
**15** The discussion of the *colores austeri* and *colores floridi* also belongs in this context. For more on this, see Karin Leonhard, "White Earth; or, How to Cultivate Color in the Field of Painting: Still Life and Baroque Color Theory," in *Vision and Its Instruments: Art, Science, and Technology in Early Modern Europe*, ed. Alina Payne (University Park, PA, 2015), pp. 190–215.
**16** See Jacob Campo Weyerman, *De levensbeschryvingen der Nederlandsche konst-schilders en konst-schilderessen*, 4 vols. (The Hague, 1729–39), pp. 2:394–95.
**17** Ibid.

# Mouth of Hell, Ravenousness, Palatal Pleasures: Incorporating as Mythical, Political, and Erotic Parallel Action

**Ralf Beil**

Eating can simply represent a means for humans to survive. In many cases, however, it plays another role. Whether cannibalism or vegetarianism, ingesting almost always has mythical or power-political dimensions, and over the course of history increasingly religious, sociological, and aesthetic ones as well. The real act of taking in nourishment becomes, in a parallel action, symbolic activity—between Eros and Death, heaven and hell, art and politics.

The oral cavity as paradigmatic passageway for internalizing food is revealed as the venue of a specific kind of semantic carousel in which the tongue becomes the vanishing point of a culinary cosmos fanned out in a perspectival view. This path of tasting and ingesting the world runs from Ithaca by way of Bern and Baku, from the Brazilian jungle by way of the park in Bomarzo, to the Tree of Knowledge of Good and Evil.

### Licking Jam from the Hood

In 1964, Allan Kaprow realized *Household*, which had been commissioned by Cornell University. This early performance took place without an audience, just the actors and actresses moving about the remote trash dump. It begins with: "Men build wooden tower on a trash mound"; then: "Women build nest of saplings and strings."[1] The roles appear to be clearly assigned. But then:

"Cars arrive, towing smoking wreck … . Women go inside nest and screech. Men go for smoking wreck, roll it into dump, cover it with strawberry jam. … Women go to car and lick jam"[2] [**fig. 1**].

Is this about a central cult of petro-modernism, ritual worship, and the sexual energy of the automobile? Is it about another level of intimacy: the ritual stretching out on the hood followed by licking its curves off with one's tongue? Is the jam just the orally experienceable extrapolation of the seductive power of the automobile, which had previously been underscored by Ödön von Horváth in his drama *Kasimir und Karoline* of 1932?[3]

The second half of the performance contradicts what in the beginning seems still to be happening in the classic way based on the system of sexual gratification: "Men destroy nest with shouts and cursing." But then: "Women destroy men's poles and tower, laughing, yelling."[4] And further: "Women jump men, rip off shirts and fling shirts into smoking trash." Then they take off their own "blouses, waving them overhead like hankies, each singing own rock-n-roll tune and twisting, dreamy-like." At the conclusion, the men "go to wreck …, begin to demolish car…, set fire to it."[5]

In addition to serving as a veritable group therapy session on gender equality and sexual

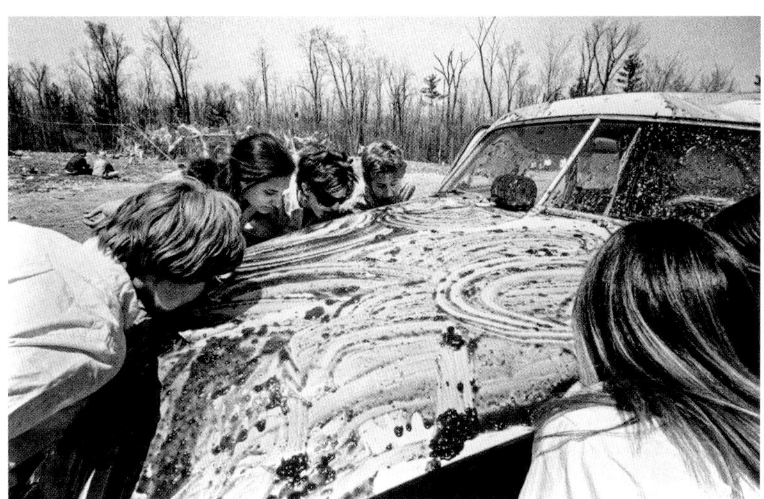

Fig. 1 Allan Kaprow
*Household, Women licking jam off a car,*
1964
Happening presented for the Festival of Contemporary Arts City dump, Ithaca, New York
Photo documentation of the performance by Sol Goldberg

liberation, Allan Kaprow's performance also deconstructs the car as the dominantly masculine object of the American "household." Five years before Woodstock, in the same year in which the United States entered the Vietnam War, art played out an uprising for the better in which the sweetness of jam became the catalyst of the action. Only today, more than fifty years later, is the dual message about human beings and machines slowly reaching the center of society.

**Lobster on Bare Skin**

Even before Eat Art became a concept in the 1960s, Meret Oppenheim initiated *Frühlingsfest* (Spring Feast) or *Le Festin* in Bern in 1959. The basic idea of this celebration among friends was simple: "Two women and three men eat from a naked woman, so three couples in all."[6] The woman is lying on a table lit by candles: "Face and neck gilded, on the right and left a mountain of candied fruit that disappears under a wreath of roses and mimosas."[7]

Oppenheim arranged the prepared foods on a girl who had been given a sedative to sleep. Steak tartare, button mushroom salad, and sweets covered her naked body, "beginning with the hors d'oeuvres on her thighs and abdomen, ending with raspberry and chocolate whipped cream on her breasts."[8] With her artist friends, Oppenheim ate the food directly from the body of the reclining girl. "It was a lovely festival. It should be celebrated every year now instead of Easter,"[9] she commented later, thereby suggesting how the eating action in the circle of friends was understood by her: as a reflection on archaic, matriarchal origins, when in the spring one celebrated the resurrection not of Christ but of the great Mother Earth. A cult rite is suggested above all by the sacred gilding of neck and face, elevating the girl to an idol of fertility. The calmly sleeping girl becomes the living altar of *Frühlingsfest*, in which eating is realized in a comprehensively energetic, mythical, and pan-erotic way.

It would become clear, already that winter, just how fragile the synesthetic utopia and the liberated Eros of the intimate festival of fertility in Bern were, when Meret Oppenheim repeated her *Festin* under other circumstances in Paris. Staged at the urging of André Breton, *Dîner sur la femme nue* (Dinner on the Naked Woman) for the opening of the *Exposition inteRnatiOnale du Surréalisme E.R.O.S.* at the Galerie Daniel Cordier, in December 1959, was primarily a social event: a gala dinner at which the imaginatively decorated woman's body was now more of a tableau vivant for langoustines and other delicacies, calling rather for the stage direction of Salvador Dalí [**fig. 2**].[10]

The shellfish, which seem to bear so clearly the signature of the Catalan artist and his "lobster eroticism," have, for that reason alone, no business being in a *Festin* signed by Oppenheim, because there everything was eaten with mouth and hands from the skin of the naked girl. By contrast, in Paris, as if for a cold buffet, they ate conventionally with plates and silverware and drank champagne from the glasses offered. The *Festin inaugural* thus became a culinary happening, restricted to male-dominated erotic fantasies. Synesthetic pleasure mutated into cannibalistically inspired lust, a private ritual into a voyeuristic spectacle.

**Cake Battle under the Swastika**

Scene change: Germany in 1933. Hitler and his minister of propaganda are having a tête-à-tête at the dining table. Joseph Goebbels is chipper and cheerful. After all, it is about propaganda for the first "Eintopfsonntag" (Stew Sunday) of the Winterhilfswerk (Winter Relief Fund) on October 1: "Stew with the Führer on Sunday!"[11] Just months after seizing power, the alimentary preparations for everything to come are starting.

"Collective self-abstemiousness every other Sunday is intended … to solidify the community of the people. 'Eighty million united by eating stew' is the slogan. But behind that [stands] the necessity to conserve meat and other high-value foodstuffs."[12] During maneuvers, too, as seen in photographs of a lunch on the battlefield in 1938,

 Ralf Beil

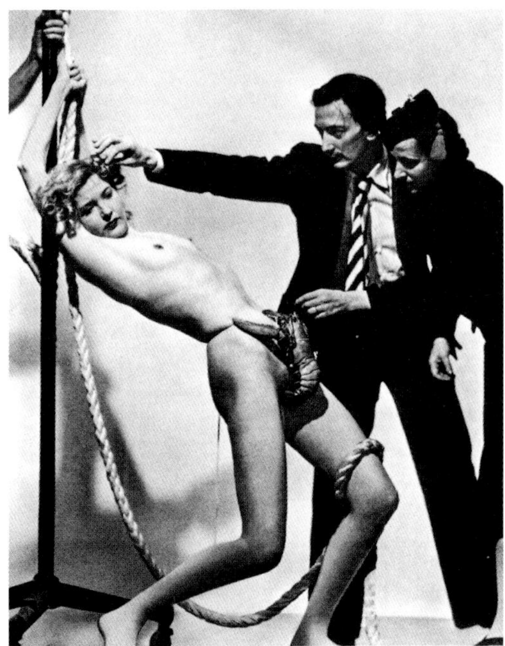

Fig. 2 Salvador Dalí Photo session in preparation for *Le Rêve de Vénus*, Murray Korman Studios, New York, 1939, photo by George Platt Lynes

the German general staff with and, around Hitler preferred to eat soup, bread, and, at most, some fruit. The series of dishes may have been due not only to propaganda but also to the Führer's irritable bowel and his constant digestion problems. He "ate after 1930 hardly any meat at all but instead lots of raw food."[13]

On September 1, 1939, the day of the invasion of Poland, by which Adolf Hitler triggered World War II, the Reichsvollkornbrotausschuss (Reich Whole-Wheat-Bread Committee) was also founded in Berlin. The idea was to make Germany self-sufficient through bread, but also through the heroic deployment on the home front: "The struggle for whole-wheat bread is a struggle for the health of the people." Aryan ideal nutrition served the purpose, according to the head of the committee and the Reich health minister, "not only of preserving the people and race in its state but also of increasing it."[14] In both reality and symbol, this was about the great "struggle" in general, which in addition to new lebensraum to the east included self-sufficiency, that is, autarky from the enemy abroad.

Fuels for human beings and machines were equally important to the war effort. Accompanied by music swelling with pathos, in a propaganda film from 1942 Hitler is seen drawing on a map the route to conquer the oil wells of Baku. His generals are enthusiastic. All of them are almost childishly joyous at the sight of a platter of cake being brought in, made euphoric by the Blitzkrieg that has already been carried out, as it were, by the stroke of a crayon [**fig. 3**].

The conquering of the Caspian Sea was staged as an almost cannibalistic devouring of territory. With chocolate frosting and sugar coating, it must have been just to the Führer's taste, who according to his diet chef, Constanze Manziarly, whom the SS guards jokingly called Frau Marzipani, was very fond of cakes and desserts. "I bake a lot, often for hours, but by the evening it's all gone,"[15] lamented the young woman from Innsbruck in a letter from the Führer's bunker.

"That 'the way to a politician's heart is through his belly' is felt by no one as much as me."[16] This note by the diet chef of the very sensitive Führer, dated October 29, 1944, takes on an especially macabre note in light of the blockade of Leningrad, with its contemptuously inhuman strategy that tolerated that hundreds of thousands would die of starvation. From September 1941 to January 1944, the city was cut off: no electricity, no water, no food—that was the motto of the German generals. "The people of Leningrad are eating nearly anything of organic origin: they are cooking leather, scraping the glue out of carpets, mixing sawdust and cotton into bread, chasing dogs, cats, rats, and sparrows. The Soviet secret service NKVD has counted up to February 1942 … more than a thousand cases of cannibalism."[17] But that was just the beginning: the blockade of the city would last 900 days. In the end, neither Leningrad nor Baku was conquered—the only evidence of the Blitzkrieg is the battle played out on the cake on celluloid.

**Human Flesh: Raw and Cooked**

In 1554, the German mercenary and cannoneer Hans Staden witnessed in the Brazilian jungle a prisoner of the Cario tribe being killed by the victorious Tupinambá. Three years later, Staden described in detail the drastic preparations for the banquet that followed: "At once he is seized by the women, who drag him to the fire, scrape all his skin off … . When the skin is scraped off, a man takes the body and cuts the legs off above the knee, and the arms. … Thereupon they cut off his back with the posterior from the fore-part: this they then divide among themselves."[18]

In a copperplate engraving by Theodor de Bry made thirty-five years later, women are literally licking their fingers. The savory taste of human flesh now far exceeded the sweetness of victory [**fig. 4**]. The flesh of the enemy was treated as a delicacy.

A second copperplate etching that Theodor de Bry added to *Warhaftige Historia und Beschreibung eyner Landschafft der Wilden Nacketen, Grimmigen Menschfresser Leuthen, in der Newenwelt America gelegen* (The True History and Description of a Country Populated by a Wild, Naked, and Savage Man-munching People, situated in the New World, America, 1557) reproduces precisely and graphically what Hans Staden described as an eyewitness: "the entrails are kept by the women, who boil them, and with the broth they make a mess called Mingau. This they and the children drink."[19]

The cultural historian Catalina Heroven sums up from a contemporary perspective the whole complex of anthropophagy described here: "Particularly when embedded in the context of colonialist practices and in a Christian understanding of morality, the cannibalistic practices of certain ethnic groups—whether real or invented—were an ideal justification for the conquest of the New World and the promotion of an idea of the 'savage.' … Already in accounts by ancient authors, anthropophagy is considered a typical feature of the foreigner."[20]

But cannibalism was by no means limited to overseas territories or antiquity; it has occurred repeatedly in Europe as well. For example, the historian and monk Rodulfus Glaber (ca. 980–ca. 1046) describes a medieval famine with cannibalistic results: "It is terrible to relate the depravity to which humanity sank. … [A]t the time, the madness of hunger drove people to devour human flesh, as had been heard in the past only rarely. People wandering past were seized by others stronger than them, butchered, cooked on a fire, and wolfed down. Many of those who had moved from one place to another to escape hunger had their throats slit at night in the homes in which they had been received to serve their hosts as food. Some tempted children with an apple or an egg, convinced them to follow them to remote places, slaughtered them, and ate them up."[21]

No one less than Lucas Cranach the Elder made a woodcut of the European cannibal in 1512, and the trail of such cannibalism by

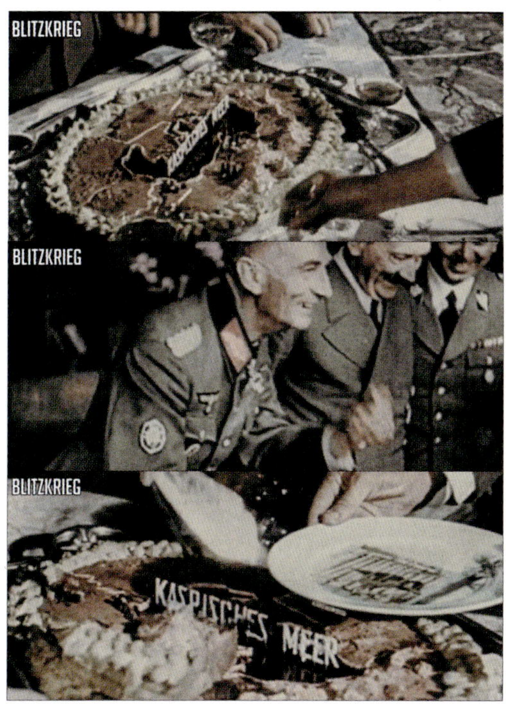

**Fig. 3** Blitzkrieg:
Hitler and his generals
celebrate the planned
capture of Baku with
a battle played out on a
cake, Vinnitsa, Ukraine,
propaganda film, 1942



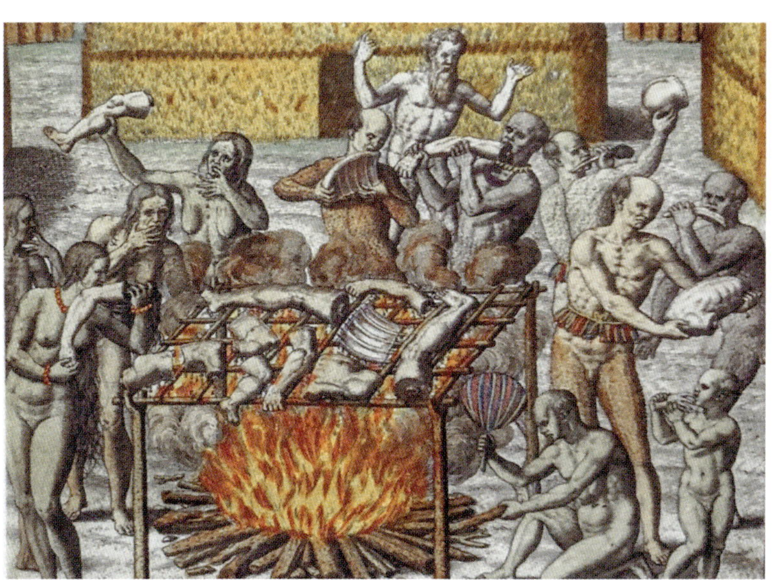

**Fig. 4** Theodor de Bry
*Cannibalism*, 1593
From Hans Staden,
*Drittes Buch Americae*,
1593, copperplate
etching, colored
Staatliche Museen
zu Berlin,
Kunstbibliothek,
Lipperheidesche
Kostümbibliothek

no means ended with the rise of the Enlightenment. One need only think of the extreme events that occurred during the sinking of the French frigate *Medusa* in 1816 when the shipwrecked sailors on a raft fed on the flesh of their comrades.

### Food for Hell, Food from God, Cycle of the Earth

Vicino Orsini, count of Bomarzo (1523–1585), did not know the hell of cannibalism from personal experience, but he did know the hell that is war. Disillusioned by the arbitrariness, violence, and double standards he had experienced, he created an alternative world with the park of Bomarzo. This *bosco sacro*, or "sacred forest," as he called it, was his place of retreat, a garden and architecture fantasy beyond compare.

This *altro mondo*, or "other world," has as one of its central architectural sculptures a walk-in fantasy of being devoured: the mouth of hell. The merciless cycle of life and death is manifested there in motifs of devouring and redemption. Ten steps of purgatory lead up to hell. Entering it is a test of courage involving the whole body, through the six-meter-tall grotesque face, with eyes nearly a meter in diameter and a mouth and lips that open more than two meters across.[22] But the tongue table with benches around it turns the oral cavity behind the jaws of hell into a veritable dining room: cool in the summer heat, protected from rain and wind in the autumn. A drawing by Giovanni Guerra from 1598 explicitly shows the mouth of hell being used for meals with musical accompaniment—the detailed drawing appears to even show a focaccia on the table [**fig. 5**].[23]

One of the main rules of Epicurus, which for Vicino Orsini ranks as a confession, is: "The beginning and root of all good is the satisfaction of the belly, and all wise and exquisite things have in this their standard of reference."[24]

The mouth of hell of Bomarzo is a special case of the worldwide phenomenon of cannibalism—going beyond any established idea of hell. The mouth of hell swallows people, but then they dine in its oral cavity, at its cost, in a sense—and piquantly on its tongue.

Whereas the gate to hell in Dante's *Divine Comedy* reads "Abandon all hope, ye who enter here," Vicino Orsini's inscription on the lips of the giant mouth inspired by it reads "Abandon all thought, ye who enter here." Replacing "hope" with "thought" is consequential. It reflects a critique of a society supposedly guided by the mind, whose true face is marked by repression of the body and hostility to pleasure. Orsini's mouth of hell, by contrast, can be read as an argument for Epicurus carved into the rock: the world may be hell, but the point is still to enjoy it, as a place for a sensory celebration of life.

Occasionally, the mouth of hell looks like a peaceful vegetarian [**fig. 6**]. But one should not be deceived: it is nevertheless a symbol of the eternal cycle of eating and being eaten, from which we do not escape and from whose immanence of guilt we cannot free ourselves. Does not every fruit of the earth eaten ultimately perpetuate, for all our secularization, the Bible's original sin of eating from the Tree of the Knowledge of Good and Evil?!

Thanks to Lucas Cranach the Elder and his painting *Adam and Eve* from the National Gallery in Prague, we are "live" witnesses of the Fall [**fig. 7**]. The painter captures the moment just a fraction of a second before Adam's bite; his lips are already starting to open. Art has never again come as close to this key moment of incorporating as it did in this painting from 1538, in which Eve, casually holding on to the Tree of the Knowledge, under the watchful eyes of the snake, guides an especially ripe fruit to Adam's mouth. And Adam looks at us as if he wanted to say: "You know what it means. Every bite will change the world from now on. Everything will become—and will perish."



Ralf Beil

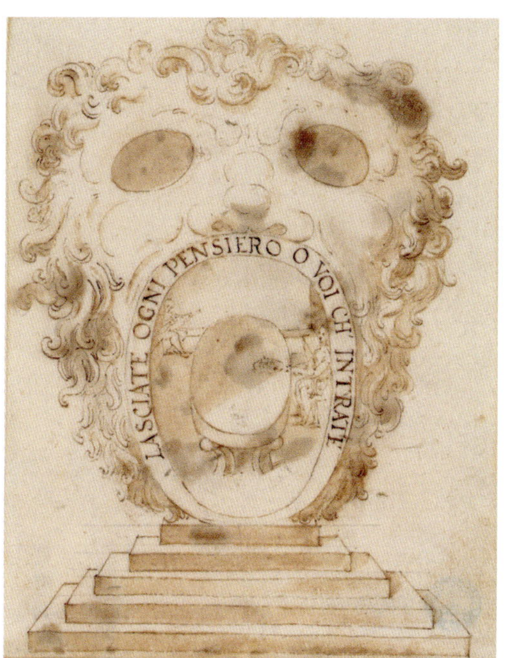

**Fig. 5** Giovanni Guerra
*Mouth of Hell with
Musician and Man
Eating*, 1598
Pen and ink, wash,
19.2 x 14.6 cm
Albertina, Vienna

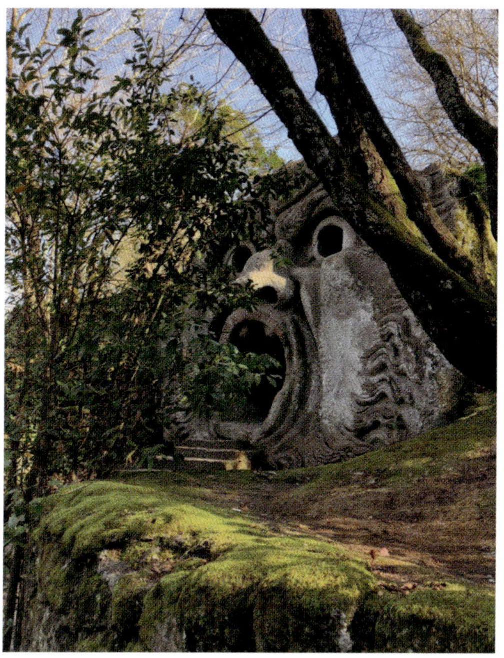

**Fig. 6** The Mouth
of Hell of Bomarzo
(1552–85) as a vege-
tarian, February 2018

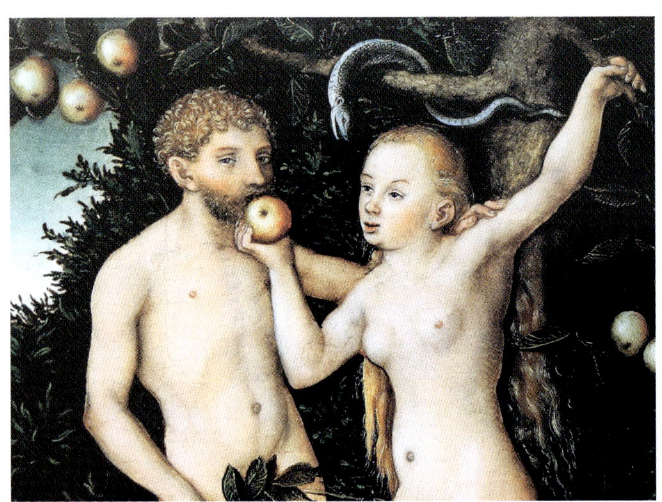

**Fig. 7** Lucas
Cranach the Elder
*Adam and Eve*, ca. 1538
Oil on wood, 49 x 33 cm
The National Gallery,
Prague (detail)

                    Ralf Beil

**1** Allan Kaprow, score for *Household* (1964), illustrated in *Allan Kaprow: Art as Life*, ed. Eva Meyer-Hermann, Andrew Perchuk, and Stephanie Rosenthal (Los Angeles, 2008), p. 174.
**2** Ibid.
**3** See Ödön von Horváth, *Kasimir und Karoline* (Frankfurt am Main, 2008).
**4** Meyer-Hermann et al. 2008 (see note 1), p. 174.
**5** Ibid.
**6** Meret Oppenheim, quoted in Ralf Beil, "Terrarium der Nudeltierchen: Meret Oppenheim," in *Künstlerküche: Lebensmittel als Kunstmaterial; von Schiele bis Jason Rhoades* (Cologne, 2002), pp. 84–101, esp. p. 93.
**7** Ibid.
**8** Ibid.
**9** Ibid.
**10** See the illustration in Beil 2002 (see note 6), p. 94, as well as the chapter "Vom Eros des Oralen: oder Der surreale Hummer – Salvador Dalí," in ibid., pp. 58–71.
**11** See Michael Sontheimer, "Hitler und der Eintopf: Suppe und Quark sollten helfen, den Krieg zu gewinnen," in "Wie Essen die Welt prägte," special issue, *Der Spiegel Geschichte* 1 (2019), pp. 126–29.
**12** Ibid., p. 128.
**13** Ibid., p. 129.
**14** Ibid., p. 127.
**15** Constanze Manziarly, quoted in Stefan Dietrich, "'Dass Politik durch den Magen geht, spürt niemand so wie ich': Vom kurzen, außergewöhnlichen Leben der jungen Innsbruckerin, die im 'Führerbunker' Hitlers Diätmahlzeiten kochte," *Zeit – Raum – Innsbruck: Schriftenreihe des Innsbrucker Stadtarchivs* 14 (2017), pp. 95–134, esp. p. 115.
**16** Ibid.
**17** "Hitlers brutaler Hunger-Plan: Leningrad-Blockade; Minus 40 Grad, Kannibalismus, überall Leichen," *Berliner Kurier*, January 14, 2014, https://www.berliner-kurier.de/news/hitlers-brutaler-hunger-plan-leningrad-blockade--minus-40-grad--kannibalismus--ueberall-leichen-3875730 (all URLs accessed in September 2019).
**18** Hans Staden, *The Captivity of Hans Stade of Hesse in A.D. 1547–1555, among the Wild Tribes of Eastern Brazil*, ed. Richard F. Burton, trans. Albert Tootal (London, 1874; orig. pub. 1557), p. 158.
**19** Ibid., pp. 158–59.
**20** Catalina Heroven, "'Ins eigene Fleisch geschnitten': Kannibalismus zwischen Gewalt und Verehrung," in *Fleisch*, ed. Stefanie Regina Dietzel et al., exh. cat. Altes Museum – Staatliche Museen zu Berlin (Cologne, 2018), pp. 52–55, esp. p. 53.
**21** Rodulfus Glaber, quoted in Johannes Saltzwedel, "'Etliche lockten Kinder an und frassen sie': Dokument: Bericht über eine Hungersnot," in "Wie Essen die Welt prägte" (see note 11), pp. 61–62, esp. p. 61.
**22** See Horst Bredekamp and Wolfram Janzer, *Vicino Orsini und der heilige Wald von Bomarzo: Ein Fürst als Künstler und Anarchist*, 2 vols. (Worms, 1985), vol. 1, p. 164.
**23** See the illustration *Höllenmaul* in ibid., vol. 2, fig. 123.
**24** Epicurus, quoted in Athenaeus, *The Deipnosophists, Books XI–XII*, trans. Charles Burton Gulick (Cambridge, MA, 1995), p. 479 (book XII, 546f).

# Food as a Medium and a Material in Art and the Kitchen

Felix Bröcker

"The emancipation of art from cuisine or pornography is irrevocable," wrote Theodor W. Adorno in his *Ästhetische Theorie* (translated as *Aesthetic Theory*),[1] with a view to the autonomy of artistic experience. In his view, it existed only if it were not about pure enjoyment, as he implied was true of the culinary, which is why he excluded it from art. As a chef who has made his roundabout way to the realm of art history, I would like to contradict Adorno and present antitheses but also parallels in the approach to food in art and in the kitchen. In both areas, implementing a craft is important, but so is reflecting on the cultural art of nutrition. Pure enjoyment is not always the focus.

**The Forward-Looking Art of Cuisine**

One famous example of a first connection between art and gastronomy is Futurist cuisine.[2] In 1932, in the context of the Futurist movement around Filippo Tommaso Marinetti (1876–1944), a Futurist cookbook was published.[3] It summarized recipes and rules that were intended to provide the foundation for a new approach to nutrition, to bring about "the abolition of everyday mediocrity from the pleasures of the palate!"[4] Their ideas combined taste impressions with those of other senses. They spoke of *conprofumo*, *conrumore*, and *conmusica* in order to identify the aroma, the taste, and the music that goes with a particular dish.[5] In dishes such as *Veal Fuselage*, *Captive Perfumes*, and *Simultaneous Ice Cream*,[6] they wanted to ring in a true revolution in nutrition and eliminate pasta in order to toughen the bodies of the Italian people for the coming wars and to give the nation, through culinary means as well, an identity that corresponded to the Futurist self-image.[7] Political considerations motivated this approach; Marinetti was enthusiastic about the war and was close to the Fascists around Mussolini.[8] The Futurists naturally declared war on traditional gastronomic cuisine as well: "Amongst the various cuisines prevalent today the one we consider the most detestable and repugnant is the international cuisine of grand hotels."[9] The cuisine mentioned here is closely associated with the French chef Auguste Escoffier (1846–1935), whose work had a crucial influence on haute cuisine and who opened restaurants in luxury hotels throughout Europe in collaboration with the hotelier César Ritz. His menus and rules formed a paradigm of cuisine, which was disseminated in Escoffier's *Guide culinaire* (1903, translated as *The Complete Guide to the Art of Modern Cookery*). Even some seventy years later, its style still dominated the hotel kitchens of Europe and America. This was opposed not only by the Futurists. In 1973, a few decades later, young chefs were proclaiming a revolution to establish the nouvelle cuisine, which combined health, creativity, and pleasure. To that end, ten commandments were formulated that took aim at Escoffier's still-valid kitchen bible. The chefs of the nouvelle cuisine combatted this heavy traditional cuisine with programmatic cookbooks such as *La grande cuisine minceur* (translated as *Great Slimming Cuisine*). As gourmet chefs, they asserted: "Our main concern is digestion."[10] Their conviction that it was necessary to cook lighter and healthier food was in line with the intentions of Futurist cuisine: "Futurist food is the realization of the general desire to renew our eating habits and of the fight against weight, big bellies, obesity."[11] There is even more that connects this first artists' cuisine to developments in top European cuisine in recent decades. The English chef Heston Blumenthal (born 1966) of the Fat Duck restaurant became known for his dish *Sound of the Sea* (2008). The sounds of the sea are served via an iPod along with a dish of shellfish, algae, and sea urchins, bringing the idea of the *conrumore* somewhat belated gastronomic fame.[12] He is also known for using the latest technology in the kitchen. For example, he employs liquid nitrogen, centrifuges, rotary evaporators, and freeze-dryers to produce his food.[13] There are far more parallels to Ferran Adrià (born 1962, chef and owner of elBulli in Roses, Spain). With a concept very similar to the one that helped the Futurists to escape

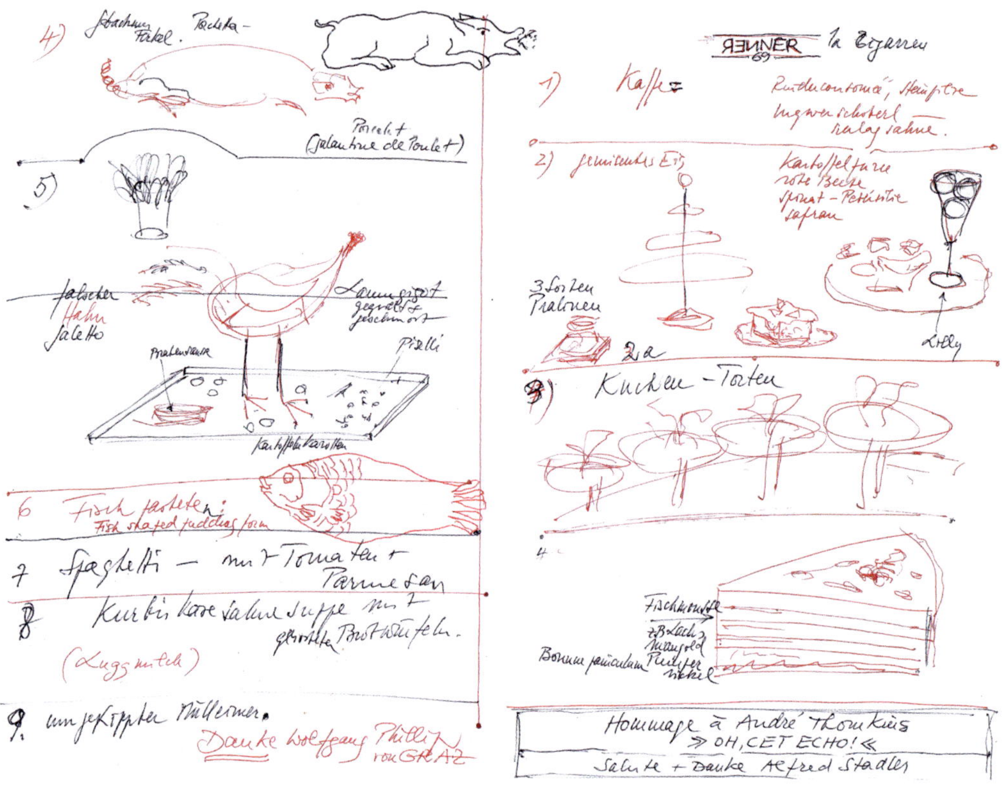

**Fig. 1** Daniel Spoerri
Preparatory sketch
for the menu of *Das
palindromische, per-
verse Travestie Essen*
(The Palindromic,
Per-verse Travesty
Dinner), 1998
Red and and black
ballpoint pen on paper,
29.7 × 42 cm
Swiss National Library,
Prints and Drawings
Department, Daniel
Spoerri Archives, Bern

          **Felix Bröcker**

the museum, he conversely made it into art institutions and was invited to Documenta in 2007. Adrià shared the enthusiasm of the Futurists for technology and as a chef integrated this radical openness into gastronomy to create new dishes using high technology.[14] He employs gristle, fish skin, and even ready-made industrial food from the supermarket, such as 3D's Bugles and Fisherman's Friend, and integrates it into his menus. By doing so, he violates the rules of classical haute cuisine and radically expands its canon of ingredients. This unreserved—with regard to the tradition of French haute cuisine—approach to diverse materials closes the gap between a cuisine oriented around high-quality products and around industrial artificial products.[15] For traditionalists, this is a provocation that was introduced to the art world in a similar way already in 1913 by the French artist Marcel Duchamp (1887–1968), whose Readymades, among other things, caused art's craft aspect to recede in favor of conceptual aspects.[16] Adrià does not simply want to satisfy desire for unusual dishes; his ambition is more far-reaching: "Cooking is a language through which all the following properties can be expressed: harmony, creativity, happiness, beauty, poetry, complexity, magic, humour, provocation, culture."[17]

**Culture in the Kitchen**

After the Futurists but long before Adrià, the Swiss artist and cofounder of Nouveau Réalisme Daniel Spoerri (born 1930) also used food as a medium and a material. In addition to using food for his art, Spoerri organized large thematic banquets that engaged with food traditions. In his *menus travestis*, for example, he subjected the traditional sequence of courses to a two-fold reversal. His first banquet of this kind, *Bananatrap-Dinner* (1970), began with a Lady Curzon Soup served in a mocca cup, and concluded with coffee presented as soup, so that the reversals turned out to be gastronomic trompe-l'oeils.[18] A later version, *Das palindromische, per-verse Travestie Essen*

(The Palindromic, Per-verse Travesty Dinner, 1998) at Schwarzenberg, began with an espresso, though in fact it was a mushroom consommé, and later included an appetizer of pasta made with vanilla ice cream [**fig. 1**]. The Restaurant Spoerri, which he founded in Düsseldorf, served dishes such as elephant trunk steak and termite omelet, which draw attention to how taste is influenced by culture. Such dishes caused a furor in a restaurant in Germany and provoked a discussion of German and foreign eating habits. Several of the ingredients, such as mango and polenta, which were unsual at the time, are now part of everyday cuisine.[19] Even ideas that still sound exotic today did not remain unique obscurities of art but are found in top-class restaurants. Ants are also served by Alex Atala (born 1968, Brazilian chef of D.O.M. restaurant in São Paulo) and René Redzepi (born 1977, Danish chef of Noma restaurant in Copenhagen).[20] Although they are offered as a local specialty, ultimately in both cases the focus is on a unique dining experience that addresses one's own cultural influence; after all, in other cultures insects are a part of the diet. Justifying this provocation gastronomically is important to chefs who point to the taste dimension. These days, chefs offer illusions like Spoerri's aforementioned culinary trompe-l'oeils in different variations.

Already a classic, and very similar to Spoerri's espresso, is the *Bouillon de champignons comme un cappuccino* (Mushroom Cappuccino) served by Alain Chapel in the 1970s: a foamed soup presented in a cup.[21] This soup cappuccino was subsequently offered in many different variations.[22] More recent illusions include the savory macaroons of Ferran Adrià and the edible stones [**fig. 2**] and vegetarian carpaccio of Andoni Luis Aduriz (born 1971, Spanish chef of Mugaritz restaurant outside of San Sebastián).[23] At Noma, butterflies are served made of flowers and edible flowerpots.[24] But everyday dishes like *Spaghettieis* (ice cream in spaghetti form) in Germany also make use of this principle.[25]

## Local Foods in the Global Context; or, The Politics of Eating

The restaurant and art project *Food*, in which Gordon Matta-Clark (1943–1978) was involved, was a place of vital interest and a workplace for many artists. Food was not just served there but was also reflected on. The open kitchen and the discussion of foods and their origins was unusual in the early 1970s and had a political dimension.[26] At nearly the same time, Alice Waters (born 1944), an American chef, gastronome, and Slow Food activist who is still very influential today, opened Chez Panisse in Berkeley, and the nouvelle cuisine in France also supported market-fresh, regional cuisine. For Waters, a gastronomic interest was the focus, but the political motifs were by all means comparable: for her, too, the point was to sensitize consumers to the origins and production of food, as a response to the growing food industry, which benefited from a decline in such knowledge. Currently, reflecting on traditional and forgotten local ingredients and techniques is the most important trend in haute cuisine, as represented most famously by the New Nordic Cuisine. Redzepi serves *Fresh Fjord Shrimp and Brown Butter* as an appetizer:[27] live shrimp served on ice. The dish is culturally justified as a traditional meal of Danish fishers, who eat live shrimp on their boats. Nevertheless, it has a strong effect that causes one to overcome personal eating habits[28] and that puts so directly before our eyes the fact that killing is an essential aspect of life (survival). This gesture was anticipated by Matta-Clark. For an event at Food, he served live shrimp in a boiled egg cut in half.[29]

For the Thai artist Rirkrit Tiravanija (born 1961), who lives and works in Chiang Mai, Berlin, and New York, traditions of foods and their political significance likewise play an important role. He addresses discourses of identity and belonging by means of foods that are culturally charged as a result of traditions and function as a medium. *Untitled 1990 (Pad Thai)* at the Paula Allen Gallery was his first solo exhibition in New

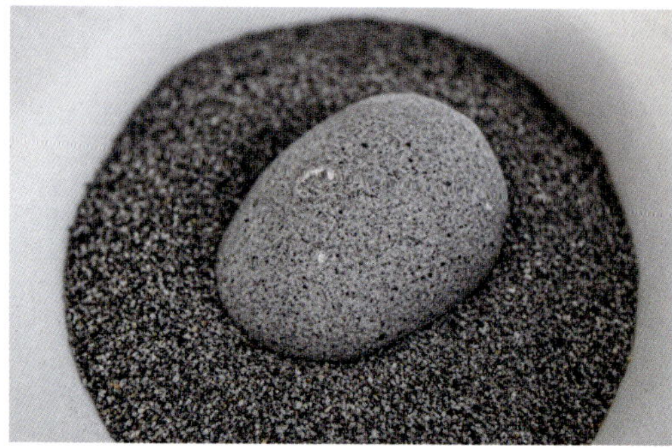

Fig. 2 Edible stone, Andoni Luis Aduriz, Mugaritz restaurant, Errenteria, Spain

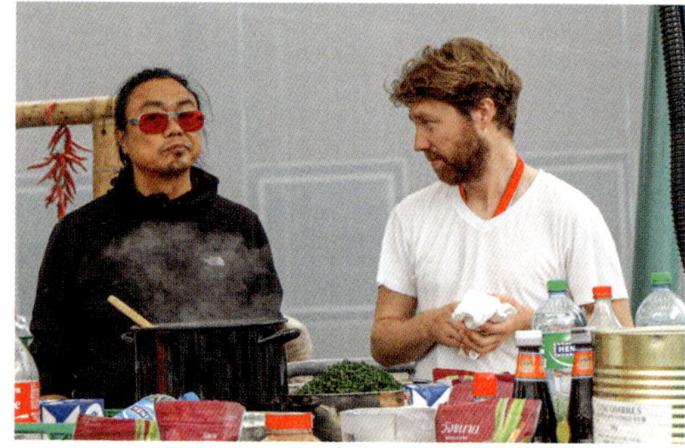

Fig. 3 Rirkrit Tiravanija with the author at Art Basel, 2015



Felix Bröcker

York. Already in this first kitchen action, food was central to understanding the work. Tiravanija has Thai roots, but he was born in Argentina, raised in Thailand, Ethiopia, and Canada, studying first in Canada and then moving to the United States. The question of one's own identity is a very personal one and part of his artistic practice.[30] The vexation of a Western understanding of art, triggered by a work in the form of a meal, takes on another level when the food served is pad thai. It is not just foreign that the works are not viewed but rather eaten; but the meal itself is also foreign. Tiravanija entered the American art system as an outsider. That Tiravanija serves pad thai as a reference to himself might be a banal observation and not yet evidence of the use of foods as a medium. But a closer look at this "typical" Thai dish reveals the complex connection between the food served and his own identity. Tiravanija is Thai, but, as described above, his cultural identity is very heterogeneous.[31] This complexity of determining identity is reflected in the "national dish" pad thai. The dish originally comes from China and was first declared the Thai national dish by Prime Minister Pibulsong-gram around 1940 to strengthen the identity of the young Thai state, which had been founded in 1939 and had previously been known as Siam, and to lend it a Western orientation.[32] Since the beginning of his career, eating as a medium has not only had a socializing function at Tiravanija's but has also raised questions revolving around identity and belonging in increasingly globalized contexts.

Although he asserts "I do not care about the craft of cooking,"[33] after many conceptual works he provided food to hundreds of visitors daily at Art Basel in 2015 [**fig.3**], and he has also recently run pop-ups and opened a restaurant—business for which skills in the craft are indeed significant.[34] Now his goal is "Making good food and good atmosphere,"[35] as Tiravanija puts it, who in this case has become a chef without any artistic-conceptual claim at all.

## Concepts and Recipes

Ferran Adrià, in turn, has moved so far from cooking as a craft that he was invited to Documenta. In 2011, he closed the restaurant elBulli and has since worked on readying his previous work as a chef for the museum. In the coming years, a visitor center / exhibition space is supposed to open its doors that will encourage creative exchange between diverse disciplines and include an exhibition.[36] Craft repetition interests him less than developing ideas and concepts. Despite the many intersections, however, Ferran Adrià emphasizes his distance from the art world: "What I find fascinating is the dialogue between both disciplines: my dishes, for instance, have nothing to do with art."[37] It is characteristic of art to use foodstuffs to negate its commodity character, to reveal aesthetic traditions, to question museums and institutions, or to deny them access to certain forms of art. Food is also used as a medium to connect art and everyday life. In addition, however, it works with the symbolic and cultural significance of dishes, though "good" taste is usually not the focus. For chefs, in turn, the medium of food is in itself nothing special; accordingly, they primarily ask questions of quality and thus seek out the material to offer a unique taste experience. It is not always about taste or concepts; sometimes, too, effects that seem to elevate cooking to an art are enough. When Grant Achatz, at his restaurant Alinea in Chicago, arranges with an artistic gesture the dessert directly on the table, which is thus turned into plate and canvas, it is certainly reminiscent of Jackson Pollock, but it by no means makes the chef an artist or the dish art. In the kitchen, too, cultural and symbolic aspects—that is, the iconography of food—offer an opportunity to enjoy foods that go beyond the purely sensory. Connecting the aesthetic and the concept, the sensory and intellectual aspects, brings together the chef-artists and the artist-chefs. That reveals, against Adorno's statement cited at the beginning, a connection of art and cuisine. What Adorno says is thus valid: "Whoever concretely enjoys artworks [also edible ones!—Auth.] is a philistine."[38]

This text is an abridged and revised version of Felix Bröcker, "Lebensmittel als Medium und Material in Kunst und Küche," in *Metabolismen: Nahrungsmittel als Kunstmaterial*, ed. Isabella Augart and Ina Jessen (Hamburg, 2019).

**1** Theodor W. Adorno, *Aesthetic Theory*, ed. and trans. Robert Hullot-Kentor (Minneapolis, 1997), p. 15.
**2** See Ralf Beil, *Künstlerküche: Lebensmittel als Kunstmaterial; von Schiele bis Jason Rhoades* (Cologne, 2002), pp. 38–57. As Cecilia Novero has noted, already in 1913 Guillaume Apollinaire had described a "cubisme culinaire" that also rethinks the culinary as art; see Cecilia Novero, *Antidiets of the Avant-Garde: From Futurist Cooking to Eat Art* (Minneapolis, 2010).
**3** Filippo Tommaso Marinetti, *La cucina futurista* (Milan, 1932); translated by Suzanne Brill as *The Futurist Cookbook*, ed. Lesley Chamberlain (London and San Francisco, 1989).
**4** Ibid., p. 38.
**5** Ibid., p. 172.
**6** Ibid., pp. 160, 147, and 152.
**7** Ibid., pp. 36–38.
**8** See Harald Lemke, *Die Kunst des Essens: Eine Ästhetik des kulinarischen Geschmacks* (Bielefeld, 2007), p. 41.
**9** Marinetti 1989 (see note 3), p. 59.
**10** The Troisgros brothers, quoted in Anonymous, "Magere Symphonie: Die fetten Jahre der französischen Grande Cuisine sind vorbei; Die neuen Spitzenköche proklamieren magere Zeiten," *Der Spiegel* 48 (1978), pp. 168–73, esp. p. 170.
**11** Marinetti 1989 (see note 3), p. 97.
**12** See Heston Blumen-

     **Felix Bröcker**

thal, *The Fat Duck Cookbook* (London, 2009), p. 206.

**13** See ibid., pp. 424–61.

**14** See Richard Hamilton and Vincente Todoli, eds., *Food for Thought, Thought for Food* (New York, 2009), p. 280.

**15** In contrast to classic cuisine, which attributes particular value to certain products such as goose foie gras and lobster, Ferran Adrià explicitly declares that diverse ingredients are of equal value. In his brief description to the cuisine of elBulli, he writes: "All the products have the same culinary value, regardless of their price." See https://elbullifoundation.com/en/synthesis-of-elbulli-cuisine (all URLs accessed in September 2019).

**16** Duchamp exhibited everyday objects as are and thus changed or expanded the existing concept of art.

**17** Adrià (see note 15).

**18** See Elisabeth Hartung, ed., *Daniel Spoerri presents Eat-Art*, exh. cat. Aktionsforum Praterinsel, Munich (Nuremberg, 2001), pp. 129 and 156–58; Klaus Taschwer, "Der Elefantenrüssel schmeckt nicht besonders gut—so wie Suppenfleisch," *Der Standard*, May 16, 2008, http://derstandard.at/3332676/Elefanten ruessel-schmeckt-nicht-besonders-gut-so-wie-Suppenfleisch.

**19** See ibid.

**20** See Alex Atala, *D.O.M.: Rediscovering Brazilian Ingredients* (London and New York, 2013), p. 40; René Redzepi, Noma Recipes, vol. 1: *A Work in Progress*, 3 vols. (London and New York, 2013), p. 204.

**21** See Aralyn Beaumont, "The Idols of Fine Dining," *Lucky Peach* 20 (Fall 2016), p. 98.

**22** See Ferran Adrià, Juli Soler, and Albert Adrià, *A Day at elBulli* (London, 2003), p. 142; Dieter Müller, *Dieter Müller* (Munich, 2005), p. 31; Bottura, Massimo, *Never Trust a Skinny Italian Chef* (London and New York, 2014), p. 28.

**23** For the stones, potatoes are covered with kaolin; the carpaccio consists of dried watermelon. See Andoni Luis Aduriz, Mugaritz: *A Natural Science of Cooking* (London and New York, 2012), pp. 94 and 168.

**24** René Redzepi (@reneredzepinoma), Instagram, June 15–18, 2019.

**25** *Spaghettieis* was probably invented in 1969 by Dario Fontanella in Mannheim, Germany. However, dishes concocted to provide guests with entertainment through visual illusions were already found in the context of Roman and medieval feasts.

**26** See Gordon Matta-Clark, *Food* (1972), http://www.ubu.com/film/gmc_food.html. He documents shopping for and preparing the products.

**27** Redzepi 2013 (see note 20), p. 72.

**28** Such dishes that are strange in the context of European habits exist in Asia, for example as *Drunken Shrimp*.

**29** See Ulrike Groos, "Optimismus bei Tisch: Zu einigen ausgewählten Künstlerlokalen," in *Eating the Universe: Vom Essen in der Kunst*, exh. cat. Kunsthalle Düsseldorf, Galerie im Taxispalais Innsbruck, and Kunstverein Stuttgart (Cologne, 2009), pp. 56–75.

**30** See Francesca Grassi and Rirkrit Tiravanija, eds., *Rirkrit Tiravanija: A Retrospective; Tomorrow Is Another Fine Day* (Zurich, 2007), p. 4.

**31** For the exhibition *Traffic* in Bordeaux in 1996, Rirkrit Tiravanija exhibited his passports and visas; see Antje Krause-Wahl, *Konstruktionen von Identität: Renée Green, Tracey Emin, Rirkrit Tiravanija* (Munich, 2006), p. 156. Travels and travel planning are constant concerns; see Thomas Kellein, ed., *Rirkrit Tiravanija: Cookbook; Just Smile and Don't Talk* (Bangkok and London, 2010), p. 11.

**32** See Alexandra Greeley, "Finding Pad Thai," *Gastronomica* 9, no. 1 (2009), pp. 78–82.

**33** Kellein 2010 (see note 31), p. 11.

**34** See Kat Herriman, "A Restaurant Where Art is on the Menu," *The New York Times Style Magazine*, November 13, 2015, https://www.nytimes.com/2015/11/13/t-magazine/rirkrit-tiravanija-gavin-brown-restaurant.html; Gisela Williams, "The Professional Pop-Up Artist," *The New York Times*, July 26, 2016, https://www.nytimes.com/2016/07/26/t-magazine/food/rirkrit-tiravanija-dottir-berlin-pop-up-restaurant.html.

**35** Williams 2016 (see note 34).

**36** See elBullifoundation, "feeding creativity," https://elbullifoundation.com/wp-content/themes/elbullifoundation/pdf/sobre_elbf_eng.pdf.

**37** Marta Represa, "Ferran Adrià on El Bulli," *AnOther Magazine*, 2013, http://origin.anothermag.com/art-photography/2887/ferran-adria-on-el-bulli.

**38** Adorno 1997 (see note 1), p. 15.

# Tasting, Not Eating

## Nur Geschmack anstatt Essen

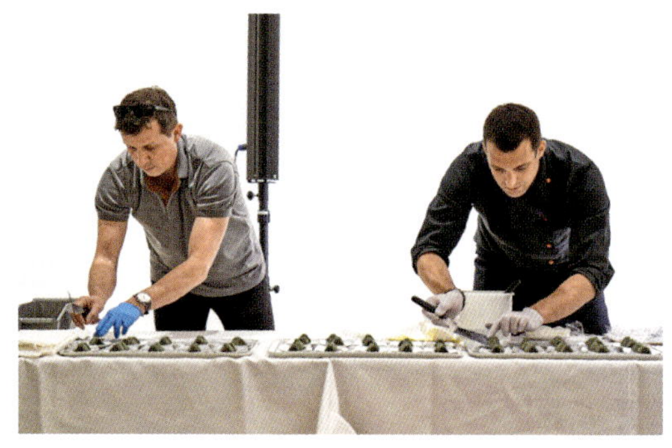

Preparation and eating of the four-course experimental menu *Tasting, Not Eating* during the *Amuse-bouche* symposium on April 6, 2019

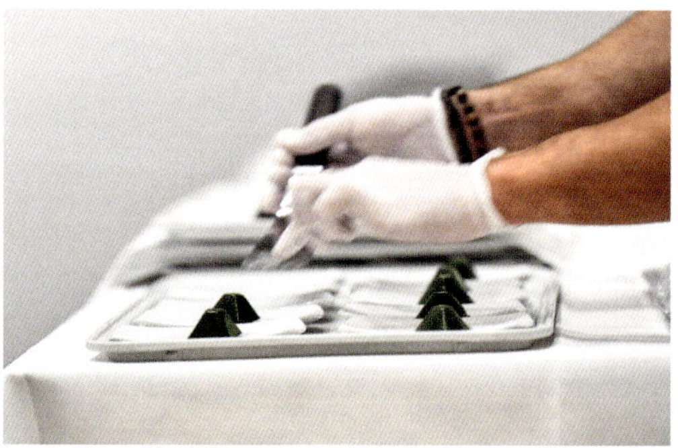

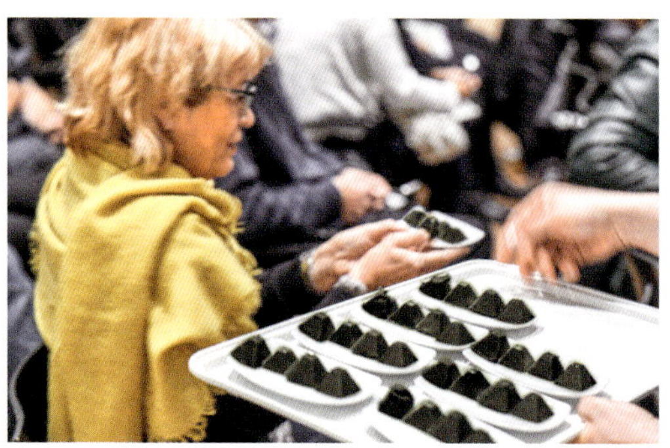

The sense of taste is in reality a very complex
phenomenon, in which several senses are involved.
Not only the optical, the sense of touch (the texture), and
the temperature (cold to hot) play a role, but it
is the interaction of all these perceptions that
determines the actual result.

A conscious altering of these impressions thus calls
perception into question!
To prove this, I have tried to confuse or exclude these
impressions.

For example: even by just coloring tomato juice black,
it becomes questionable whether you can taste it immediately as though it were its original red. For this reason,
I imagined dissolving only concentrated essences in
gelatine and serving them in the form of cubes. Only the
sequence takes place in the correct order. In a more complicated version, the normal order could also be changed:
for example, backward!

We could begin with an appetizer of chicken stock in
cube form; as a first course, a fish cube, a spinach cube,
and a tomato cube are served together. As a main course,
we take game, lamb, or beef cubes, and as a side dish
potato, leek, celery, beetroot, mushrooms, paprika
(a selection of these flavor carriers)—all in cube form.
As a dessert, you can imagine fruit or chocolate flavors.
Experience will show how many of these tastes will
be deduced immediately and unambiguously.

PS: This idea has been newly developed—
thus there is no experience yet.

Daniel Spoerri, February 20, 2019

# Tasting Harmony in the World

**Paul Stoller**

Haam'issa fumbu ga doonu hassara
"(A piece of) Rotten fish will spoil millet porridge"
—Songhay proverb

I first heard the "rotten fish" proverb in 1984 at the end of a rather "rotten" meal that I had shared with my teacher, Adamu Jenitongo, in his West African compound in Tillabéri, a town in the western region of the Republic of Niger. After a two-year hiatus, I was back to engage in anthropological fieldwork in Tillabéri, where I had long conducted ethnographic research on the religion of the Songhay people. As always, Adamu Jenitongo and his family—a sister, two wives, two sons, a motley crew of cousins, and many scantily clad grandchildren—welcomed "the white man who speaks Songhay" into their home. Among Songhay people, a stranger is "God" in your house. In an uncomfortably poor land, the sages say that the stranger should be given the best "accommodations" and fed with sumptuous meals replete with meat, chicken, and copious amounts of sauce laced with butter oil. If these sauces are sweetened with juice squeezed from the *burgu* plant, a grass that grows in the shallows of the Niger River, family pride is reinforced. Songhay elders like Adamu Jenitongo tend to say that treating the stranger with generosity and respect brings harmony and balance to the world.

With that set of expectations, the rancidly sour taste of rotten sauce, which was served on the last night of the visit, created a moment of disharmony and imbalance, which compelled Adamu Jenitongo to recite the "rotten fish" proverb. What set of conditions created the context for the preparation and presentation of rotten sauce?

The next morning, Adamu Jenitongo said the obvious: social life had grown tense in his Tillabéri compound. A young woman from another ethnic group, the Fulani, had married Adamu Jenitongo's youngest son. During that stint of fieldwork in 1984, no one seemed particularly pleased with Djenaba, whose appearance—tall, thin, with an aquiline nose and copper-colored skin—underscored her social and cultural difference. As the youngest in-law in the compound, people expected her to do the lion's share of the household work—fetching water,

cleaning pots and pans, sweeping the compound of debris, trekking into town to buy condiments, not to forget cooking lunch and dinner. Djenaba performed these incessant chores with quiet dignity. During that period of time in the compound, hardly anyone expressed appreciation for her efforts. What's more, people did not often call her by her name. Instead, they called her *djebbo*, which in the Fulani language means "woman." Indeed, during my time in the compound, I rarely saw her smile or laugh.

What might a young Fulani woman in a Songhay compound do to improve her social situation? In a society in which women, especially women who are "other," can exercise few, if any, rights, how might Djenaba express the poignancy of her alienation? She could divorce her husband and return to her family—a shameful act, the emotional costs of which would far outweigh the social benefits. She could verbally object to her treatment, but given her marital status and her gender, such protest would fall upon deaf ears and probably deepen her alienation.

When guests arrived in the compound, Djenaba may well have understood that a perfect storm of social factors had formed on the horizon. When that storm moved through the compound, she might be able to express herself in a forceful manner. Consider these factors. As the most junior spouse in the compound, Adamu Jenitongo's wives asked her to prepare special meals for honored guests. These meals, she knew, should be of the previously mentioned highest quality—good cuts of beef, thick sumptuous sauces filled with aromatic spices and laced with butter oil. These are known as "thick sauces," which should be served in "thick" situations like feeding an honored guest. During this one-month sojourn in 1984, which would be considered a "thick" situation, Djenaba, who was not passionate about cooking, produced thick sauces that were acceptable, but hardly sumptuous. What would happen, if, at the right moment, she delivered a profoundly "thin" sauce? Would people in the compound feel a degree of empathy for the sourness of her alienation?

The last night of the visit, Djenaba decided to prepare *fukko hoy*, a "thin" sauce lacking meat, made from the dried leaves of the *fukko* plant, which, if prepared correctly, produces a slightly sour taste that Songhay people covet. If the *fukko* sauce is not prepared correctly, it turns so rancidly sour that it is impossible to eat. Knowing these culinary particulars, Djenaba produced a profoundly "thin" sauce, the sourness of which brought shame to Adam Jenitongo's Tillabéri compound and provoked the recitation of the "rotten fish" proverb.

The rotten sauce scene disrupted social life in the Tillabéri compound. A dust cloud of shame settled over Adamu Jenitongo's compound. Djenaba had expressed her discomfort and displeasure. In a moment of social defiance, she had undermined the social harmony of the compound. Through the powerful sense of taste, she had attracted the attention of all of her in-laws who the next day didn't miss an opportunity to insult her insolence and castigate her ethnicity.[1]

What can we take away from the gustatory experience of rotten sauce in a remote compound in West Africa? The ethnographic richness of this minor incident demonstrates powerfully how taste is much more than a culinary exercise. Indeed, the sensuous experience of taste can shape our social relations and configure the emotional contours of our well-being, which, as I'll attempt to suggest in this essay, is a central theme in the anthropological approach to taste-in-the-world.

**Tasting Social Life in the World**

There are many challenges to confront when one sets out to explore taste in the world. It is almost impossible for people in the more visually oriented societies in Europe and North America to contemplate such a refined gustatory analysis. In Europe and North America, most people "see" the truth and "envision" reality. It is hard to imagine how to smell, feel, or taste "truth" or "reality." Even so, for more than a generation a relatively small group of anthropologists has attempted—with no small amount of success—to incorporate elements of the sensorium, including taste, into anthropological descriptions of social worlds.

Such a tack, of course, makes a great deal sense. No matter the society, when people confront the world in which they live, they use all of their senses. Curiously, much social science description has been devoid of sensory description or sensorial analysis. Aside from the pioneering work of Walter Ong, whose *The Presence of the Word* (1967) would set the foundation for a future study of the non-visual senses,[2] in most social science representation scholars have tended to spatialize the non-visual senses. In so doing, they have adhered themselves to the bloodless prose of plain style, which has long been the foundation of (social) scientific discourse. Guided by Ong's contribution and also by the provocative work of Victor Zuckerkandl (1956) on the philosophical dimensions of sound in the world,[3] Steven Feld published the first sensorially contoured anthropological work, *Sound and Sentiment* (1982), an ethnography about the existential importance of sound in a highland New Guinea environment in which vision is limited.[4] Other anthropological works on sound followed.[5]

In time, image-conscious anthropologists refined their approach to vision and set the parameters for visual anthropology, which for a very long time focused almost entirely on the production and analysis of ethnographic film. A number of visual anthropologists, however, refined their approach to the visual and put forward thoughtful books and essays about how human beings see the world.[6]

As this early work progressed, a group of anthropologists at Concordia University in Montreal began to compare and contrast all the senses across a wide variety of societies. David Howes, an important scholar of sensorial anthropology and the director of the Concordia Sensoria Research Group, became interested in sensorial ratios. Why might

                                                           **Paul Stoller**

vision, sound, smell, or taste be more primary in a group's sensorial organization of experience? That work launched a more sustained analysis of sensoria around the world.[7]

There have been two approaches to the anthropological analysis of the sensorium: a theory-building analytical orientation to the senses and a more descriptively ethnographic representation of sensoria. There is no shortage of analytical works on vision, smell, sound, touch, and taste. Many of these works focus upon an attempt to isolate sensorial principles of universal application. During these developments, other scholars, including several anthropologists, have considered the science of sensation—the chemistry of taste and smell,[8] the phenomenology of sound,[9] and dimensions of visual culture.[10] These works have enhanced our comprehension of the human sensorium.

A second group of scholars has taken a more phenomenological approach to the representation of sensoria. They have attempted to use ethnographic description to evoke the senses in prose, art installations, and film. Anthropologists like Ruth Behar, Michael Taussig, Michael Jackson, Robert Desjarlais, Piers Vitebsky, and Kirin Narayan have used sensuous prose to evoke the sensory dimensions of people and the places in which they live.[11]

Like these ethnographically orientated authors, I, too, believe that form and style can provide powerfully evocative representations of sensory worlds. In my own ethnographic work, which has always foregrounded narrative, I have attempted to evoke the distinctive sounds, smells, texture, vistas, and tastes of social life in West Africa and among West Africans in New York City.[12] In the attempt to give the reader a sensory feel of a place, I have tried to weave these sensuous descriptions of social life into the fabric of my books.

### Tasting Culture

Within the context of a multifaceted sensorial anthropology, taste is perhaps the most

difficult sense to describe. In many languages there is a dearth of words that one can use to describe tastes, which has both physiological and symbolic dimensions. In the words of Carolyn Korsmeyer:

"Recorded opinions about the sense of taste are filled with ambivalence and paradox. Some theorists consider it beneath consideration; others recommend its cultivation. Some regard taste as a mere matter of physical sensation, unworthy of extensive attention; others devote a lifetime to its exploration. Some classify taste as a 'lower' bodily sense, along with smell and touch; others consider it as complex and informative as vision and hearing. Approaches to taste may be ascetic or sybaritic, dismissive or obsessed—and all attitudes in between."[13]

The literature on taste is therefore broad and diverse. There are many studies on the physiology of taste and flavoring practices, in particular culinary traditions.[14] There are historical studies on the development of culinary tastes into high and low cuisines and how they create social distinction.[15] The gustatory properties of food have also been associated with religious practices. In some societies, food is linked to deities, saints, and is part and parcel of fasting and feasting events.[16] Perhaps the most common association of taste devolves from Kant's *Critique of Judgment* (1790) in which the gustatory sense becomes aestheticized as it is removed from the complex and messy elements of its production.[17] From the Kantian perspective, taste becomes a standard of refined distinction in art and in social life. Beyond Kantian dimensions of taste, writers have published studies on cultivation of taste[18] and essays on how taste is linked to emotion and memory.[19]

Where do ethnographically contoured anthropological works fit into the broad and vast literature on taste? Very few anthropologists have considered the physiology of taste in the classic tradition of Brillat-Savarin. Fewer still have engaged in exploring the science of taste and smell or the flavoring practices of distinctive cuisines. The vast literature on the history of gustation in society has sparked some anthropological interest, as in Jack Goody's sociocultural analysis of high and low cuisine in which he charts the connection between presence of high cuisine and social hierarchy—a concrete manifestation of social inequality. Taste has also prompted some of the more important anthropological investigations of social memory.

Perhaps the most focused anthropological takes on taste underscore how it can be extended into the realm of cultural symbolism. Several anthropologists have focused on particular aspects of taste (strong/bitter/sweet and sour/spicy [hot] and mild). Following the careful ethnographic analysis of Mary Weismantel, we know that among Quichua-speaking people who live in Zumbagua in the Ecuadorian Andes, local terms that reference the taste sensations of strong/bitter and hot/sweet enable people "to place foods in a cultural context that shapes how people know them, creating implicit connections between sensory experience, cultural knowledge and the political and economic structures of social life."[20] Weismantel goes on to suggest that the taste sensations of sweetness and saltiness cut to the heart of gender relations in that society. Consider the specificity of taste in Weismantel's contrast of "bitter" or "strong" foods, or in Quichua, *jayaj* to *mishqui*, which is sweet and tasty. Strong bitter foods are eaten raw and linked to male domains outside the household, whereas sweet and tasty foods are prepared (cooked) and eaten in the house. In essence, the gustatory properties of foods are associated with gendered classifications and relate to gendered productive activities. Put another way, taste in Zumbagua is used symbolically to create and reinforce ordered cosmological categories that give shape to social practices and to social life.[21]

In the celebrated work of the late Sidney Mintz, taste becomes an active ingredient of political and economic distinction. Unlike the orientation of Bourdieu, or, for that matter, Kant, Mintz considers how the properties of one gustatory element—sweetness—have had an impact on social identity and changes in the perception of social class and modern consumerist individualism. As he wrote: "The first sweetened cup of hot tea to be drunk by an English worker was a significant historical event, because it prefigured the transformation of an entire society, a total remaking of its economic and social basis."[22] In his state-of-the-art paper on food, taste, and the senses, David Sutton comments on Mintz's contribution to an anthropology of taste:

"Mintz develops these ideas in tracing the relationship of sugar and sweetness to moral ideas. The addictive taste of sugar made it difficult to give up, and, thus, a contentious item of anti-slavery boycott, whereas its taste once again led commentators to suggest it would lead the working classes into idleness and women into other desires and illicit pleasures."[23]

As Sutton suggests, Mintz focused on a particular flavor as a jumping off point for understanding society and its transformations. He goes on to demonstrate how this important orientation connects with the work of C. Nadia Seremetakis and Jane Cowan, both of whom considered the impact of sweetness in Greek social life.[24]

The anthropological study of taste also compels us to consider synesthesia—the dynamic blending of the senses. Barbara Kirshenblatt-Gimblett has stressed how synesthesia is central to the human experience of taste. "From color, steam rising, gloss and texture, we infer taste smell and feel. Taste is something we anticipate and infer from how things look, feel to the hand, smell (outside the mouth), and sound. Our eyes let us 'taste' food at a distance by activating the sense memories of taste and smell."[25]

In the end what can one say about the anthropology of taste? It does analyze the history and aestheticization of taste and also the relation of taste (and flavor) to social identity and to social change. It also considers the sensuous dynamics of taste and how they relate to phenomena like synesthesia. And yet, the anthropologists of taste have not fully developed their work. As Sutton concluded:

"The deployment of recent, intertwining approaches from the anthropology of the senses, phenomenology, materiality studies, and theories of value, among others, provides exciting opportunities for rich ethnographic elaboration. And the focus on sensory aspects experienced like few other things both inside and outside of bodies (and transformed in the crossing of bodily boundaries) means that these approaches have much to gain from an engagement with food. But our theoretical progress has yet to be matched by any corpus of rich ethnographies that make the sensory aspects of food central to an understanding of lives and experiences; many of the writings on this topic remain in the form of short, suggestive articles or snippets of ethnography in larger works on other topics."[26]

**Savoring Taste in Slow Ethnography**
Like Sutton, I believe that anthropologists have just begun to sample the tastes of social worlds. In order to write tasteful ethnographies, anthropologists need to engage in what I like to call slow anthropology, which is increasingly difficult to practice in a fast world. Slow anthropology devolves from the Slow Food movement, which was initially a protest against the opening of a McDonald's, the icon of fast-food establishments, near the Spanish Steps in Rome. In 1986, Carlo Petrini, an Italian activist and journalist, informally organized the Slow Food movement. In Paris in 1989, Petrini and others formally founded their international movement. From its very beginnings, the Slow Food movement was less a platform for recipes of sumptuous slow cooking than a sustained cultural critique of life in the fast lane of contemporary society. It has been a critique of the endless array of "taste-less" offerings in fast food restaurants, the widespread anonymity Facebook "friendships," the dearth of face-to-face conversations, and the global corporatization of social relations.[27]

Enter the anthropology of taste, which is well suited to fit into the ever-expanding matrix of slowness—especially when it comes to studies of taste-in-culture. As the work of Mary Weismantel, Steve Feld, Sidney Mintz, C. Nadia Seremetakis, and David Sutton has demonstrated, it takes many years to develop the ethnographic sensitivities to understand the significant symbolic social and political dynamics of taste-in-the world. It is through a slowly developed anthropology that one can understand how taste can bring both harmony and disharmony to social worlds.

My slow approach to anthropology gave me the time to develop the sensitivities needed to understand how playing with sauces could create and undermine social harmony in Adamu Jenitongo's Tillabéri compound. On subsequent visits to Tillabéri, the quality of the food did not improve. Still the principal compound cook, Djenaba continued to produce mediocre food, but given the stubborn strictness of Songhay cultural protocols about family life, no one dared to take her place. During one of my visits, Adamu Jenitongo's older son, Moussa, ate his dinners in town and arranged for his father's sister's daughter, Ramatu, to prepare afternoon meals. He made sure that that food was shared with me and his father. For Moussa, marriage seemed like the only solution to the family's food problem. When he soon thereafter got married, his new wife, now the youngest in-law in the compound, replaced Djenaba as the family cook. Her thick savory sauces brought tasteful harmony and a long-absent sense of well-being to the Tillabéri compound.

**1** Paul Stoller and Cheryl Olkes, "Bad Sauce, Good Ethnography," *Cultural Anthropology* 1 (1986), pp. 336–52; Paul Stoller and Cheryl Olkes, "La sauce épaisse: Remarques sur les relations sociales songhaïs," *Anthropologie et Sociétés* 14, no. 3 (1990), pp. 57–76.
**2** Walter Ong, *The Presence of the Word* (New Haven, CT, 1967).
**3** Victor Zuckerkandl, *Sound and Symbol: Music and the External World*, trans. W. Trask (Princeton, 1956).
**4** Steven Feld, *Sound and Sentiment* (Philadelphia, 1982).
**5** Ellen Basso, *A Musical View of the Universe: Kalapalo Myth and Ritual Performances* (Philadelphia, 1985); Anthony Seeger, *Why Suyá Sing: A Musical Anthropology of an Amazonian People* (1987; repr., Urbana, IL, 2014); Paul Stoller, *The Taste of Ethnographic Things* (Philadelphia, 1989); Paul Stoller, *Sensuous Scholarship* (Philadelphia, 1997); see also Louise Meintjes Samuels, Ana Maria Ochoa, and Thomas Porcello, "Soundscapes: Toward a Sounded Anthropology," *Annual Review of Anthropology* 39, no. 1 (2010), pp. 329–45, and Thomas Porcello, Louise Meintjes, Ana Maria Ochoa, and David W. Samuels, "The Reorganization of the Sensory World," *Annual Review of Anthropology* 39 (2010), pp. 51–56.
**6** Jean Rouch and Steven Feld, *Cine-Ethnography* (Minneapolis, 2003); Paul Stoller, *The Cinematic Griot: The Ethnography of Jean Rouch* (Chicago, 1992); Paul Henley, *The Adventure of the Real: Jean Rouch and the Craft of Ethnographic Cinema* (Chicago, 2010); David MacDougall, *Transcultural Cinema* (Princeton, 1998); David MacDougall, *The Corporeal Image: Film, Ethnography and the Senses* (Princeton, 2005); Jay Ruby, *Picturing Culture: Explorations of Film and Anthropology* (Chicago, 2000).
**7** David Howes, *Empire of the Senses: The Sensual Culture Reader* (Oxford and New York, 2005); David Howes and Constance Classen, *Ways of Sensing:*

Paul Stoller

*Understanding the Senses in Society* (New York, 2013); Constance Classen and David Howes, *The Book of Touch* (Oxford and New York, 2005).

**8** Linda Bartoshuk and Valerie Duffy, "Chemical Senses," in *Comparative Psychology: A Handbook,* ed. Gary Greenberg and Maury Haraway (New York, 1998).

**9** Don Ihde, *Listening and Voice: The Phenomenology of Sound* (1975; repr., Albany, NY, 2012).

**10** Martin Jay and Sumathi Ramaswamy, eds., *Empires of Vision* (Durham, NC, and New York, 2014); Nicholas Mirzoeff, *Visual Culture Reader* (New York, 2012).

**11** Ruth Behar, *An Island Called Home* (New Brunswick, NJ, and New York, 2009); Ruth Behar, Traveling Heavy (Durham, NC, and New York, 2013); Michael Taussig, *Mimesis and Alterity: A Particular History of the Senses* (New York, 1993); Michael D. Jackson, *In Sierra Leone* (Durham, NC, and New York, 2004); Michael D. Jackson, *The Work of Art* (New York, 2016); Robert Desjarlais, *Body and Emotion* (Philadelphia, 1992); Robert Desjarlais, *Shelter Blues: Sanity and Selfhood among the Homeless* (Philadelphia, 1997); Piers Vitebsky, *The Reindeer People* (New York, 2005); Kirin Narayan, *Storytellers, Saints and Scoundrels* (Philadelphia, 1989); Kirin Narayan, *My Family and Other Saints* (Chicago, 2007).

**12** Paul Stoller, *Fusion of the Worlds: An Ethnography of Possession among the Songhay of Niger* (Chicago, 1989); Stoller 1989 (see note 5); Stoller 1997 (see note 5); Paul Stoller, *Money Has No Smell: The Africanization of New York City* (Chicago, 2002); Paul Stoller, *The Power of the Between: An Anthropological Odyssey* (Chicago, 2008); Paul Stoller, *Yaya's Story: The Quest for Well-Being in the World* (Chicago, 2014).

**13** Carolyn Korsmeyer, ed., *The Taste Culture Reader: Experiencing Food and Drink* (Oxford and New York, 2005), p. 1.

**14** Jean-Anthelme Brillat-Savarin, *The Physiology of Taste,* trans. Fayette Robinson from the last Paris edition (1854; repr., Adelaide, 2014); Bartoshuk/Duffy 1998 (see note 8); Elizabeth Rozin and Paul Rozin, "Culinary Themes and Variations," *Natural History* 90, no. 2 (February 1981), pp. 6–14.

**15** Jack Goody, Cooking, *Cuisine and Class* (Cambridge, 1982); Pierre Bourdieu, *Distinction,* trans. Richard Nice (Cambridge, MA, 1984).

**16** Sarah Peterson, *Acquired Taste: The French Origins of Modern Cooking* (Ithaca, NY, 1994); R. S. Khare, ed., *The Eternal Food: Gastronomic Ideas and Experiences of Hindus and Buddhists* (Albany, NY, 1994); Elizabeth Carmichael and Chloe Sayer, *The Skeleton at the Feast: The Day of the Dead* (Austin, 1991).

**17** Immanuel Kant, *The Critique of Judgment* (1790; repr., New York, 1966).

**18** Ella Butler, "'Taste Environments': Theorizing the Contemporary," *Fieldsights* (2019), https://culanth.org/fieldsights/taste-environments (all URLs accessed in July 2019); Jukka Gronow, *Caviar with Champagne: Common Luxury and the Ideals of the Good Life in Stalin's Russia* (Oxford and London, 2003); Emile Peynaud, *The Taste of Wine* (New York, 1987).

**19** Marcel Proust, *Swann's Way,* vol. 1: *Remembrance of Things Past* (Adelaide, 2003); C. Nadia Seremetakis, *The Senses Still* (Boulder, CO, 1994); David Sutton, "Food and the Senses," *Annual Review of Anthropology* 39 (2010), pp. 209–23; Rosabelle Boswell, "Sensuous Stories in the Indian Ocean Islands," *The Senses and Society* 12, no. 2 (2017), pp. 193–208.

**20** Mary Weismantel, "Tasty Meals and Bitter Gifts," *Food and Foodways* 5, no. 1 (1991), pp. 79–94, esp. p. 87.

**21** Ibid.

**22** Sidney Mintz, *Sweetness and Power* (New York, 1985), p. 214.

**23** Sutton 2010 (see note 19), p. 212.

**24** Seremetakis 1994 (see note 19); Jane Cowan, "Going Out for Coffee? Contesting the Grounds of Gendered Pleasures in Everyday Sociability," in *Contested Identities: Gender and Kinship in Modern Greece*, ed. Peter Loizos and Evthymios Papataxiarchis (Princeton, 1991), pp. 180–202.

**25** Barbara Kirshenblatt-Gimblett, "Playing to the Senses: Food as a Performance Medium," *Perform Research* 4, no. 1 (1999), pp. 1–30, esp. p. 3.

**26** Sutton 2010 (see note 19), p. 220.

**27** Carlo Petrini, *Slow Food Nation: Why Our Food Should Be Good, Clean and Fair* (New York, 2007).

# When Noodles Surprise: An Encounter with Changing Cultures of Taste in the Andes

Antje Baecker

Peru's rich culinary culture is influenced by the geographical, climatic, and cultural diversity of the country, whereby the numerous regional and "traditional" cuisines are constantly changing. Some culinary traditions are forgotten, and some are preserved, while various others are reinvented. I find the latter particularly fascinating. During my field research from 2007 to 2008 in Coporaque, a village community located in the southern Peruvian Andes in the Colca Valley [**fig. 1**], I noticed the frequent use of noodles for the preparation of everyday meals, mostly soups, but also *segundos* (main courses), together with local agricultural products or as a substitute for them. Until the 1980s, local staple foods, such as corn, barley, potatoes, and quinoa, formed the basis of nutrition in the Colca Valley. Noodles, mostly brought home from the city by family fathers, were generally prepared for festive occasions in the immediate family circle. The extension of the road to Arequipa, which began in the mid-1970s, changed this.[1] Arequipa's relative proximity and growing importance are closely linked to the change in life in Coporaque and its culinary culture.

This essay focuses on the acculturation of noodles in the Andes from the perspective of the anthropology of tasting. With this, I follow Paul Stoller, who, in *The Taste of Ethnographic Things,* was one of the first to draw attention to the importance of sensual experiences both as a theme and a method of anthropological research.[2] In the following, I will examine the extent to which sensual eating experiences influence cultural processes of appropriation of foreign foods, their integration into the local culinary culture, and thus the transformation of culinary cultures. In doing so, I would like to stimulate a discussion that goes beyond economic considerations of changing eating habits. In this context, I shall illustrate the extent to which bodily and sensual experiences are shaping judgments of taste and hierarchies of values.

Allow me to begin with a brief anecdote: Once I asked Anita,[3] wife and mother of four children between the ages of seven and twenty, why she so often uses noodles for family meals. She answered:

"I cook noodles for the children. They like them. They like the way they taste. They get bored eating our harvested products every day. They prefer food that has been purchased at the store, modern food."

This explanation was provided by many other people whom I interviewed in the course of my field research. I see one important reason for the fact that noodles are also the favorite food of many children in Coporaque in their sensual qualities. Children's preference for sweet-tasting food is a worldwide phenomenon. From an ethnological point of view, it results from the emotions of comfort and safety associated with this taste first experienced during breastfeeding.[4] In the Andes, a sweetish, viscous porridge called *api* in Quechua is children's first staple food. They easily adapt to this food, traditionally made from corn and today often made from oats, because it has sensuous properties that are similar to breast milk. The porridge, like breast milk, has a whitish-yellow color, is soft and creamy, pleasantly warm, mild and sweet in taste. It even produces a similar mouth feel.[5] My observation is consistent with that of Janet Carsten, who conducted research at the other end of the world: the Malay people living on Langkawi consider cooked rice and breast milk as similar and therefore use rice as a baby food.[6] Also in Coporaque and in the Andes region in general, breast milk and starchy foods form a kind of sensual–substantive continuum. The tuber called *oca* (Oxalis tuberosa) is thus described as producing mother's milk,[7] and *chicha*, a slightly alcoholic beverage drink made from corn, barley, or quinoa, is considered to be very similar to breast milk.[8] In addition, there are certain traditional soups—so-called white dishes with alpaca or sheep meat, fresh and white freeze-dried potatoes (*tunta*), barley or corn, today sometimes refined with a dollop of canned evaporated milk—which are said to stimulate the

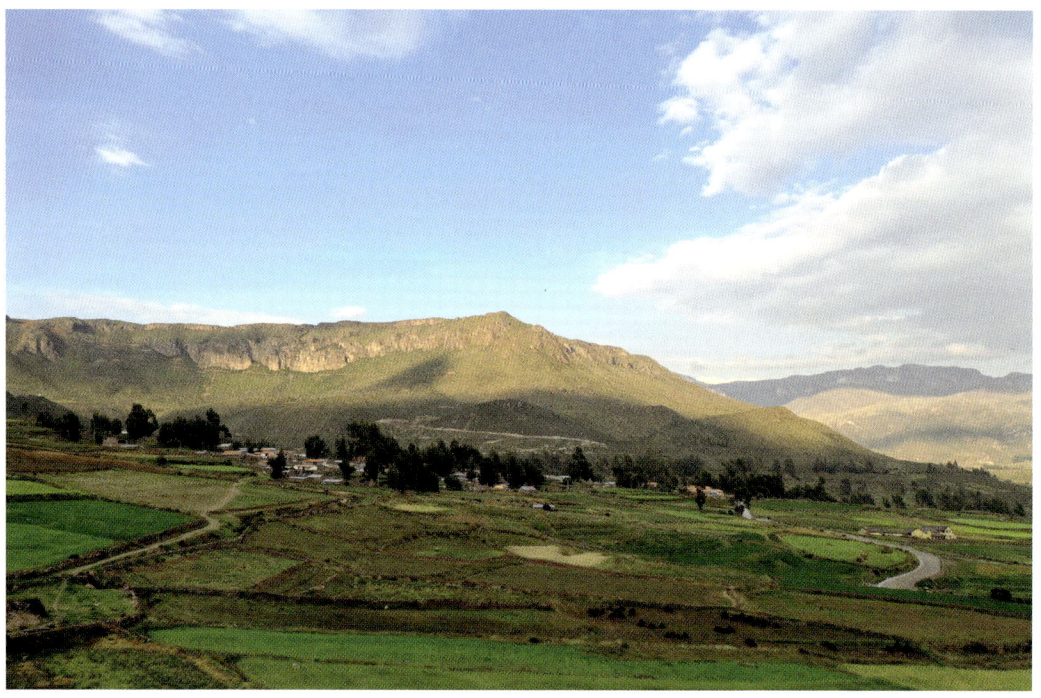

**Fig. 1** Coporaque
in the department of
Arequipa, Peru, 2019

    **Antje Baecker**

production of breast milk. They are said to work like medicine.

With predominately starchy foods, mothers not only feed their children, but also themselves. The food that the women prepare also serves as a means of self-identification. While many eldery women prefer food from grain and tuber products grown on their own fields, such as corn and barley, women of the younger generation often show a preference for noodles. They also regard them to be the product of their labor, albeit of their monetary, mostly non-agricultural activities. In addition, they associate their consumption with a mestizo, modern, and urban way of life, which forms part of their translocal identity.[9] Elderly women, who often organize their households in keeping with an agrarian culture and perform physically demanding daily work in one of the fields, perceive the daily use of noodles as a threat to their own identity and health.[10] This can be explained by the fact that food is regarded as something that constitutes both the body and the person.[11]

In the traditional world view of their ancestors, health is based on the humoral balance of the body. "Humoral" refers to the internal thermic effect that a food product has on the body. This principle is based on the idea of the body as a permeable material object—sensual properties of food products are transferred to the body when consumed.[12] Here, the objectively perceptible and measurable temperature of the food plays a role, too. Thus, food can have a warming and a cooling effect on the body.[13] A "lukewarm" state between "hot" and "cold" is considered ideal. This flexible balance is maintained by the diet. Hot, cold, dry, and liquid food is thus consumed in balanced quantities. Moist, liquid, and hot food such as soup serves the circulation of blood. Dry or dried, solid grain, and tuber products, for example *chuños*, give the body a firm structure, produce a hard and disease-resistant body, because they keep it closed.[14] The source of health, of *animu* (vitality) and *fuerza* (physical strength), is local food.[15]

Physical strength manifests itself as solid, high-quality body fat.[16] It forms the foundation of the body of a "true" Andean person, a *runa* (in Quechua: human, person).[17] Local food products and methods of preparation are called *mishqui* in Quechua, which means sweet or tasty. The epitome of *mishqui* is *api*, the aforementioned mild, sweet, lukewarm, and viscous porridge of barley, corn, or similar cereals. The local cereals used are also considered *mishqui*. In the sense of "tastes good," "tasty," the term also refers to savory dishes: mild in taste, adequately salted, and often very satiating.[18] *Mishqui* is associated with the female sphere and refers to homemade food with local ingredients in a traditional way. *Mishqui* dishes form the basis of the family's diet in the Colca Valley as a whole, but especially that of women and children[19] [**fig. 2**]. One of the reasons for this that it is based on the concept of the female body as being more open than the male body, and therefore more vulnerable.[20]

In contrast, non-local, purchased food products cause *debilidad* (weakness),[21] and illness.[22] They are considered humorally unbalanced.[23] Critics describe them as low in nutrients, but also as too rich, too watery, too spicy, too hot, or too easily perishable. Skeptics also have reservations about raw or uncooked food products that are suitable for immediate consumption.[24] "Too dry" and "too cold" are characteristics associated with aging, dying, and death.[25] The traditional Andean conviction is that the excessive consumption of non-local food products— not only occasionally on festive occasions or as a snack, but regularly as an everyday meal—is perceived as threatening. The body first loses good fat and then produces soft, inferior body fat. As a result, those affected become unable to perform "real" work, that is to say, work in the fields.[26] These are the characteristics of the body of the others: the *mistis* (mestizos), people who live in the city, "whites," foreigners, and all those who feed mainly on these food products.[27] People with a more conservative world view occasionally also see the poor health of some migrant workers as an indication that non-local food makes people weak and ill.[28] They often attribute this to the improper diet of the people concerned—meaning the consumption of predominantly urban food: *segundos* with rice as a filling accompaniment.[29]

Nevertheless, the cultural appreciation of "non-local" food products and dishes has a long tradition in the Andes. Although these foods are not said to have a nourishing effect on the body, they have another important function. They bring culinary variety, "joy of the body," or they are used to give others "culinary pleasure."[30] Since they are generally more difficult to access than local agricultural products, as they cost money, and are a product of the dominant market economy, such foods are also associated with an elevated social status. They thus function as a "gift" for establishing and maintaining social networks. With them, one recognizes an existing relationship and shows both respect and affection. Gifts of food products brought home by a husband to his wife are part of his obligatory contribution to the maintenance of the household.[31] And adult children who are engaged in monetary economic activities also contribute to the maintenance of their parents' household by buying basic food, including pasta.

Purchased and non-local foods therefore form a separate category. In Coporaque, as in the whole of Peru, besides the expression *comida de fiesta* (festival food), there are other terms: *comida moderna* (modern food), *comida para el paladar* (food for the palate), and *golosina* (delicacy). Also "snacks" and *comida rapida* (fast food), as well as *comida ligera* (light food), are common. Critics often call them *comida chatarra* (junk food).[32] They are partially attributed to the Andean taste category of *jayaj* (bitter, spicy, and strong). Sour and very salty dishes are also described as *jayaj*.[33] On the one hand, the term stands for the spiced, complete world.[34] On the other hand, as the opposite of *mishqui*, it refers to certain threats. Besides "bitter," *jayaj* also has the connotation of "inedible," "over-salted," and "raw." The term refers to the male sphere, to the world of "others"—the *mistis* (mestizos), the whites, and the spirits.[35] "Non-local foodstuffs" or "modern food" and "bitter/spicy" nevertheless form different categories.[36] The former refers to the type of production and origin, while the latter primarily forms a taste category. In addition to the "bitter," "non-local," or "modern" food products or drinks such as beer, which are regarded as *jayaj*, there are also edibles of non-local origin which actually taste sweet, that is to say, *mishqui*, but which are not *mishqui* in the conservative sense because of their non-local origin. This includes bread, biscuits, flour,

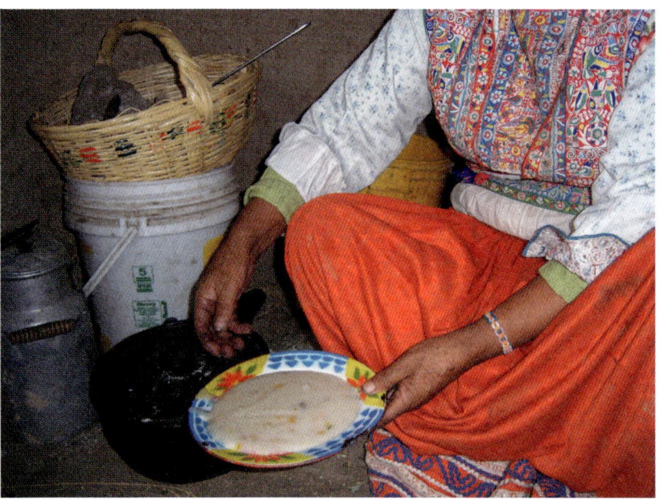

**Fig. 2** *Mishqui* dish *lawa de maiz*—cream of corn soup, prepared with alpaca fat and *charki* (freeze-dried alpaca meat), greens, and ground corn. Coporaque, Arequipa, Peru, 2008



**Antje Baecker**

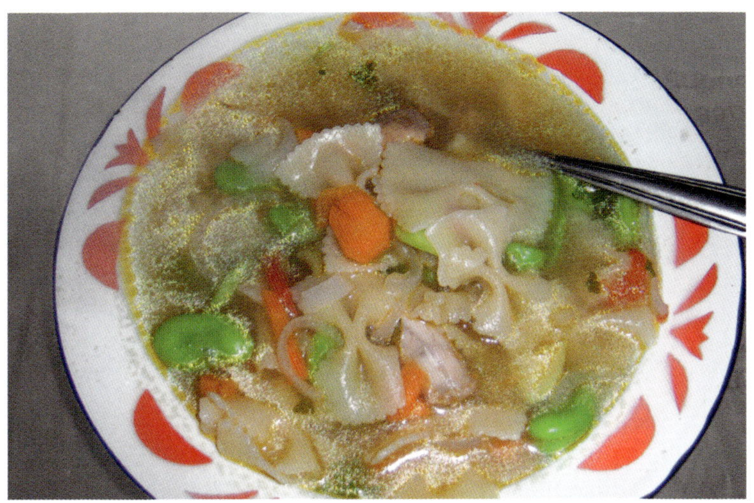

Fig. 3 *Sopa de fideo*— noodle soup, has prepared with chicken giblets, onions, tomatoes, noodles, potatoes, rice, stalk celery, carrots, and broad beans. Coporaque, Arequipa, Peru, 2008

noodles, and industrially produced sweets such as candies. While men bring male relatives and friends "bitter" beer and share this with them, these "sweet" purchased foods serve as gifts for women and children.[37] Such staple foods—which have the same sensual qualities as local *mishqui* products and are therefore also associated with childhood, motherhood, and family, and thus generally with comfort, security, and security—fit well into the culinary grammar of the local cuisine, that is to say, into everyday cuisine as well.[38] Noodles are also suitable for integration into the local culinary culture as an everyday foodstuff because they are bought uncooked, thus subjecting them to the cultural transformation process of cooking. Together with local ingredients, noodles are used, for example, in traditional soups. When prepared using familiar cooking methods such as roasting[39] and traditional cooking utensils such as clay pots and mud hearths,[40] noodles are given the locally appreciated individual taste called *sazón*.[41] *Sazón* stands for the culinary signature of a cook [**fig. 3**]. In this way, the non-local noodles are "Coporaquenized"; they become, in a sense, "one's own" noodles, a dish associated with one's own culture and home. Yannis Hamilakis calls this procedure a process of "familiarizing."[42] In the way in which non-local food products are used in Copo-

raque, I see Fernando Santos-Granero's view confirmed that the inhabitants of the Andes, as well as societies of the Amazon, see the "foreign" ("non-local food") as part of their own identity. Cooking, eating, and tasting represent sensual processes of embodiment through which the "other" loses its threatening quality because it becomes a part of the self.[43] Food is also understood in the Andes as a social substance.[44] Over time, people who eat together, who share the same meals and food substances together, become socially related by forming a collective body, which is, in this case, the family.[45] During common meals, relationships are formed and experienced through tasting.[46] The social changes in the Colca Valley make interpersonal relationships more fragile in general. They are challenged when the children leave the valley and become migrants, because there is a possibility that they may not return. Noodles counteract this fragility, I assert, because they are an ideal vehicle for mothers to show their children affection and love—also in anticipation of a corresponding "return gift," namely, that the children come home on a regular basis. They do this by serving noodles as a "gift," also in the context of everyday dishes. Pasta is treated as a culinary extra, as a delicacy, because it costs money. Mothers use different variations of noodles. On special occasions, such as

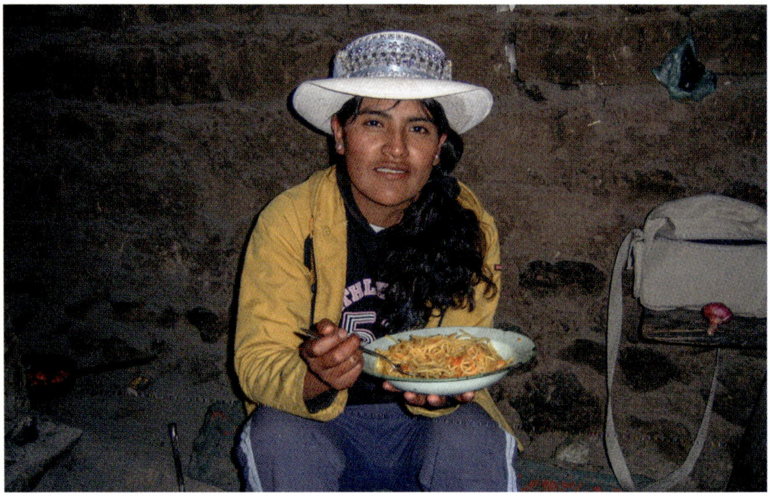

**Fig. 4** On the occasion of her birthday, a young woman has prepared her favorite dish *tallarines rojos con atun* (red spaghetti with canned tuna), which she shares with her parents and siblings. Coporaque, Arequipa, Peru, 2008

birthdays or when the adult daughter comes home from the city to visit her family, mothers often prepare spaghetti, *tallarines*, the favorite dish of many children and young women [**fig. 4**]. For everyday meals, they tend to use smaller noodles called *fideos*.

Mothers apparently integrate pasta into their everyday cooking in order to prepare their children for a life beyond Coporaque. They accustom their children to a non-Andean sensuous world and equip them with cosmopolitan eating and living habits even before they begin their lives as city dwellers. Local dishes prepared with noodles can be seen as "sensorial interfaces"[47] that bring together at least two forms of sensual knowledge: that of the local Andean world, Coporaque, and that of the translocal non-Andean world, cities and other places. With pasta dishes, mothers create a new Andean "tastescape"[48] for their children.

This living environment offers them the chance to experience different times and places as a whole in a sensual way. The simplicity of the local pasta dishes often proves to be a great advantage in a foreign place. Since they are prepared from universally available and relatively inexpensive ingredients, they can be easily cooked. They make it possible to experience the *sazón* of the mother—or at least a hint of it. Taste brings back memories of home and childhood, no matter where you are. Especially in difficult times, experiencing pasta that tastes like home can evoke feelings of comfort. With their pasta dishes, mothers in Coporaque have established noodles, a global food, as a new comfort food[49] that fits into the everyday life of the young generation of Coporaqueños, because tasting noodles can be seen as a way to experience both the world "out there" and the world back home as a whole in a sensual-emotional way.



Antje Baecker

**1** See Paulo Andrzej and Gałaś Andrzej, "La Minería y Otras Inversiones en la Vecindad del Cañón del Colca," in *Expedición Cientifica Polaca: Cañón del Colca*, ed. Zaniel Novoa Giocochea (Lima, 2009), pp. 139–69, esp. p. 163.
**2** Paul Stoller, *The Taste of Ethnographic Things: The Senses in Anthropology* (Philadelphia, 1989), pp. 7, 9, and 29; see also Lydia Maria Arantes, "Kulturanthropologie und Wahrnehmung: Zur Sinnlichkeit in Feld und Forschung," in *Ethnographien der Sinne: Wahrnehmung und Methode in empirisch-kulturwissenschaftlichen Forschungen*, ed. Lydia Maria Arantes and Elisa Rieger (Bielefeld, 2014), pp. 23–28, esp. p. 27.
**3** She and her husband live primarily from the cultivation and sale of agricultural products. Part of the harvest is used to feed the family.
**4** Deborah Lupton, *Food, the Body and the Self* (London, 1996), p. 7.
**5** Ibid., p. 31.
**6** Janet Carsten, "The Substance of Kinship and the Heat of the Hearth: Feeding, Personhood, and Relatedness among Malays in Pulau Langkawi," *American Ethnologist* 22, no. 2 (1995), pp. 223–41, esp. p. 228.
**7** Margaret A. Graham, "Food, Health and Identity in a Rural Andean Community," in *Medical Pluralism in the Andes*, ed. Joan D. Koss-Chioino, Thomas Leatherman, and Christine Greenway (London and New York, 2003), pp. 148–65, esp. p. 156.
**8** Ibid.; also see Mary Weismantel, "Have a Drink, Chicha, Performance and Politics," in *Drink, Power, and Society in the Andes*, ed. Justin Jennings and Brenda J. Bowser (Gainesville, FL, 2008), pp. 257–77, esp. p. 272.
**9** Juana Camacho, "Good to Eat, Good to Think: Food, Culture and Biodiversity in Cotacachi," in *Development with Identity: Community, Culture and Sustain-*

*ability in the Andes,*
ed. Robert E. Rhoades
(Cambridge, MA, 2006),
pp. 156–72, esp. p. 159.
**10** According to Claude
Fischler, humans are
neophiliac, that is to
say, curious about new
things, and yet at the
same time cautious, sus-
picious, and conservative
in their eating habits:
"Any new, unknown food
is a potential danger."
Claude Fischler, "Food,
Self and Identity," *Social
Science Information* 27,
no. 2 (1988), pp. 275–92,
esp. p. 277.
**11** Julian López García,
"Q'aras y Jaquis:
Comida e Identidad en
el Altiplano de Bolivia,"
*Folklore Americano* 59
(1998), pp. 187–209,
esp. pp. 187 and 191.
**12** Lauris A. McKee,
"Ethnomedicine and
Enculturation in the
Andes of Ecuador," in
Koss-Chioino et al. 2003
(see note 7), pp. 131–47,
esp. pp. 136–37.
**13** See Joseph W.
Bastien, "Qollahuaya-
Andean Body Concepts:
A Topographical-Hydrau-
lic Model of Physiology,"
*American Anthropologist*
87, no. 3 (1985), pp.
595–611, esp. pp. 607–8.
An excess of "heat" is
considered less harmful
than a humorous state
that is too "cold."
For more information,
see Edita Vera Vokral,
*Küchenorganisation und
Agrarzyklus auf dem Al-
tiplano: Nahrungsgewin-
nung, Zubereitung und
Konsum in der ländlichen
Gesellschaft bei Juliaca
(Südperu)* (Bonn, 1989),
p. 251.
**14** Chilli is considered
hot, soups are hot and
moist, and fresh meat is
both moist and hot (in
a humoral sense). See
Gerardo Fernández
Juárez, "Comida,
Cuerpo y Enfermedad:

Referentes Etnicos en
el Altiplano Aymara,"
*América Indígena* 57,
nos. 3–4 (1997),
pp. 99–132, esp.
pp. 118–19.
**15** Graham 2003
(see note 7), p. 155.
**16** López García 1998
(see note 11), p. 191;
Francis Ferrie, "A Diet of
Fat Connecting Humans
and Nonhumans (in
the Bolivian Foothills
between the Andes and
Amazonia)," *Tipití: Journal of the Society for the
Anthropology of Lowland
South America* 13, no. 2
(2015), pp. 105–18,
esp. p. 113.
**17** Mary Weismantel,
*Cholas and Pishtacos:
Stories of Race and Sex
in the Andes* (Chicago,
2001), pp. 190 and
199–200.
**18** A meal salted with
precision is the food of a
"true" person. The pinch
of salt stands for human-
ity, for a complete world
that strives for harmony
and connectedness.
For more on this, see,
among others: Francis-
co M. Gil García, "La
Cocina de los Chullpas:
Representaciones del
pasado e identidades en
el presente a partir de
la alimentación en los Andes," *Revista Española
de Antropología Amer-
icana* 44, no. 1 (2013),
pp. 191–215, esp. p. 195;
López García 1998 (see
note 11), pp. 190 and
196. According to Vokral,
salt is a regulator in the
hot-cold system: Vokral
1989 (see note 13),
p. 135.
**19** Mary Weismantel,
*Food, Gender, and
Poverty in the Ecuador-
ian Andes* (Philadelphia
1988), p. 92.
**20** Anne C. Larme,
"Environment, Vulnerabil-
ity and Gender in Andean
Ethnomedicine," *Social
Science & Medicine* 47,

no. 8 (1998), pp. 1005–15,
esp. pp. 1005 and
1009–10.
**21** We are dealing here
with a pathology of eth-
nomedicine in the Andes.
*Debilidad* can be recog-
nized by certain physical
symptoms, which are
treated with specific
local healing methods.
See Graham 2003 (see
note 7), p. 155; Larme
1998 (see note 20).
**22** See Fernández Juárez
1997 (see note 14),
p. 119; Mary Weismantel,
"Making Kin: Kinship
Theory and Zumbagua
Adoptions," *American
Ethnologist* 22, no. 4
(1995), pp. 685–704,
esp. p. 695.
**23** Fernández Juárez
1997 (see note 14),
pp. 99 and 118; McKee
2003 (see note 12),
pp. 136–37; Weisman-
tel 1995 (see note 22),
p. 695; Weismantel
2001 (see note 17),
pp. 191–92.
**24** Mary Weismantel,
"The Children Cry for
Bread: Hegemony and
the Transformation of
Consumption," in *The
Social Economy of Con-
sumption IV*, ed. Henry
J. Rutz and Benjamin
S. Orlove (Lanham,
MD, 1989), pp. 105–24,
esp. pp. 90, 92, and
136–37; Weismantel 1995
(see note 22), p. 695;
Weismantel 2001 (see
note 17), pp. 191–92;
López García 1998 (see
note 11); Fernández
Juárez 1997 (see note
14), pp. 99 and 118; Mc-
Kee 2003 (see note 12),
pp. 136–37.
**25** Graham 2003 (see
note 7), p. 155.
**26** Ibid., p. 158.
**27** Fernández Juárez
1997 (see note 14),
p. 119; López García
1998 (see note 11),
p. 191.
**28** Graham 2003 (see
note 7), p. 156.

**29** From the point of view of the rather conservative-thinking Andeans, rice has no nourishing and invigorating effect on the body, but rather a weakening effect. Critics also describe urban dishes as very rich in fat and sweet. See Fernández Juárez 1997 (see note 14), pp. 107 and 119.

**30** Mary Weismantel, "Tasty Meals and Bitter Gifts," in *The Taste Cultural Reader: Experiencing Food and Drink*, ed. Carolyn Korsmeyer (Oxford and New York, 2005), p. 93. See also Weismantel 1988 (see note 19), p. 139, and López García 1998 (see note 11), p. 191.

**31** Weismantel 1988 (see note 19), p. 139; Weismantel 2001 (see note 17), p. 111; Weismantel 2005 (see note 30), pp. 87–88 and 92.

**32** In Zumbagua, Ecuador, there is also an independent term for purchased, culturally foreign foods: *wanlla*, which means "extra portion." See Weismantel 2005 (see note 30), p. 91; Rachel Corr, "Reciprocity, Communion, and Sacrifice: Food in Andean Ritual and Social Life," *Food and Foodways* 10, nos. 1–2 (2002), pp. 1–25, esp. p. 9.

**33** *Uchu* (chilli) and *cachi* (salt) belong together in a certain sense and have a similar significance. See Weismantel 1988 (see note 19), pp. 92 and 137.

**34** López García 1998 (see note 11), p. 196.

**35** A world without salt and sugar is also associated with the world of the "others," the spirits. See ibid., pp. 195–96.

**36** *Jayaj* is first and foremost a taste category. *Comida para el paladar* (food for the palate),

*comida moderna* (modern food), and *golosina* (delicacy) are synonyms of *wanlla* (extra portion). See Weismantel 2005 (see note 30), p. 91.

**37** In fact, the term *mishqui* is not used exclusively for local food, but also for some market-based products, such as sweets and *sabor*, a flavor enhancer with a bit of salt. See Weismantel 1988 (see note 19), p. 107.

**38** Marin Trenk, "Chicken McNuggets: 500 Jahre Kulinarische Globalisierung," in *Die Welt im Löffel: Kochen, Kunst, Kultur*, ed. Sebastian Schellhaas (Bielefeld, 2012), pp. 46–60, esp. p. 55.

**39** Noodles are often roasted raw before being cooked in boiling water.

**40** They produce a smoky and an earthy taste, a *sabor a tierra*. See Benjamin S. Orlove, "Down to Earth: Race and Substance in the Andes," *Bulletin of Latin American Research* 17, no. 2 (1998), pp. 207–22, esp. p. 213; Camacho 2006 (see note 9), p. 166. The propane gas stove is, however, becoming increasingly popular in the preparation of everyday foods. The mud hearth is mainly used for the preparation of large banquets. However, only a few inhabitants still cook with clay pots. They serve as a gift for women at weddings. In most cases, they are not replaced if they get broken.

**41** *Sazón* means "taste" in the sense of "flavor." *Sazón* is also the knowledge of cooking. Meredith Abarca describes it as a physical knowledge: Meredith E. Abarca, *Voices in the Kitchen: Views of Food and the World from Working Class Mexican and Mexican

American Women* (College Station, TX, 2006), p. 51.

**42** For more on the term "familiarizing process," see Yannis Hamilakis, *Archaeology and the Senses: Human Experience, Memory, and Affect* (Cambridge, 2013), p. 83.

**43** Fernando Santos-Granero, "Hybrid Bodies: A Visual History of Yanesha Patterns of Cultural Change," *Current Anthropology* 50, no. 4 (2009), pp. 477–512, esp. pp. 477–78.

**44** Sidney Mintz, *Sweetness and Power: The Place of Sugar in Modern History* (New York, 1985).

**45** Weismantel 1995 (see note 22), p. 695.

**46** Geneviève Teil and Antoine Hennion, "Discovering Quality or Performing Taste? A Sociology of the Amateur," in *Qualities of Food*, ed. Mark Harvey, Andrew McMeekin, and Alan Warde (Manchester and New York, 2004), pp. 19–37, esp. p. 25; Stoller 1989 (see note 2).

**47** On the term "sensorial interface," see Kelvin E. Y. Low and Devorah Kalekin-Fishman, "Afterword: Towards Transnational Sensescapes," in *Everyday Life in Asia: Social Perspectives on the Senses* (London, 2016), pp. 195–203, esp. pp. 198 and 200.

**48** In line with Low's concept of the "sensescape," see Kelvin E. Y. Low, "The Social Life of the Senses: Charting Directions," *Sociology Compass* 6, no. 3 (2012), pp. 271–82, esp. p. 279.

**49** Charles Spence, "Comfort Food: A Review," *International Journal of Gastronomy and Food Science* 9 (2017), pp. 105–9, esp. p. 105.

# The Taste of the Foreign: Eating and Migration

Thomas Macho

The philosophical tradition tried to define "being"—*to ón* in ancient Greek, *ens* in Latin—as a unity based on categories of quality, quantity, relation, place, time, and position. Being is, as it were, whole, unmixed, and undivided—"ens et unum convertuntur," as scholasticism taught, alluding to Aristotle's *Metaphysics*, and Martin Heidegger was still asking in *Sein und Zeit* (translated as *Being and Time*) about the possible "Being-a-whole" of Dasein, which is said to be foreshadowed in the "anticipation of death." These discourses are rather remote from our daily lives. After all, it is one of the most elementary preconditions of existence to have to mix with the foreign. For anyone who wishes to remain alive has to eat and drink every day, ingest juices and parts of other animals or plants, and incorporate them. Not even the strictest ascetics live only from themselves. Reason is therefore never "pure" but rather constantly reliant on metabolism, dependent on cycles of acquiring and excreting—in short, it is a metabolic reason.

Our life already begins that way: with hunger for the other, for the foreign. Milk is the first concrete gift, after life itself, that is offered to us, as it is so often said. Yet all gifts and presents are ambiguous: milk provides peace, satiety, and sleep, but it also threatens us with flatulence, stomachaches, and vomiting. It divides the world into nourishing and denying, good and evil objects. Melanie Klein analyzed these dividing processes and related them to the conflict between life instincts and death instincts, Eros and Thanatos[1]—as if the newborn in particular would constantly vacillate over whether to accept the gift of life. It replaces the blood of motherly provision with the navel cord, then the air breathed in with the first cry, when the stage of breathing—*Le stade du respir* according to Jean-Louis Tristani[2]—begins. Not coincidentally, the plagues of sucked milk result from their relationship to the air that is often swallowed along with it and then hampers digestion; the oral sadistic aggression that forces the infant to bite its mother's nipple transforms the milk

back into blood, as it were. Yet this blood no longer nourishes, and the attack of rage quickly gives way to new neediness and fiery hunger. As late as the Renaissance, by the way, a distinction was still commonly made between "blood mothers" and "milk mothers," that is, wet nurses.[3]

In *Masse und Macht* (translated as *Crowds and Power*), Elias Canetti identifies the motherly with food—and borders on a misogynistic misjudgment: "A mother is one who gives her own body to be eaten. She first nourishes the child in her womb and then gives it milk. This activity continues in a less concentrated form throughout many years; her thoughts, in so far as she is a mother, revolve around the food the growing child needs. It does not have to be her own child; a strange child may be substituted for her own, or she may adopt one. Her passion is to give food, to watch the child eating and profiting by the food it eats."[4] To Canetti, mothers seem to be desiring machines of feeding, who admittedly seem to follow their own desire more than that of the child: the hunger of the wicked witch in the Grimms' fairy tale *Hansel and Gretel* who fattens the boy up in order to roast and eat him—that is to say, to be able to lead him back into her own stomach. Famously, the children are lured with gingerbread and confectionery, but the bread of life is the bread of death, in the end for the evil mother witch herself, who is shoved by her female rival into the oven, that is, forced back into the hot belly of prenatal life. The oral sadistic aggression is projected onto the evil mother, while the children identify with the air: "The wind, the wind, the heavenly child." Canetti, too, consoled himself about the feeding passions of mothers with the memory of air: "He no longer wants thoughts that bite. He wants thoughts that make it easier to breathe."[5]

Metabolic practices transform the foreign into the own and back into the foreign. Using the example of milk again: only around a quarter of the human population can drink and tolerate milk even after childhood; more than 90 percent of Asian populations are lactose-intolerant. According to the latest anthropological studies, the ability to digest lactose without problems emerged very late as a genetic effect resulting from a settled way of life, agriculture, and cattle breeding. Nevertheless, even those of us in lactose-tolerant zones are disgusted by milk skin: skin on the milk, milk on the skin, as Julia Kristeva explains on the very first pages of her theory of abjection.[6] And Maud Ellmann, in an inspiring essay called *The Hunger Artists*, even asserted that: "Our first experience of eating [and drinking] is force-feeding: as infants, we were fed by others and ravished by the food they thrust into our jaws." Only later do we begin to eat "in order to avenge ourselves against this rape inflicted at the very dawn of life." What tastes good to us seems to heal the "wound of feeding."[7] This takes place in the form of the other, who can now be perceived as one's self, having been appropriated.

Another of the mythical narratives that revolve around eating and drinking is the idea that eaters and drinkers take in the energies and qualities of that being eaten and drunk, of the animals and plants in question. They enrich themselves from the other, possibly even from an enemy in war. Using the example of the ritual cannibalism of the Tupi, a precolonial ethnic group in Brazil, Eduardo Viveiros de Castro examines the practices of metabolic reason in his *Métaphysiques cannibales* (2009, translated as *Cannibal Metaphysics* in 2014). He explains it as the "transmutation of perspectives," whereby "the 'I' is determined as other through the act of incorporating this other, who in turn becomes an 'I'…but only ever *in* the other—literally, that is, *through* the other." Viveiros de Castro asks what is really devoured from the enemy, and he answers: "What was eaten was the enemy's relation to those who consumed him; in other words, *his condition as enemy*. In other words, what was assimilated from the victim was the signs of his alterity, the aim being to reach his alterity as a point of view on the Self. Cannibalism and the peculiar form of war with which it is bound up involve

a paradoxical movement of reciprocal self-determination through the point of view of the enemy."[8] And he defines the Western ontology of the whole, of the one, of the unmixed and undivided being, as the source and origin "of every colonialism," which denies the metabolic conversion of perspectives. "But the wind turns, things change, and alterity will eat through even the thickest walls of identity and thus cause them to fall."[9]

The shift in metabolic perspective that Viveiros de Castro analyzes is not foreign to other traditions and practices either. Admittedly, this shift in perspective often appears as a kind of cycle of guilt. The classical scholar and anthropologist Walter Burkert has claimed that ancient Greek animal sacrifices—such as the sacrifice of oxen in Athens, the Buphonia—can be traced back to the hunting rituals of European ethnic groups that are often described as "comedies of innocence" in literature. The point is to reassure the dead animal that the hunters regret its death but bear no guilt for it. As additional evidence, Burkert cites an ancient Babylonian text that precisely describes the rituals necessary to sacrifice an ox: "The ox stands bound on a reed mat; its mouth is washed; evocations are whispered into its right and left ear; it is sprayed with water, cleaned with a torch, surrounded with a circle of flour. After prayer and song, the ox is killed, its heart immediately burned; its skin and left shoulder tendon are removed to use to cover the tympanum [hand drum]. More libations [drink offerings] and offerings; the priest bows before the severed head and speaks: 'This act—all the gods performed it; I did not perform it.' One text version says that the cadaver is buried; another version prohibits the main priest, at least, from eating the meat."[10]

Roberto Calasso described similar metabolisms of guilt several years ago in his study of the ancient Indian vedas.[11] More than half a century ago, Elias Canetti emphasized the experience of transformation as a central element of eating, alluding to the field research conducted by Carl Strehlow and his son, Ted Strehlow, among the aborigines in central Australia. *"The thing which is eaten eats back,"* Canetti remarks, since the "transformations which link man with the animals he eats are as strong as chains. Without transforming himself into animals he would never have learnt to feed himself…. In later societies the memory of the way in which food was originally gained, that is, through transformation, is still preserved in later sacred communions. The flesh which is communally eaten is not what it seems to be; it stands for some other flesh and becomes it whilst it is being eaten."[12]

The transformations from the pleasure of eating and drinking remain precarious, threatened by the possibility of the tables turning at any time: *"The thing which is eaten eats back."* Therein lies the essence of melancholy, according to Canetti: the melancholic "is resigned to his fate and sees himself as prey; first as prey, then as food, and finally as carrion or excrement. The process of depreciation, which makes his own person some more and more worthless, is figuratively expressed as feelings of guilt. … The melancholic does not want to eat and, as a reason for his refusal, may say that he does not deserve to. But the real reason is that he sees himself as being eaten and, if forced to eat, is reminded of this. His own mouth turns against him; it is as though a mirror were held before him and he saw that something was being eaten. But this is himself. The terrible penalty for always having eaten is suddenly and ineluctably there before him."[13] A final transformation: pleasure in and craving for food and drink appear as lethal self-consumption, which almost seem to compel refusals to eat, a kind of collective hunger strike. In our culture of eating and consumption today, guilt cycles dominate. Every day, the forgotten metabolism is brought to mind again: in reports on the increase of plastic trash in the oceans; on the transcontinental migration of fruit, vegetables, fish, and meat; on the climate-critical emission of carbon dioxide from mass livestock breeding and industrial agriculture; on fires being set to clear the rain forest for cattle grazing or the production of soy and palm oil. Clearly, we are in the process of swallowing up our own future on this planet.

Almost exactly a hundred and fifty years ago, the Estonian cultural historian Victor Hehn—Nietzsche studied him closely—analyzed the migration paths of domesticated plants and animals;[14] and more than thirty years ago, the American historian Alfred W. Crosby, who died on March 14, 2018, published his study *Ecological Imperialism*, in which he impressively demonstrated that the colonial conquests were only possible with the aid of cattle and wheat.[15] Even as recently as the early 1970s, stores that sold basic foodstuffs were called, in German, *Kolonialwarenläden* (colonial goods stores). In the meanwhile, it has long been forgotten that it was only the spice trade with the East Indies and later the importation of potatoes, sugar, tomatoes, coffee, and cocoa from the New World that enriched our menus. And while we debate a restrictive asylum policy and the building of new border barriers, we have long since given no more thought to the fact that in the 1950s it was still nearly impossible to visit a pizzeria or a Chinese or Japanese restaurant in German-speaking countries, for instance. Exotic cuisines were established only after World War II ended—the result of countless migration movements by guest workers, who were, of course, not perceived as guests but were often supposed to serve tourist guests.[16] Recently, the Italian journalist Marco d'Eramo, in his *Il selfie del mondo: Indagine sull'età del turismo* (Selfie of the World: Investigation into the Age of Tourism, 2018), emphasized this connection between migration and tourism: "A specter is haunting, avoided by all the discourses on tourism. And this specter is the migrant. Not only because the migrant and the tourist are in the first instance the complementary, symmetrical sides of modern travel: the tourist is the foreigner whom the native serves, while the migrant is the foreigner who comes to serve the native."[17]

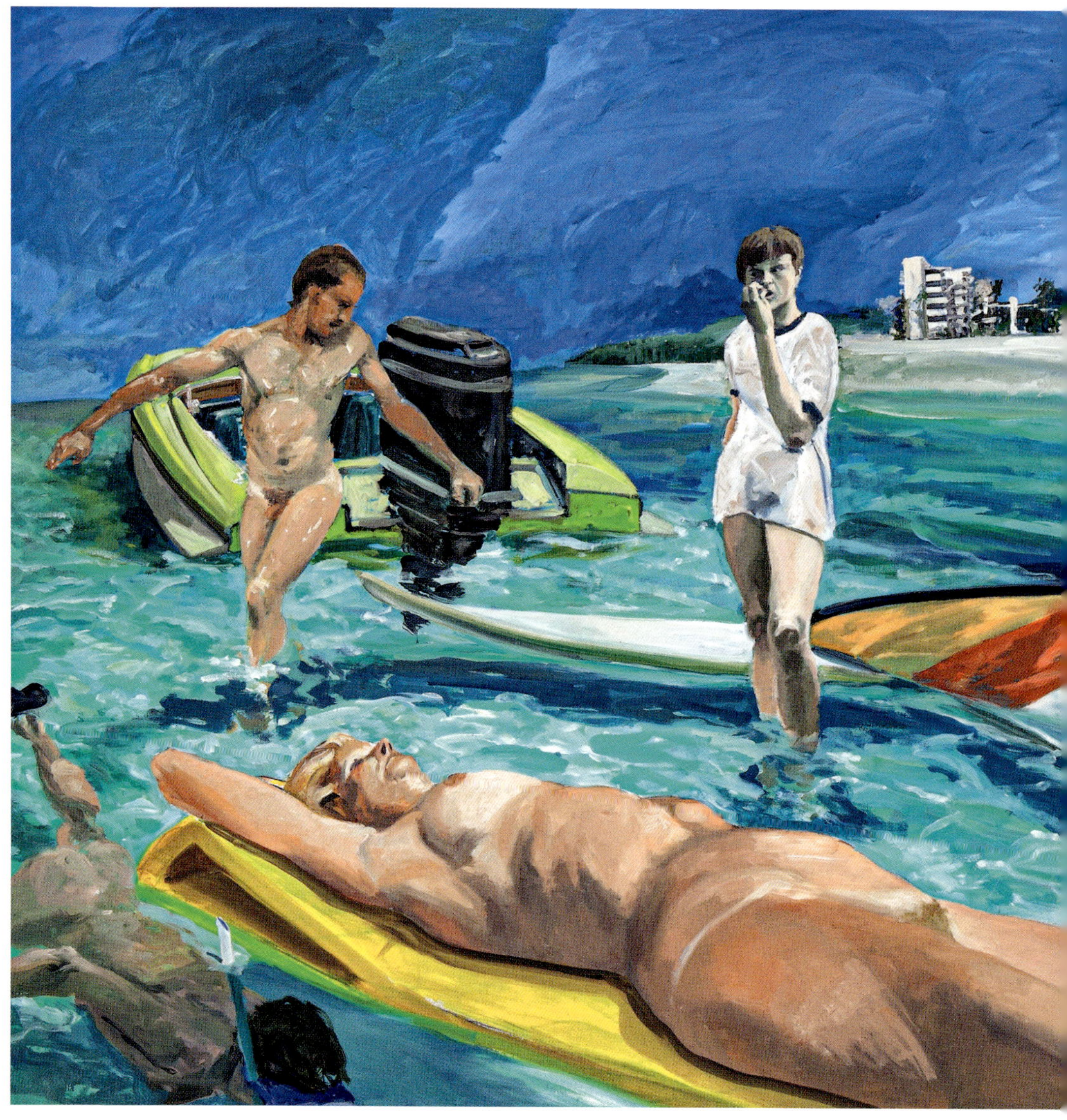

Fig. 1 Eric Fischl
*A Visit To / A Visit From /*
*The Island*, 1983
Oil on canvas,
213.4 × 426.7 cm
Whitney Museum of
American Art, New York

                    Thomas Macho

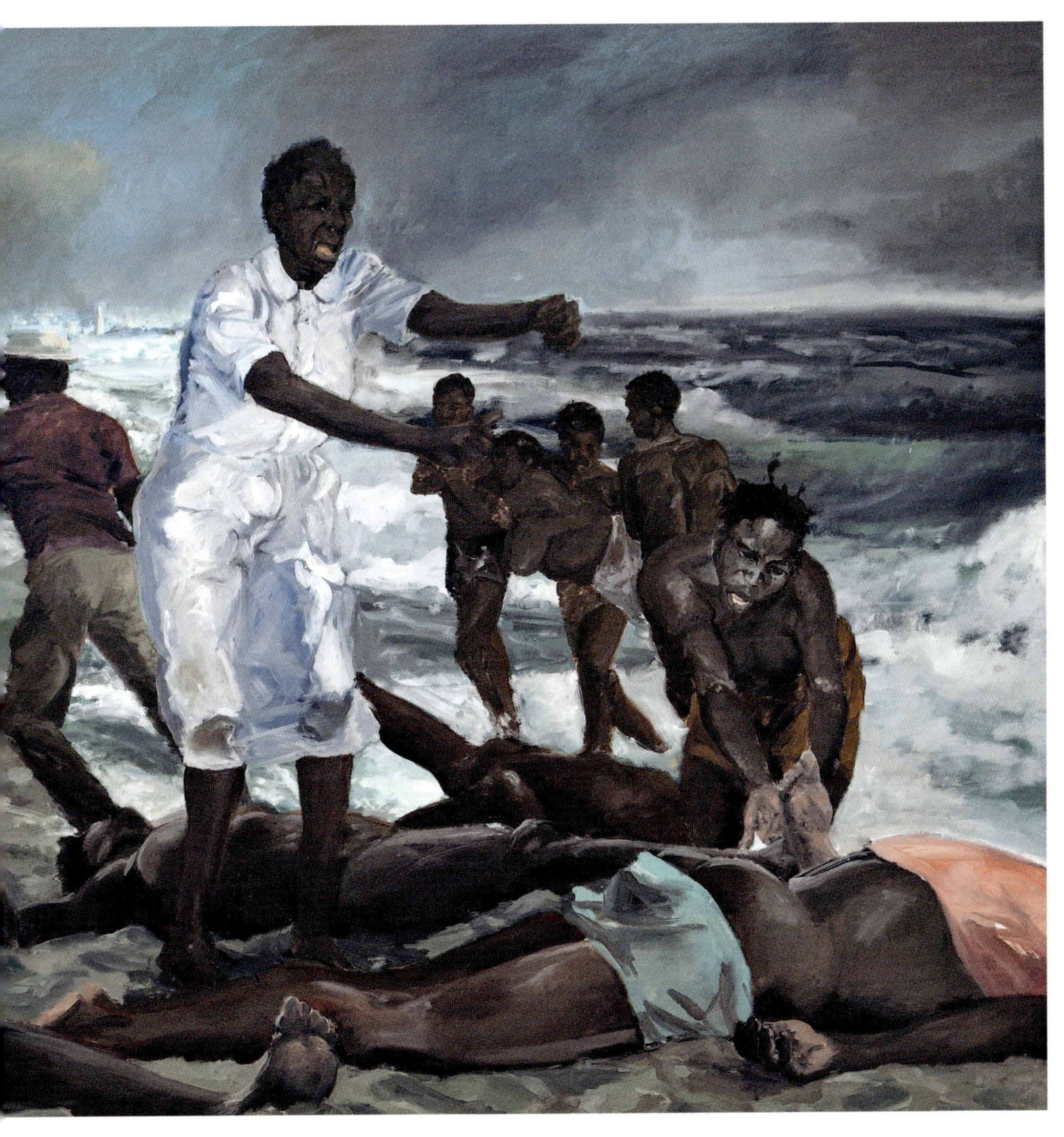

Briefly, the current numbers for comparison: in 2018, according to the United Nations High Commissioner for Refugees (UNHCR), around 70.8 million people were put to flight and exiled; in that same time period, 1.5 billion tourist entries were recorded. Around thirty-five years ago—before any rubber boats were crossing the Mediterranean—the American artist Eric Fischl painted a pair of large-format, realistic oil paintings now hanging in the Whitney Museum of American Art in New York. [**fig. 1**]. The moods of the two pendants could not be more different. In the left-hand painting, we see a beach scene with a motorboat pilot and a woman sunning herself on an air mattress; the water is calm, the sky blue. In the right-hand painting, stormy weather appears to rage; the sky is dark, the sea churning. We see a group of dark-skinned men and women pulling one another out of the sea. The painting is based on a photograph showing refugees from Haiti arriving on Florida's coast. The compositions of the two pendants are similar: naked bodies lying in the foreground; the borders between sky and sea are at the same height. The painting on the left shows a family on a beach vacation in Haiti; the painting on the right, people who have risked their lives to flee the same island. *A Visit To / A Visit From / The Island*: relaxation corresponds visually with the profoundest exhaustion. This double image confronts not only the rich with the poor, but also the migration streams of tourism and flight.

Marco d'Eramo has observed that our pictures of multicultural societies are eminently influenced by metaphors from cuisine. He quotes one example from Finland: "Spices are the colours that different cultures bring to the Finnish society and the salt in the bottom is support and help for each other."[18] And he commented on a remark by Angela Davis: "The metaphor that has displaced the melting pot is the salad. A salad consisting of many ingredients is colorful and beautiful, and it is to be consumed by someone."[19] Finally, he quotes Amartya Sen, who reminded us that Indian cuisine first encountered the chili when "the Portuguese brought it to India from America, but it is effectively used in a wide range of Indian food today and seems to be a dominant element in most types of curries. It is plentifully present in a mouth-burning form in vindaloo, which, as its name indicates, carries the immigrant memory of combining wine with potatoes. Tandoori cooking might have been perfected in India, but it originally came to India from West Asia. Curry powder, on the other hand, is a distinctly English invention, unknown in India before Lord Clive, and evolved, I imagine, in the British army mess."[20]

A cuisine of the foreign, a cuisine of melting and appropriation, a cuisine of forgetting and guilt-plagued renunciation? How can we engage in the practice of metabolic reason, giving and taking in eating and drinking, that does not risk suddenly turning into the melancholy of self-consumption and hopelessness? Jacques Derrida once reminded us that good food always presumes an attitude of hospitality, since eating well does not mean primarily "taking in and grasping in itself, but *learning* and *giving* to eat, learning-to-give-the-other-to-eat," since the law of "infinite hospitality" is simply: "One never eats entirely on one's own."[21] A touching example of this attitude is offered by Ilija Trojanow in his reflections *Nach der Flucht* (After the Escape). He tells the story of his mother who only really arrived in a new country when she had the first opportunity to invite others to a meal: "Not other refugees, who exchange stories like cigarettes, but natives whom she had met without intention and free of purpose. She has to overcome herself to invite them; she scrapes the money together for a meal that satisfies her own very modest expectations. She plunges into the opportunity. She is entirely present. She forgets for several happy moments the grammatical mistakes that creep into her labored jokes. Glowing, she serves up her arrival."[22]

**1** See Melanie Klein, *The Psychoanalysis of Children*, trans. Alix Strachey with H. A. Thorner (New York, 1975), p. 124.
**2** See Jean-Louis Tristani, *Le stade du respir* (Paris, 1978).
**3** See Christiane Klapisch-Zuber, "'Blutseltern' und 'Milcheltern,'" in *Das Haus, der Name, der Brautschatz: Strategien und Rituale im gesellschaftlichen Leben der Renaissance* (Frankfurt am Main, 1995), pp. 94–119.
**4** Elias Canetti, *Crowds and Power*, trans. Carol Stewart (New York, 1978), p. 221.
**5** Elias Canetti, *The Secret Heart of the Clock: Notes, Aphorisms, Fragments, 1973–1985*, trans. Joel Agee (New York, 1989), p. 51.
**6** See Julia Kristeva, *Powers of Horror: An Essay on Abjection*, trans. Leon S. Roudiez (New York, 1982), pp. 2–3.
**7** Maud Ellmann, *The Hunger Artists: Starving, Writing, and Imprisonment* (Cambridge, MA, 1993), pp. 35–36.
**8** Eduardo Viveiros de Castro, *Cannibal Metaphysics: For a Post-Structural Anthropology*, ed. and trans. Peter Skafish (Minneapolis, 2014), pp. 142–43.
**9** Eduardo Viveiros de Castro, *Kannibalische Metaphysiken: Elemente einer post-strukturalen Anthropologie*, trans. Theresa Mentrup (Leipzig, 2019), p. 24. (This sentence does not appear in the original French or the English translation—Trans.)
**10** Walter Burkert, *Homo Necans: Interpretationen altgriechischer Opferriten und Mythen* (Berlin, 1972), pp. 18–19.
**11** See Roberto Calasso, *Ardor*, trans. Richard Dixon (New York: Farrar, Straus and Giroux, 2014).
**12** Canetti 1978 (see note 4), p. 357.
**13** Ibid., pp. 347–48.
**14** See Victor Hehn, *Kulturpflanzen und Hausthiere in ihrem Übergang aus Asien nach Griechenland und Italien sowie in das übrige Europa (Historisch-linguistische Skizzen)* (Berlin, 1870).
**15** See Alfred W. Crosby, *Ecological Imperialism: The Biological Expansion of Europe, 900–1900* (Cambridge, 1986).
**16** See Maren Möhring, *Fremdes Essen: Die Geschichte der ausländischen Gastronomie in der Bundesrepublik Deutschland* (Munich, 2012).
**17** Marco d'Eramo, *Il selfie del mondo: Indagine sull'età del turismo* (Milan, 2019), p. 220.
**18** Ibid., pp. 203–4. English translation quoted in: Salla Tuori, "Cooking Nation: Gender Equality and Multiculturalism as Nation-Building Discourses," *European Journal of Women's Studies* 14, no. 1 (2007), pp. 21–35, esp. 27.
**19** d'Eramo 2019 (see note 17), pp. 203–4. English translation quoted in: Angela Y. Davis, "Gender, Class and Multiculturalism: Rethinking 'Race' Politics," in *Mapping Multiculturalism*, ed. Avery F. Gordon and Christopher Newfield (Minneapolis, 1996), pp. 40–48.
**20** Amartya Sen, *Identity and Violence: The Illusion of Destiny* (London, 2006), pp. 156–57.
**21** Jacques Derrida, "'Eating Well,' or The Calculation of the Subject," trans. Peter Connor and Avital Ronell, in Jacques Derrida, *Points …: Interviews, 1974–1994*, ed. Elisabeth Weber (Stanford, CA, 1995), pp. 255–87, esp. p. 282.
**22** Ilija Trojanow, *Nach der Flucht* (Frankfurt am Main, 2017), p. 18.

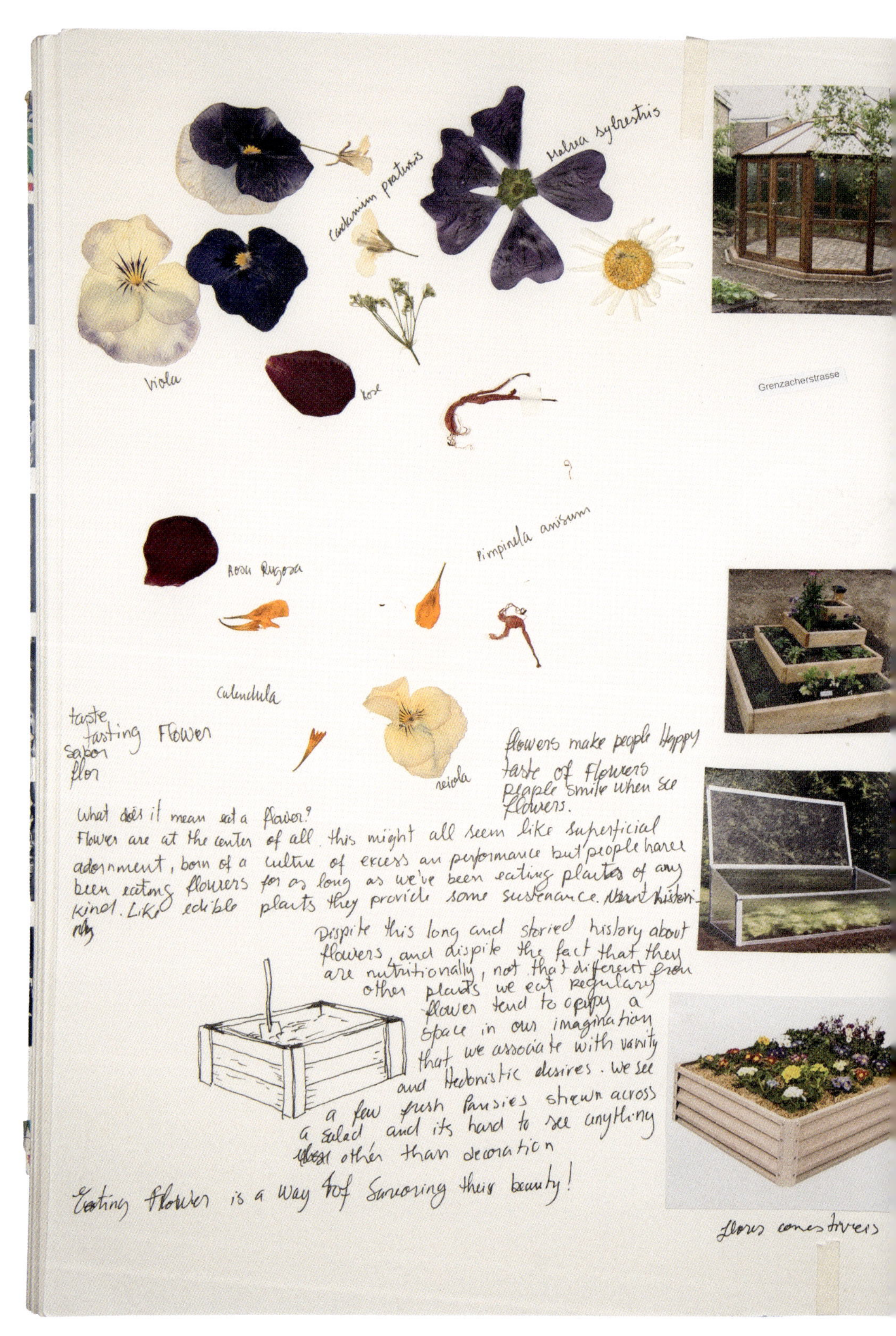


Marisa Benjamim
Preparatory sketches
for *Hortus Deliciarum*
at Museum Tinguely
(February 19 to May 17
2020), 2019
Collage and ink on paper,
21 × 29.7 cm
Courtesy of the artist

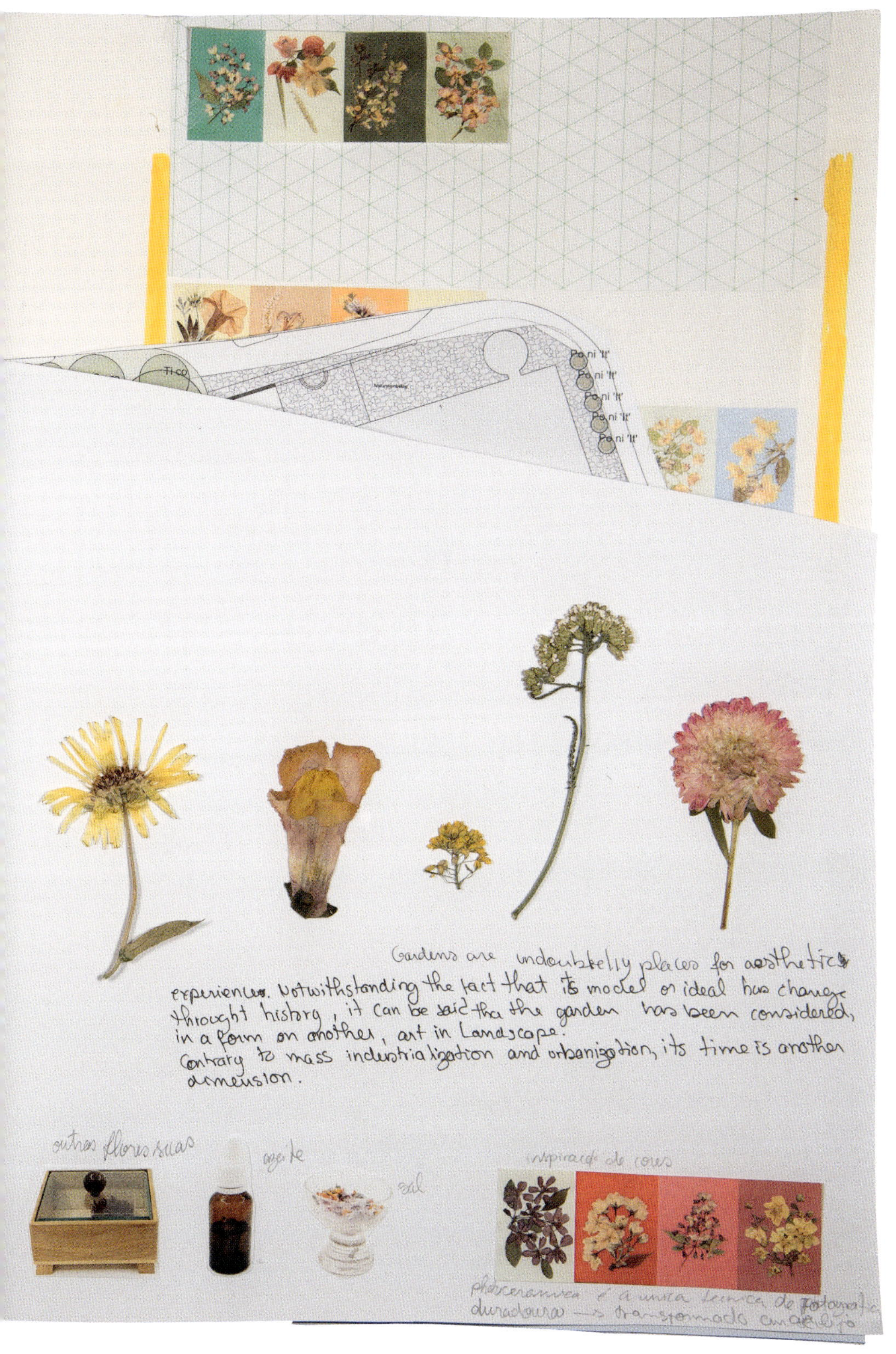

Gardens are undoubtelly places for aesthetic experiences. Notwithstanding the fact that its model or ideal has change throught history, it can be said tha the garden has been considered, in a form on another, art in Landscape.
Contrary to mass industrialization and urbanization, its time is another dimension.

outras flores suas
azeite
sal
inspiração de cores
Fotocerâmica é a única técnica de fotografia duradoura — transformada em azulejo

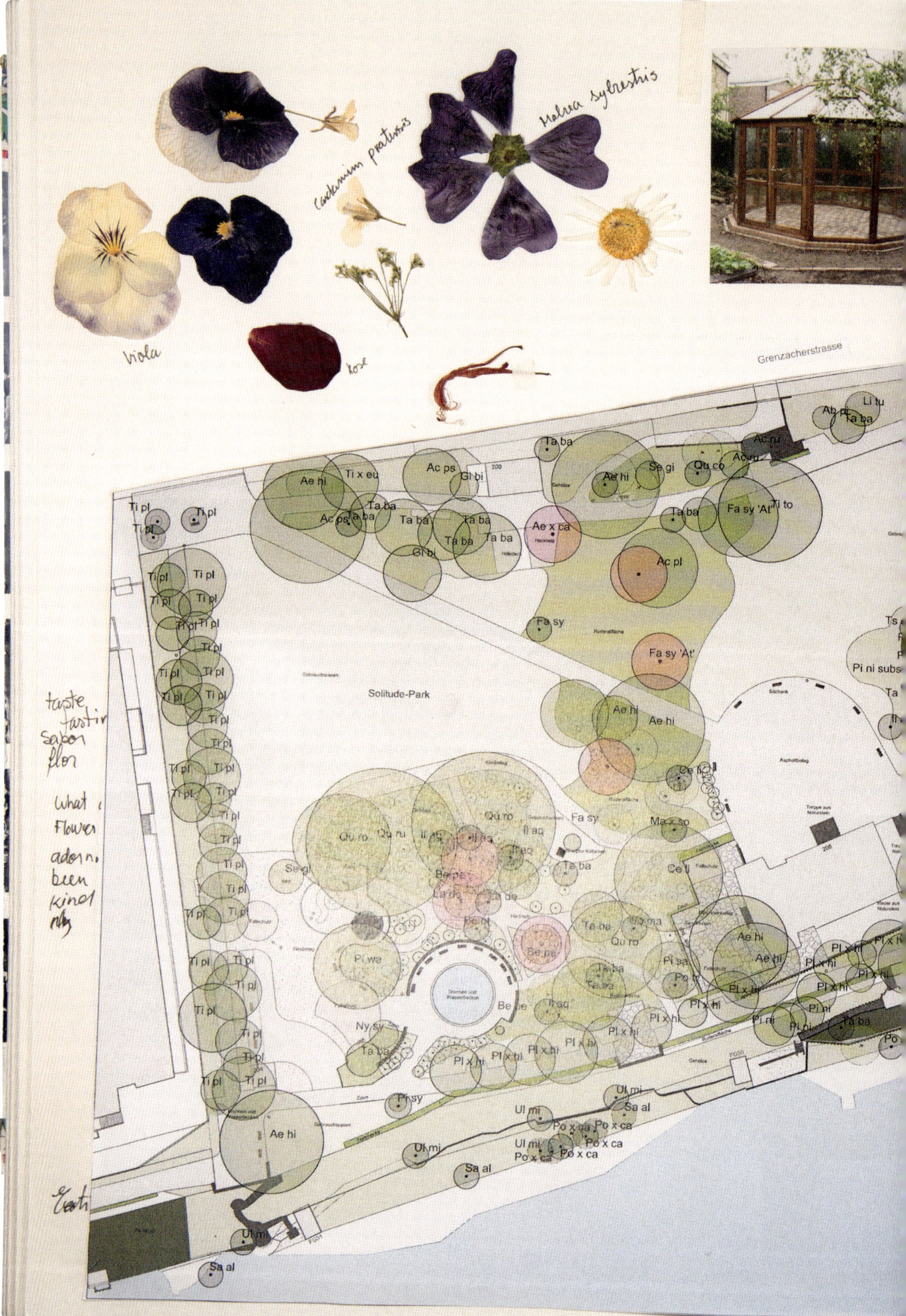

Cardamium pratensis
Malva sylvestris
viola
rose
Grenzacherstrasse
Solitude-Park

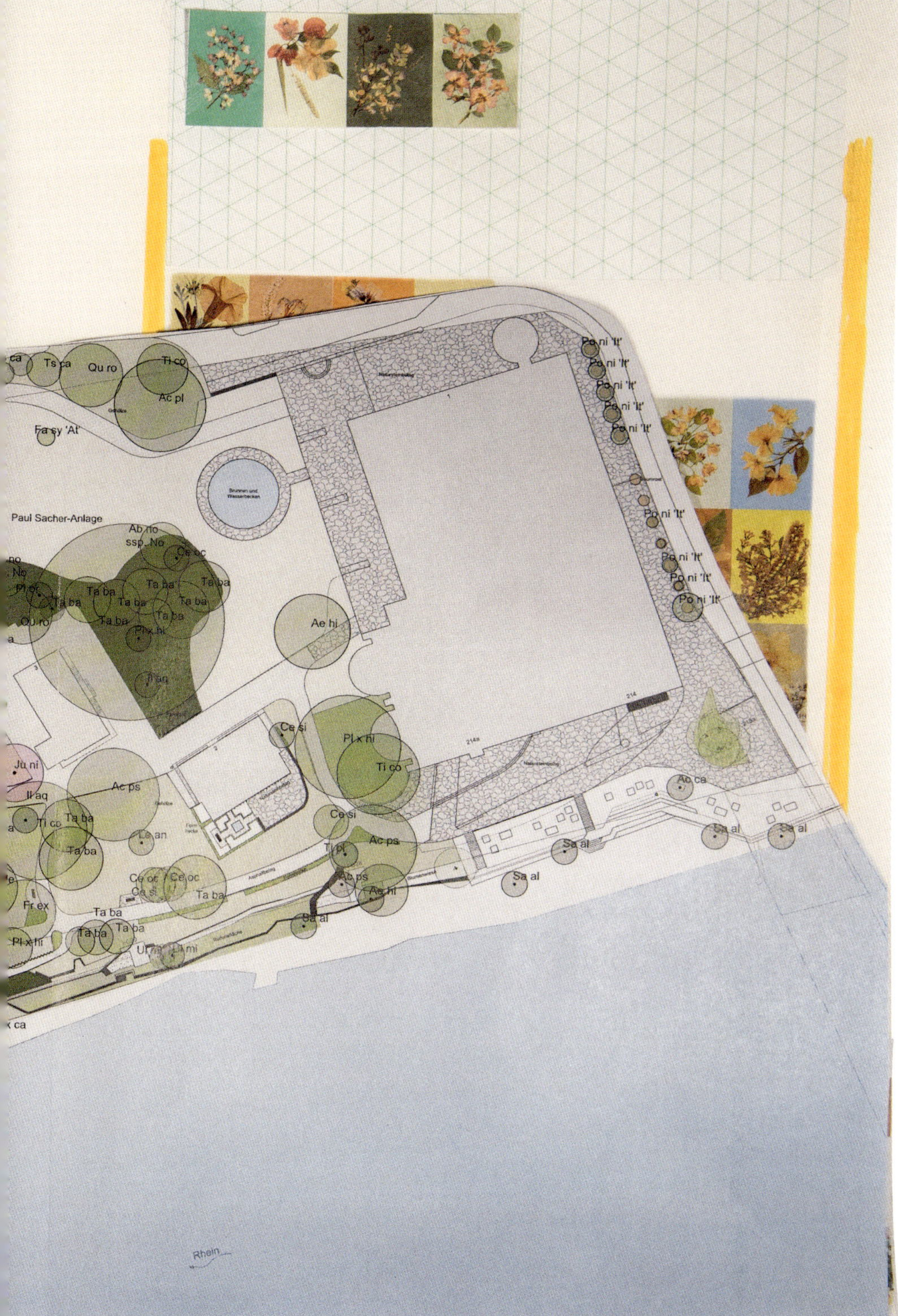
Paul Sacher-Anlage
Rhein
Brunnen und
Wasserbecken
Ts ca
Qu ro
Ti co
Ac pl
Fa sy 'Al'
Ab no
ssp. No
Ce oc
Ta ba
Ta ba
Ta ba
Ta ba
Ta ba
Ta ba
Ta ba
Pl x hi
 Il an
Ae hi
Qu ro
Ju ni
Il aq
Ac ps
Ti co
Ta ba
Ta ba
Lo an
Ce si
Pl x hi
Ti co
Ce si
Ac ps
Ti pl
Ac ps
Ae hi
Ce oc / Ce oc
Ce si
Ta ba
Fr ex
Ta ba
Ta ba
Ta ba
Pl x hi
Sa al
Ul mi / Ul mi
Po ni 'It'
Po ni 'It'
Po ni 'It'
Po ni 'It'
Po ni 'It'
Po ni 'It'
Po ni 'It'
Po ni 'It'
Ac ca
Sa al
Sa al
Sa al
Sa al

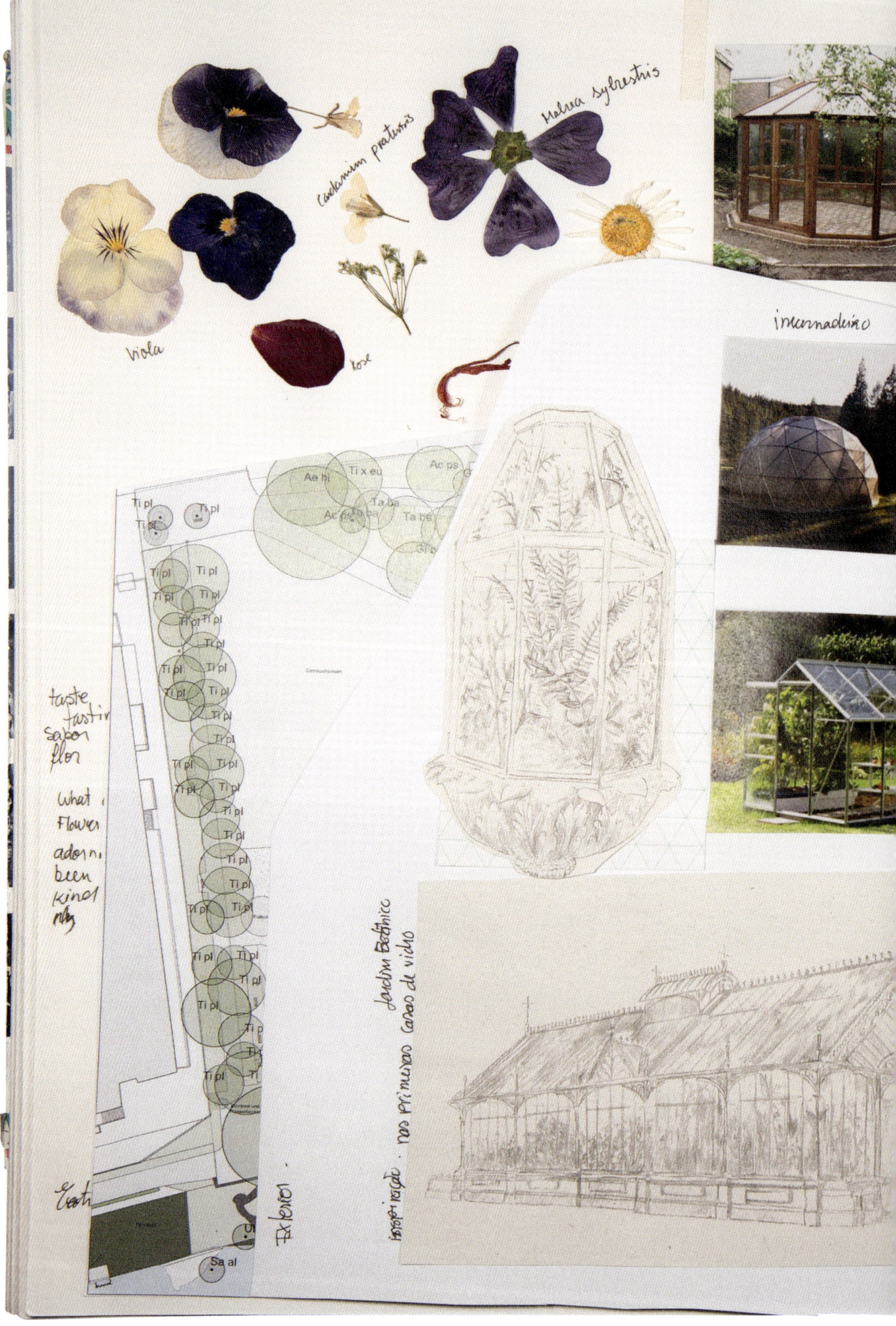
Malva sylvestris
Cardamium pratensis
viola
rose
incernadeiro
taste
tasting
sabor
flor
What
Flower
adorn
been
kind
Exterior
Jardim Botânico
inspirado . nas primeiras casas de vidro

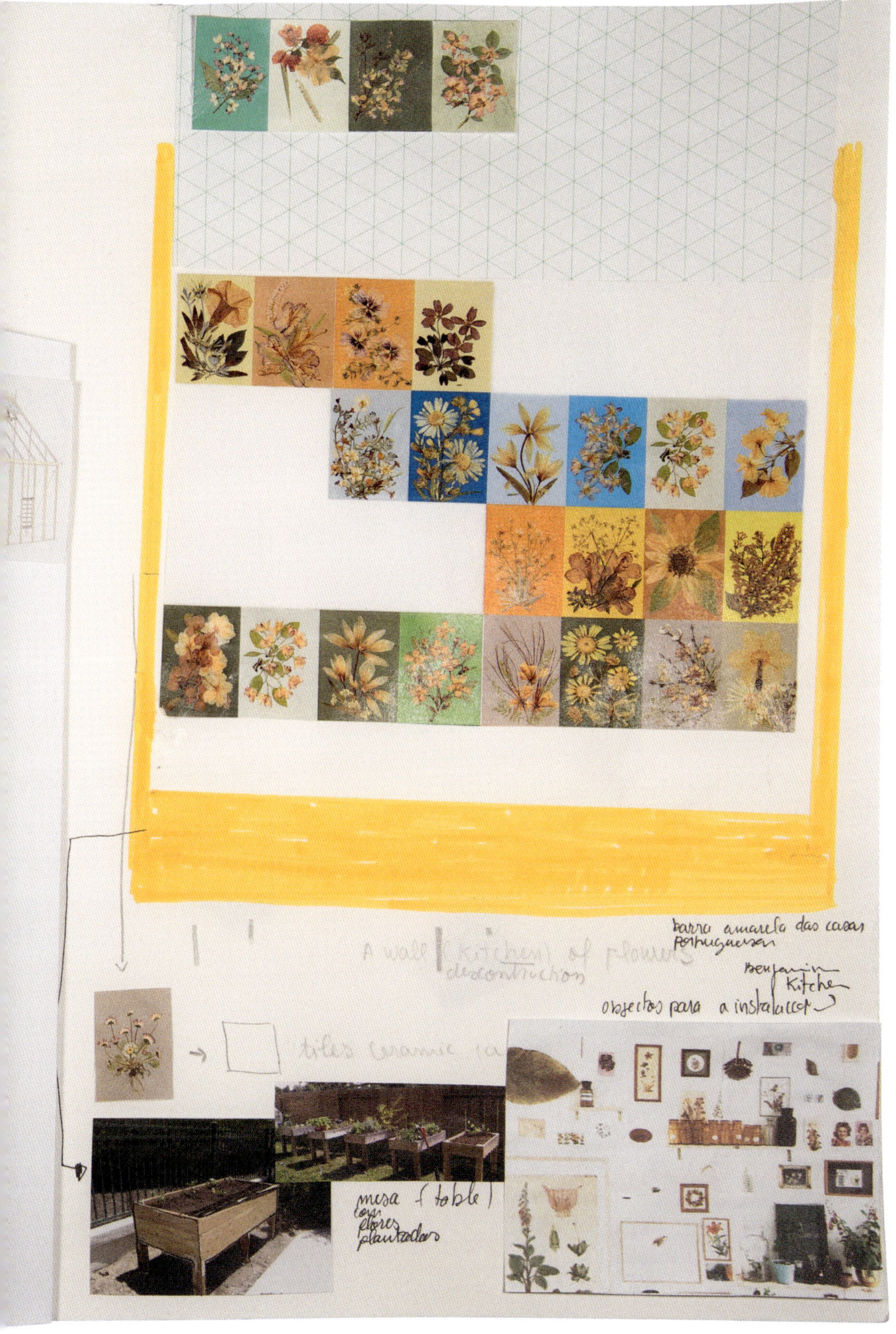

A wall [kitchen] of flowers
deconstruction
barra amarela das casas
Portuguesas
Benjamin
Kitchen
objectos para a instalacão
tiles ceramic ic
mesa (table)
com
flores
plantadas

# Authors

**Antje Baecker** is a PhD candidate at the University of Leipzig's Institute of Anthropology. She writes about food, taste, and cultural change in the context of concepts of the body and of the person in the Peruvian Andes. She became acquainted with Peruvian food culture and cuisine in the course of several lengthy study trips to Peru undertaken over a period of twenty years. As a trained chef, her academic work is always closely tied to practice. Her sensory experiences have inspired artistic projects such as the installation *Home Scents*, at the show *Grassi invites#2: dazwischen /in/ between*, held in 2016 at the Grassi Museum of Ethnology in Leipzig. She has been a tutor for the hands-on module *Museum on the Couch* since 2015 and is offering a teach-and-learn project on sensory ethnography in 2019.

**Ralf Beil** is an exhibition curator and cultural historian. After studying art history, German literature, and philosophy in Freiburg and Paris, he worked initially as a freelance curator and art critic for *Artefactum*, *Neue Zürcher Zeitung*, *Kunst-Bulletin*, and *Kunstforum International*. His doctoral dissertation examines how artists from Egon Schiele to Jason Rhoades have used food as an art material. He was curator and conservator at Kunstmuseum Bern from 1999 to 2003, and in the same function at the Musée cantonal des Beaux-Arts Lausanne from 2004 to 2005. Then he headed the Institut Mathildenhöhe Darmstadt from 2005 to 2015. It was there, in 2012, that he was awarded the Justus Bier Prize for Curators. From 2015 to 2018 he was director of the Kunstmuseum Wolfsburg.

**Marisa Benjamim** is currently enrolled in the Art in Context master's degree program at the Berlin University of the Arts, where she is supported by a grant from the Calouste Gulbenkian Foundation in Portugal. She also holds a bachelor's degree in sculpture and a degree in visual arts from the ESAD, Academy of Fine Arts in Caldas da Rainha, Portugal. Recent exhibitions include: *Endangered Plants*, Haber Space in collaboration with the New York Academy of Medicine, New York (2017), *Floristaurant*, Riga International Biennial of Contemporary Art, Riga (2018), *Green Edible Installation*, Gallery Nord – Kunstverein Tiergarten, Berlin (2018), *Eau Florale*, Roskilde Festival, Roskilde (2019), and *Plant Cure*, Humanity Gallery at LIU, in collaboration with the Brooklyn Botanic Garden (2019).

**Felix Bröcker** is now, after several years of work as a chef, researching cooking and eating as an aesthetic practice in both art and the kitchen. After completing his master's degree at Goethe University and the Städelschule, both in Frankfurt am Main, he has been working on his doctorate at Offenbach University of Art and Design since 2016, investigating strategies of visual presentation in European haute cuisine. In addition to his theoretical examination of the subject, Bröcker works as a chef and project coordinator at the interface of art and the kitchen, as well as in research projects focusing on gastronomy. He also regularly gives lectures on the development of European haute cuisine.

**Elisabeth Bronfen** is a professor of English and American Studies at the University of Zurich and the Global Distinguished Professor at New York University. A specialist in American literature and visual culture, she has published numerous books on a range of subjects, including representations of femininity and death, nocturnal spaces in philosophy, literature, and film, and the imaginary geography of Hollywood. She is currently researching Shakespeare's return and revival in contemporary television drama. Her recent collection of cooking memories, *Obsessed: The Cultural Critic's Life in the Kitchen* (New Brunswick, NJ, 2019), is steeped in her passion for food.

**Karin Leonhard** studied art history, modern German literature, and theater studies at Ludwig Maximilian University in Munich from 1988 to 1995. In 2001, the art historian submitted her dissertation titled *Zur Interieurmalerei Jan Vermeers* (On the Interiors of Jan Vermeer). From 2004 to 2011, she was a research assistant at the Catholic University of Eichstätt-Ingolstadt; from 2009 to 2011, a fellow at the Art History Institute in Florence (Max Planck Institute); and from 2011 to 2013, a senior research fellow at the Max Planck Institute for the History of Science, Berlin. From 2013 to 2015, she held a professorship at the University of Bonn, followed by a professorship at the University of Constance. Since 2014, she has also been Honorary Curator of the Rijksmuseum Amsterdam. Her research focuses on the connection between theories of art and nature in the early modern period, the methodology of art history, and, most recently, the dialogue between art history and restoration sciences.

**Thomas Macho** heads the Vienna-based International Research Centre for Cultural Studies (IFK) run by Linz University of Art and Design, having previously been professor of cultural history at the Humboldt University of Berlin from 1993 to 2016. He earned his doctorate with a dissertation on the philosophy of music at the University of Vienna and wrote his habilitation thesis on metaphors of death at the University of Klagenfurt. His most recent monographs include: *Das Leben ist ungerecht* (Life Is Unfair, St. Pölten and Salzburg, 2010), *Vorbilder* (Paragons, Munich, 2011), *Schweine: Ein Portrait* (Pigs: A Portrait, Berlin, 2015), *Das Leben nehmen: Suizid in der Moderne* (To Take One's Own Life: Suicide in Modernity, Berlin, 2017).

**Wolfgang Meyerhof** is currently guest professor at Saarland University, having retired as head of the Department of Molecular Genetics at the German Institute of Human Nutrition Potsdam-Rehbrücke, where he investigated the molecular and cellular basis of the sense of taste. He received his academic training in developmental biology and neuroendocrinology at the Free University Berlin and the University Hospital Hamburg-Eppendorf. He has won several prizes and is an elected member of the Leopoldina, the German National Academy of Science.

**Annja Müller-Alsbach** is curator of the exhibition *Amuse-bouche. The Taste of Art*. She studied art history, classical archaeology, and medieval history in Basel and Vienna. In 1996, she worked as a research trainee at the Kunstmuseum Basel, and from 1998 to 1999 as a freelance research assistant at Museum Tinguely. Since 2000, she has worked at the latter museum as a conservator and has also contributed to various projects revolving around the permanent collection and special exhibitions. She has curated exhibitions on, among others, Kurt Schwitters (2004), Max Ernst (Museum Tinguely, Basel, and the Menil Collection, Houston, 2007–08), Robert Rauschenberg (2009–10), and Arman (together with Jean-Michel Bouhours, Centre Pompidou, Paris, 2011). In 2015, she curated *Belle Haleine – The Scent of Art*.

**Jeannette Nuessli Guth** is a food scientist specialized in food sensory science. She has been a lecturer in this field at the ETH Zurich since 2000 and has worked on the sensory interactions of taste and aroma, time-dependent methods, and consumer studies. Her current research revolves around the question of how different linguistic communities and cultures describe their perceptions when eating and drinking. Among her partners in this interdisciplinary field are the Zurich University of Applied Sciences and the University of Zurich.

**Maren Runte** teaches linguistics in the Department of Applied Linguistics at the Zurich University of Applied Sciences. She wrote her doctoral dissertation on a lexicographical subject at the University of Duisburg-Essen, and her current research focus is in the field of corpus linguistics. The linguistic analysis of descriptions of taste has preoccupied her since 2009, initially through the research project *Sensory Language and the Semantics of Taste* and then in a continuation of the same project undertaken in collaboration with the food sensory scientist Jeannette Nuessli Guth at the ETH Zurich.

**Charles Spence** is a tenured professor at Oxford University and heads the Crossmodal Research Laboratory there. He has worked with a number of the world's top chefs, including Heston Blumenthal (The Fat Duck) and Ferran Adrià, in his research kitchen. Spence is currently collaborating with the next generation of modernist chefs, with molecular mixologists, chocolatiers, culinary artists, designers, and composers, on multisensory experience design. He has published more than 850 articles as well as authoring and editing twelve books, including the prizewinning *The perfect meal*, together with Betina Piqueras-Fiszman in 2014. His latest book *Gastrophysics: The new science of eating* (London 2017) deals, in part, with the translation of the latest neuroscience-inspired design for food from the modernist restaurant to the healthcare / airplane / home setting, et cetera, and has just been awarded the 2019 Le Grand Prix de la Culture Gastronomique from the Académie Internationale de la Gastronomie.

**Daniel Spoerri** attracted notice as an artist mainly on account of his "snare pictures" of the 1960s. He began his career in the 1950s as a dancer in Bern. In the 1970s, Spoerri made a name for himself by running a restaurant and founding Eat Art (and the Eat Art gallery in Düsseldorf with its numerous banquets). In the 1990s, he created a large sculpture park, Il Giardino di Daniel Spoerri, in Tuscany which since 1997 has been a foundation open to the public. The Ausstellungshaus Spoerri in Hadersdorf am Kamp near Krems in Lower Austria opened in 2009. Spoerri's long list of recent exhibitions reflects both his ongoing development as an artist and the unbroken interest in his work.

**Paul Stoller** has been conducting anthropological research for over thirty years. His early work concerned the religion of the Songhay people who live in the Republics of Niger and Mali in West Africa. Since 1992, Stoller has pursued studies of West African immigrants in New York City. Those studies have concerned such topics as spirit possession, the anthropology of the senses, and the politics of immigration. Stoller's work has resulted in the publication of fifteen books, including ethnographies, biographies, memoirs, and also three novels. He has won many awards for his work, including a Guggenheim Fellowship (1994), the Anders Retzius Gold Medal in Anthropology (2013), and the American Anthropological Association's Anthropology in Media Award (2015) in recognition of his blogs for *The Huffington Post*. He is currently writing a blog on culture and well-being for *Psychology Today*. His most recent book, published in 2018, is *Adventures in Blogging: Public Anthropology and Popular Media*.

**Roland Wetzel** has been the director of Museum Tinguely in Basel since April 2009. Wetzel studied art history, business management, and musicology in Zurich. The emphases of his research efforts and interests lie in the transdisciplinary art forms of the period from the 1910s to the 1960s and in contemporary art. From 2000 to 2009, he was employed at Kunstmuseum Basel. At Museum Tinguely, he has conceptualized an exhibition program that primarily distinguishes between Tinguely's role models, his contemporaries, and his topicality in the contemporary era. In 2016, he curated *Prière de toucher. The Touch of Art*.

**Stefan Wiesner** is a Michelin-starred chef with seventeen Gault & Millau points. After completing his apprenticeship and working in various establishments, he returned to his parents' restaurant, the Rössli in Escholzmatt, which he and his wife Monica took over in 1989. Among Switzerland's top chefs, he is regarded as a visionary, an experimentalist in the vanguard of "natural cuisine," and as a sensuously poetic food artist. Sometimes he is dubbed the "alchemist" or the "wizard in the kitchen." Wiesner is a guest lecturer at the University of Applied Sciences Northwestern Switzerland and the author of several cookbooks. His gourmet menus mingle philosophy with pleasure; and while ethics, ecology, culture, architecture, aesthetics, and art are all essential ingredients, the real staples are knowledge and skill.

# List of Exhibited Works

**Sonja Alhäuser**
*Schokoladenmaschine II*, 1999
Steel, white liquid chocolate
(tempered), motor, silicone
(figurine), 102 × 60 × 59 cm
Courtesy of the artist

**Farah Al Qasimi**
*Pomegranate*, 2015
Archival inkjet print
(exhibition copy), 35 × 45 cm
Courtesy of the artist, The Third
Line, Dubai, and Helena Anrather
Gallery, New York

**Farah Al Qasimi**
*Butterfly Garden*, 2016
Archival inkjet print
(exhibition copy), 70 × 95 cm
Courtesy of the artist, The Third
Line, Dubai, and Helena Anrather
Gallery, New York

**Farah Al Qasimi**
*Lunch*, 2018
Archival inkjet print (exhibition
copy), 102 × 74 cm
Courtesy of the artist, The Third
Line, Dubai, and Helena Anrather
Gallery, New York
[Book cover]

**Anonymous**
Menu for the Futurist Taverna del
Santo Palato in Turin, 1931
Printed menu, 18.5 × 13.5 cm
Collezione Guido Andrea Pautasso

**Janine Antoni**
*Lick and Lather*, 1993
Chocolate and soap, 57 × 38 × 27 cm,
50 × 35 × 25 cm
"la Caixa" Collection.
Contemporary Art

**Janine Antoni**
*Mortar and Pestle*, 1999
C-print, 121.9 × 121.9 cm
Courtesy of the artist and Luhring
Augustine, New York
[p. 12]

**Marisa Benjamim**
*Hortus Deliciarum*, 2019
Installation with various materials
(wood, floral tiles, paint, greenhouse, plants), dimensions variable
Courtesy of the artist
[pp. 126–31]

**Joseph Beuys**
*1a gebratene Fischgräte (Hering)*,
1970
Cardboard, fish bone, string,
34.8 × 17.8 × 5.8 cm
Kunstpalast, Düsseldorf

**Joseph Beuys**
*Ich kenne kein Weekend*, 1972–73
Book: 15 × 10 × 3 cm,
bottle: 15 × 4.5 × 4.5 cm,
case lid: 50 × 64 × 6 cm
Edition Block Berlin

**Joseph Beuys**
*Gib mir Honig*, 1979
Tin honey pail, labeled and
stamped, ca. 16 cm × 13 cm Ø
Edition of 12
Galerie Heinz Holtmann, Cologne

**Joseph Beuys**
*Capri-Batterie*, 1985
Light bulb with plug socket in
wooden box, lemon, 8 × 11 cm
Edition 62/200, signed and
numbered on certificate
Rusterholtz Galerie, Basel

**George Brecht**
*Sonnensalz (from the Anthology of
Misunderstanding)*, 1969
Cardboard box with salt with two
labels, 14 × 7 × 4 cm
mumok – Museum moderner Kunst
Stiftung Ludwig Wien, Vienna, on
loan from the Austrian Ludwig
Foundation, Vienna, since 1993

**Pol Bury**
*Bratpfanne mit Eiern*, 1972
Frying pan with eggs, 53 × 32 × 20 cm
Kunstpalast, Düsseldorf

**Raffaele Carrieri**
"Rivoluzione in cucina, ovvero: culi-
narian futurista," *Il Secolo Illustrato*,
no. 25, June 24, 1933
Newspaper, 40.5 × 30 cm
Collezione Guido Andrea Pautasso

**Costantino Ciervo**
*Global Gene*, 2007
7-channel video installation,
aluminum, 7 TFT/LCD monitors,
7 HDD players, 7 videos (color,
sound), each ca. 20',
each 39 × 44.5 × 12 cm
Sammlung Carola und Günther
Ketterer-Ertle

**Jan Davidsz. de Heem**
*Fruchtstilleben mit gefülltem
Weinglas*, undated (17th century)
Oil on oak, 35 × 53 cm
Staatliche Kunsthalle, Karlsruhe

**Crispijn de Passe (the Elder)**
"Taste," plate 5 from the series
*The Five Senses*, printed between
1590–1637
Copper engraving and etching
on paper, 9.9 cm Ø
Graphische Sammlung, ETH Zurich,
gift of Heinrich Schulthess-von
Meiss (1894/1898)

**Bea de Visser**
*Blowup*, 2002
Video (color, no sound), 23' (loop)
Courtesy Bea de Visser and
LIMA Amsterdam

**Marcel Duchamp**
*Menu de réveillon*, 1907
Drypoint on paper, 24.5 × 15.5 cm
Métropole Rouen Normandie –
Musée des Beaux-Arts

**Hans-Peter Feldmann**
*Ein Pfund Erdbeeren*, 2005
34 color photographs,
each ca. 10 × 10 cm
Ariane Piëch, courtesy
Galerie Hans Mayer, Düsseldorf

**Urs Fischer**
*Noisette*, 2009
Hole in the wall, silicone, motion
sensor, electric motor, mechanism,
dimensions variable
Edition of 3 & 2 artist's proofs, AP 2
Private Collection, Courtesy
of the Artist
[p. 12]

**Fischli Weiss**
*Bei den Höhlenbewohnern*, 1979
*Der Brand zu Uster*, 1979
*Der Unfall*, 1979
*Eitles Pack*, 1979
*In Anos Teppichladen*, 1979
*In den Alpen*, 1979
*In der Arktis*, 1979
*Moonraker*, 1979
*Pavesi*, 1979
*Untergang der Titanic*, 1979

From: *Wurstserie*, 1979
C-prints, each 24 × 30.2 cm
Sammlung Fotomuseum
Winterthur, gift of George Reinhart

**Karl Gerstner**
*Taste Perceptor*, 1970
13 labeled vials, rubber pins,
fragrance, wooden box with
glass window, adhesive letters,
metal handle and hinge, rubber,
42 × 39.4 × 20.4 cm
Collection Museum Haus
Konstruktiv, donated by Hermann
Strittmatter GGK Zurich

**Hendrick Goltzius,**
**after Peter Overadt**
"Taste," plate 4 from the series
*The Five Senses*, printed in 1596
Copper engraving on paper,
25.7 × 17.5 cm
Graphische Sammlung, ETH Zurich,
gift of Heinrich Schulthess-von
Meiss (1894/1898)

**Damien Hirst**
*Chicken*, 1999
*Dumpling*, 1999
*Steak and Kidney*, 1999

From: *The Last Supper*, 1999
Screenprints on paper,
each 153 × 101.5 cm
Ex. 127/150
Kunstmuseum Wolfsburg

**Roelof Louw**
*Soul City (Pyramid of Oranges)*,
1967/2020
Wood, 8,000 oranges,
1,524 × 1,667 × 1,667 cm
Richard Saltoun Gallery, London

**Sarah Lucas**
*Eating a Banana*, 1990
Black-and-white photograph,
74.9 × 81.9 cm
M. van der Mey-Tcheng, Amsterdam

**Sarah Lucas**
*Sausage Film*, 1990
Video (Betacam SP, color,
sound [mono]), 8'
Sarah Lucas, Courtesy
Sadie Coles HQ, London

**Filippo Tommaso Marinetti**
"La cucina futurista e pasta asciutta:
S.E. Marinetti Lancia il nuovo verbo
per la Cucina Futurista," *La Cucina
Italiana*, no. 1, January 15, 1931
Newspaper, 56.5 × 42.5 cm
Collezione Guido Andrea Pautasso

**Filippo Tommaso Marinetti/Fillia**
*La cucina futurista*, Sonzogno,
Milan, 1932
Book, 18.4 × 12 cm
Collezione Guido Andrea Pautasso

**Cildo Meireles**
*Inserções em circuitos ideológicos:
1-projeto Coca-Cola*, 1970
Coca-Cola bottles, transferred text,
each 24.5 × 6 × 6 cm
Unlimited edition
Daros Latinamerica Collection,
Zurich

**Alexandra Meyer**
*Geschmacklos*, 2012
Video (color, sound), 5'11"
Courtesy of the artist

**Alexandra Meyer**
*Butter*, 2019
Multimedia installation: animal and
human butterfat, video (color, no
sound), 1'10" loop, digital picture
frame showing the painting *Caritas
Romana* (1620–30) by Caspar de
Crayer, dimensions variable
Courtesy of the artist

**Antoni Miralda & Dorothée Selz**
*Pain Surprise*, 1971
Bread (dyed green), wood,
43.3 × 19.2 cm
Kunstpalast, Düsseldorf

**Nicolas Momein**
*Incomplete Closed Cube, Aliboron
l'a digéré*, 2011
9 salt licks, each 25 × 25 × 25 cm
Fonds cantonal d'art contemporain,
Geneva

**Anca Munteanu Rimnic**
*My Dear*, 1999
C-print, 80 × 100 cm
Private Collection, Courtesy
of the artist

**Anca Munteanu Rimnic**
*Pizza*, 2009
Sound piece, 3'4"
Courtesy of the artist

**Otobong Nkanga**
*Contained Measures of a Kolanut*,
2012–ongoing
Variable sizes of tables, handmade
100% cotton paper, inkjet printed
photographs on Forex, wood, kola-
nuts, extract of kolanut, glass plates,
knife, gloves, cushions, decanter
and stand, dimensions variable
Courtesy of the artist
[p. 20]

**Otobong Nkanga**
*Kolanut Tales – Dismembered*, 2016
Woven textiles and yarns
(polyester, bio cotton, linen, acrylic),
220 × 180 cm
Courtesy of the artist

**Emeka Ogboh**
*Sufferhead Original–Basel Edition*,
2020
Multimedia installation with beer
bottles, printed text, HD video
(color, sound), 1'24"
Courtesy of the artist

**Opavivará!**
*Aguardente*, 2019
Bidet, ceramic tiles, wood, cachaça,
glasses, fountain system with
submerged pump, 80 × 80 × 47 cm
A Gentil Carioca, Rio de Janeiro

**Dennis Oppenheim**
*Gingerbread Man*, 1970
digitalized 16 mm film (b/w,
no sound), 3'
Dennis Oppenheim Estate,
New York

**Meret Oppenheim**
*Chuchi-Cahier*, undated
(c. 1937/38/43)
Handwritten notes, various
materials and collage in notebook,
22×19×1 cm
Private collection

**Meret Oppenheim**
*Bon appétit, Marcel!*
*(Die weisse Königin)*, 1966–78
Baked dough with spine of par-
tridge, silverware, plate, glass with
wine remnants, oil cloth chess-
board, napkin, 32×32×10 cm
Collection Foster Goldstrom

**Peter Overadt**
"'Gustus' or Taste", plate from the
series *The Five Senses*, ca. 1600–50
Copper engraving on paper,
25.2×29 cm
Graphische Sammlung, ETH Zurich,
gift of Heinrich Schulthess-von
Meiss (1894/1898)
[p. 15]

**Georg Pencz**
"Taste ('Gustus')," plate 4 from
the series *The Five Senses*, printed
ca. 1544
Copper engraving on paper,
sheet: 7.6×5 cm
Graphische Sammlung, ETH Zurich,
gift of Heinrich Schulthess-von
Meiss (1894/1898)
[Back cover]

**Tobias Rehberger**
*Familie Strychnin (Die nächste Gen-*
*eration)*, 2020
Unglazed porcelain, paint,
beetroot juice, strychnine,
dimensions variable
Courtesy Galerie Bärbel Grässlin,
Frankfurt

**Torbjørn Rødland**
*The Thousand Dollar Sandwich*, 2019
Color photograph, C-print on Kodak
Endura paper, 62×78×4 cm
Collection Erling Kagge, Oslo

**Dieter Roth**
*Grosses Schimmelbild*, 1969
Wooden frame covered with glass
on both sides, layers of moldy
organic materials of different colors,
121×82×8.5 cm
Kunstmuseum Basel, gift of
Emil Wartmann, Basel, 1986
[p. 17]

**Dieter Roth**
*Literaturwurst "Die Welt,"* 1969
Shredded copy of the newspaper
*Die Welt* in a plastic bag shaped
into the form of a sausage, label,
40×10 cm
Bündner Kunstmuseum Chur, gift of
Hans and Hildi Müller, Pontresina

**Jan Pietersz. Saenredam,**
**after Hendrick Goltzius**
"Tasting," plate 4 from the series
*The Five Senses*, printed after 1595
Copper engraving on paper,
sheet: 11.5×7.7 cm
Graphische Sammlung, ETH Zurich,
gift of Heinrich Schulthess-von
Meiss (1894/1898)

**Carlo Schröter**
*Restaurant Spoerri Suppen*,
undated
8 soup tin cans, paper labels,
cardboard display:
each 5.1 cm×5.9 cm Ø,
display: 31.5×31.5×8.2 cm
Kunstpalast, Düsseldorf

**Cindy Sherman**
*Untitled #182*, 1987
Chromogenic color print,
232.7×156.8 cm
Ex. 3/6
Kunstmuseum Wolfsburg

**Shimabuku**
*Sakepirinha*, 2008
Neon sign, 98×228 cm
Galerie Barbara Wien, Berlin
Recipe (inkjet print),
framed, 75×50 cm
Edition 3/3
Courtesy of the artist

**Shimabuku**
*Ice Cream with Salt*, 2010
Screenprint on paper, 100×70 cm
Courtesy of the artist; Air de Paris

**Shimabuku**
*Ice Cream with Pepper*, 2010
Screenprint on paper, 100×70 cm
Courtesy of the artist; Air de Paris

**Roman Signer**
*Lebkuchen/Gingerbread*, 2003
Wooden table, gingerbread,
70×100×40 cm
Courtesy Galerie Martin Janda,
Vienna

**Slavs and Tatars**
*Open Mic*, 2018
Plexiglass, digital print, LED lights,
stainless steel, aluminium,
95×29×20 cm unique
Courtesy the artist; Kraupa-Tuskany
Zeidler, Berlin

**Slavs and Tatars**
*Pickle Tits*, 2018
Poster (Offset print), 70×50 cm,
unlimited edition
Courtesy the artist; Kraupa-Tuskany
Zeidler, Berlin

**Slavs and Tatars**
*Underage Page (extended-*
*turquoise)*, 2018
Stainless steel, faux leather, foam,
105×156×60 cm
unique
Courtesy the artist; Kraupa-Tuskany
Zeidler, Berlin

**Slavs and Tatars**
*Brine & Punishment*, 2019
Vending machine with Sauerkraut
juice *Brine & Punishment*, Vinyl
stickers, 183×99×88 cm
Courtesy the artist; Kraupa-Tuskany
Zeidler, Berlin

**Daniel Spoerri**
*Le Pétit Déjeuner de Kichka*, 1961
Assemblage on wood, 57×57 cm
Beth Rudin DeWoody

**Daniel Spoerri**
*Meal Variation No. 2 Eaten by*
*Marcel Duchamp*, 1964
Screenprint on linen, 66×80 cm
mumok – Museum moderner Kunst
Stiftung Ludwig Wien, Vienna,
former Hahn Collection, acquired
in 1978

**Daniel Spoerri**
*Variations on a Meal Eaten by*
*Bob Rosenblum*, New York, 1964
Assemblage on painted wood,
54.5×64×23 cm
Galerie Ziegler SA, Zürich

**Daniel Spoerri**
*Achtung Kunstwerk (Attention œuvre d'art)*, 1968
Jar with pickled herring, glass, herring, paper, plastic, 12 × 7.5 cm
Vice-Versand edition, ex. no. 3
Centre Pompidou – Musee national d'art moderne – Centre de creation industrielle, Paris
[Frontispiece]

**Daniel Spoerri**
*Wenn alle Künste untergehn, die edle Kochkunst bleibt bestehn*, 1969
Assemblage, 120 × 63 × 10 cm
Private collection, Milan

**Daniel Spoerri**
"Menu Travesti: Kartoffelbrei-Eis mit Fleischpralinen," *Twen*, no. 9, September 1970
Magazine, 22 × 23.5 cm
Swiss National Library, Prints and Drawings Department, Daniel Spoerri Archives, Bern

**Daniel Spoerri**
*Daniel Spoerri presents Eat Art, Claude et François Lalanne "Le Dîner Cannibale,"* 1970
Poster (probably screenprint), 30,5 × 43 cm
Swiss National Library, Prints and Drawings Department, Daniel Spoerri Archives, Bern

**Daniel Spoerri**
*The Banatrap-Dinner*, banquet during the Edinburgh International Festival, as part of the exhibition *Art and Anti-Art: Strategy. Gets Art*, August 23, 1970
Poster (probably screenprint), 59.5 × 46.2 cm
Swiss National Library, Prints and Drawings Department, Daniel Spoerri Archives, Bern

**Daniel Spoerri**
*Das palindromische, per-verse, Travestie Essen*, chef: Sarah Wiener, during *MAHLZEIT VAKANZ 98!*, Schwarzenberg, Vorarlberg, July 1, 1998
Preparatory sketch for menu, copperplate engraving on paper, 16.2 × 20.1 cm
Red and black ballpoint pen on paper, 29.7 × 42 cm
Swiss National Library, Prints and Drawings Department, Daniel Spoerri Archives, Bern
[p. 90]

**Mladen Stilinović**
*Secer (Sugar)*, 1992
Sugar on a wooden board, 18 × 26 cm
Courtesy Branka Stipančić and Galerie Martin Janda, Vienna

**Mladen Stilinović**
*Seflja – secer (Ladle – Sugar)*, 1993
Acrylic, sugar, chewing gum in a ladle, 30 × 9 × 9 cm
mumok – Museum moderner Kunst Stiftung Ludwig Wien, Vienna, on loan from the Austrian Ludwig Foundation, Vienna, since 2014

**Mladen Stilinović**
*Stolica – secer (Chair – sugar)*, 1993
Acrylic, b/w photograph, sugar on a wooden board, 32 × 31.5 × 0.5 cm
mumok – Museum moderner Kunst Stiftung Ludwig Wien, Vienna, on loan from the Austrian Ludwig Foundation, Vienna, since 2014

**Sam Taylor-Johnson**
*Still Life*, 2001
One-channel video (color, no sound) on monitor, 3'44" loop
Edition 5/6
Courtesy Sammlung Goetz, Munich
[p. 18]

**André Thomkins**
*Zuckerhut*, 1971
Licorice branches, sugarloaf, sugar cubes, 24 × 24 × 24 cm
Museum Kunstpalast, Düsseldorf

**Mario Valli**
"Nella cucina futurista," *Pro Familia*, no. 17, April 26, 1931
Newspaper, 38 × 18.5 cm
Collezione Guido Andrea Pautasso

**Claudia Vogel**
*Tastescape*, 2019–20
Installation and performance with pedestal, copper distillery, laboratory glassware and tools, various plants, dimensions variable
Courtesy of the artist

**Jorinde Voigt**
*Eat me*, 2019
140 g honey from Schliersee and CBD extract in a glass, signed and numbered
Edition of 100
Klosterfelde Edition, Jorinde Voigt

**Andy Warhol**
*Mario Banana #1*, 1964
16 mm film transferred to digital file (color, no sound), digitized, 4' (at 16 frames per second)
Collection of The Andy Warhol Museum, Pittsburgh
Contribution The Andy Warhol Foundation for the Visual Arts, Inc

**Andy Warhol**
*Campbell's Soup II*, 1969

*Old Fashioned Vegetable Soup – Made with Beef Stock*
*Scotch Broth Soup (A Hearty Soup) – One of the Manhandlers*
*Vegetarian Vegetable Soup – The Alphabet Soup*
*New England Clam Chowder Soup – Important! Add whole Milk*
*Chicken 'n Dumplings Soup – Stout Hearted Soup*
*Hot Dog Bean Soup – Tender Beans and little Franfurter slices – Stout Hearted Soup*
*Oyster Stew (with Grade AA Butter) – Important! Add whole Milk*
*Tomato-Beef Noodle O's Soup*
*Golden Mushroom Soup – Rich in sliced Mushrooms – Great for Gravies and Sauces!*
*Cheddar Cheese Soup – Great as a Sauce, too!*

Series of 10 screenprints on paper, sheet: each 89.9 × 58.4 cm, image: each 81 × 47.6 cm
Staatsgalerie Stuttgart, Graphische Sammlung, acquired in 1988 with lottery funds
[p. 19]

**Tom Wesselmann**
*Still Life #3*, 1962
Mixed media and collage on board, 76.2 × 76.2 cm
The Estate of Tom Wesselmann, New York, Courtesy Gagosian

**Elizabeth Willing**
*Lick*, 2009
HD video (color, sound), 8'14" (original 29')
Courtesy of the artist and Tolarno Galleries, Melbourne

**Elizabeth Willing**
*Goosebump*, 2011–ongoing
Pfeffernüsse (frosted gingerbread) and icing on a wall, dimensions variable
Courtesy of the artist and Tolarno Galleries, Melbourne
[p. 13]

**Elizabeth Willing**
*Pick-me-up (kinder)*, 2016–ongoing
Pieces of Kinder chocolate in wrappers, glue, dimensions variable
Courtesy of the artist and Tolarno Galleries, Melbourne

**Elizabeth Willing**
*Pick-me-up (Icekonfekt)*, 2016–ongoing
Pieces of Icekonfekt chocolate in wrappers, glue, dimension variable
Courtesy of the artist, and Tolarno Galleries Melbourne

**Erwin Wurm**
*A portrait of the artist as a young man*, 2011
Acrylic, paint, iron, 6.5 × 2 × 1.8 cm
The artist and KÖNIG GALERIE, Berlin, London, Tokyo

**Erwin Wurm**
*A portrait of the artist as a young man*, 2011
Acrylic, paint, iron, 6.3 × 2.1 × 2.1 cm
The artist and KÖNIG GALERIE, Berlin, London, Tokyo

**Erwin Wurm**
*A portrait of the artist as a young man*, 2011
Acrylic, paint, iron, 8 × 2.7 × 2.7 cm
The artist and KÖNIG GALERIE, Berlin, London, Tokyo

**Erwin Wurm**
*A portrait of the artist as a young man*, 2011
Acrylic, paint, iron, 8.3 × 3.8 × 3.8 cm
The artist and KÖNIG GALERIE, Berlin, London, Tokyo

**Erwin Wurm**
*A portrait of the artist as a young man*, 2011
Acrylic, paint, iron, 4.5 × 3.5 × 1.5 cm
The artist and KÖNIG GALERIE, Berlin, London, Tokyo

**Erwin Wurm**
*A portrait of the artist as a young man*, 2011
Acrylic, paint, iron, 7 × 2.7 × 2 cm
The artist and KÖNIG GALERIE, Berlin, London, Tokyo

**Erwin Wurm**
*A portrait of the artist as a young man*, 2011
Acrylic, paint, iron, 7.4 × 5.7 × 2.3 cm
The artist and KÖNIG GALERIE, Berlin, London, Tokyo

**Rémy Zaugg**
*UND, WENN ICH EINEN UNREIFEN APFEL ESSE, DAS GIFTIGE GRÜN NICHT MEHR VORHANDEN WÄRE.*, 1978–91
Stove enamel on aluminum, 241 × 219.5 × 4.4 cm
MUSEUM MMK FÜR MODERNE KUNST, Frankfurt am Main

This book is published in conjunction
with the exhibition
*Amuse-bouche. The Taste of Art*

Museum Tinguely, Basel
February 19 – May 17, 2020

**Editor**
Museum Tinguely, Basel

**Managing editor**
Lisa Anette Ahlers

**Graphic design and typesetting**
Neil Holt

**Copyediting**
Dawn Michelle d'Atri

**Translations**
Gérard Goodrow (pp. 6, 96, 108)
Steven Lindberg (pp. 10, 22, 40, 48, 68, 78, 88, 118)
John Wheelwright (p. 56)

**Production**
Stefanie Kruszyk, Hatje Cantz

**Project management**
Juliane Eisele, Hatje Cantz

**Reproductions**
Repromayer GmbH, Reutlingen

**Printing and binding**
Livonia Print, Riga

**Paper**
Arctic Volume White, 150 g/m²

**Typefaces**
Le Monde Journal Pro
Neuzeit S

**Published by**
Hatje Cantz Verlag GmbH
Mommsenstraße 27
10629 Berlin
www.hatjecantz.de
A Ganske Publishing Group Company

English edition:
ISBN 978-3-7757-4639-7
German edition:
ISBN 978-3-7757-4638-0

Printed in Latvia

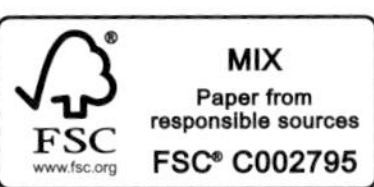


**Exhibition**

**Director**
Roland Wetzel

**Deputy director**
Andres Pardey

**Curator**
Annja Müller-Alsbach

**Curatorial Assistants**
Anja Seiler, Laura Haak

**Registrar/Exhibition manager**
Daniel Boos

**Restoration and conservation**
Jean-Marc Gaillard, Olivia Mooser

**Technical supervisor**
Matthias Fluri

**Communications**
Isabelle Beilfuss, Hannah Schelly

**Art education**
Beat Klein, Sarah Stocker

**Administration**
Nathalie Gaillard, Heidi Juen, Céline Strässle,
Céline Studer

Museum Tinguely
Paul Sacher-Anlage 1
CH – 4002 Basel
Tel.: +41 61 681 93 20
infos@tinguely.ch
www.tinguely.ch

**MUSEUM TINGUELY**
EIN KULTURENGAGEMENT VON ROCHE

**Cover illustration**
Farah Al Qasimi, *Lunch*, 2018
Courtesy of the artist, The Third Line,
Dubai, and Helena Anrather Gallery

**Frontispiece**
Daniel Spoerri, *Achtung Kunstwerk*, 1968
Centre Pompidou – Musée national d'art moderne –
Centre de création industrielle, Paris

**Back cover**
Georg Pencz, "Taste (Gustus),"
plate 4 from the series *The Five Senses*, ca. 1544
Graphische Sammlung ETH Zurich

## Acknowledgments

The Museum would especially like to thank the lenders for their generous support of the exhibition.

*Hortus Deliciarum* by Marisa Benjamim was supported by:

 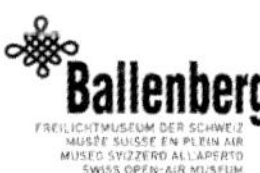

Bau- und Verkehrsdepartement des Kantons Basel-Stadt
**Stadtgärtnerei**

*Sufferhead Original – Basel Edition* by Emeka Ogboh was supported by:

**Ballenberg**
FREILICHTMUSEUM DER SCHWEIZ
MUSÉE SUISSE EN PLEIN AIR
MUSEO SVIZZERO ALL'APERTO
SWISS OPEN-AIR MUSEUM

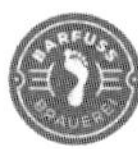

Barfuss Brauerei, Wuppenau

H A N I M A N N S

⊦ **JENSEN
HEITZ**

Alphornbau Stocker, Kriens

Balthasar Streiff - Streiffalphorn, Basel

Selavy Music Production, Basel

Theater Basel

## Copyright



## Photo Credits